SMALL
GIANTS

SMALL GIANTS

Companies That Choose to Be Great Instead of Big

BO BURLINGHAM

Dear Paul,
Go for the mojo!
All the best,
Bo B

PORTFOLIO

PORTFOLIO

Published by the Penguin Group

Penguin Group (USA) Inc., 375 Hudson Street, New York, New York 10014, U.S.A.

Penguin Group (Canada), 90 Eglinton Avenue East, Suite 700, Toronto, Ontario, Canada M4P 2Y3
(a division of Pearson Penguin Canada Inc.)

Penguin Books Ltd, 80 Strand, London WC2R 0RL, England

Penguin Ireland, 25 St. Stephen's Green, Dublin 2, Ireland
(a division of Penguin Books Ltd)

Penguin Books Australia Ltd, 250 Camberwell Road, Camberwell, Victoria 3124,
Australia (a division of Pearson Australia Group Pty Ltd)

Penguin Books India Pvt Ltd, 11 Community Centre, Panchsheel Park,
New Delhi – 110 017, India

Penguin Group (NZ), Cnr Airborne and Rosedale Roads, Albany, Auckland 1310,
New Zealand (a division of Pearson New Zealand Ltd)

Penguin Books (South Africa) (Pty) Ltd, 24 Sturdee Avenue, Rosebank,
Johannesburg 2196, South Africa

Penguin Books Ltd, Registered Offices: 80 Strand, London WC2R 0RL, England

First published in 2005 by Portfolio, a member of Penguin Group (USA) Inc.

7 9 10 8

Publisher's Note

This publication is designed to provide accurate and authoritative information in regard to the subject matter covered. It is sold with the understanding that the publisher is not engaged in rendering legal, accounting, or other professional services. If you require legal advice or other expert assistance, you should seek the services of a competent professional.

LIBRARY OF CONGRESS CATALOGING-IN-PUBLICATION DATA

Burlingham, Bo.
    Small giants : companies that choose to be great instead of big / Bo Burlingham.
       p.   cm.
    Includes index.
    ISBN 1-59184-093-7
    1. Small business—United States—Management.   2. Private companies—United States—
Management.   3. Close corporations—United States—Management.   4. Success in business—
United States.   I. Title.

HD62.7.B835   2005
658.4'09—dc22   2005051487

Printed in the United States of America
Set in Goudy
Designed by Helene Berinsky

For my grandson,
Owen Dimitri Burlingham,
and any others who, by the grace of God,
will join us in the future

ACKNOWLEDGMENTS

Movies have credits, and books have acknowledgments, but I feel as though many of the people involved in the production of this one deserve something more—say, a standing ovation. Let's start with the people who came up with the idea. Credit for that goes to Patrick Nolan, the director of trade paperback sales for Penguin, who had the original inspiration, and Adrian Zackheim, founder and publisher of the Portfolio division of Penguin, who contacted me after reading a cover story I had written in *Inc.* magazine on Zingerman's, entitled "The Coolest Small Company in America." He said he saw the possibility of a book growing out of the article. I didn't get it at first, but I agreed to meet with him. Over breakfast at Pershing Square Restaurant in Manhattan, he articulated the idea so clearly and so brilliantly that, by the time I left, my involvement was a foregone conclusion. After conferring with my wife, Lisa, and my literary-agent-head-cheerleader-guardian-angel, Jill Kneerim, I got started.

By then, a whole bunch of other people had already had an impact on what would eventually become *Small Giants:* former *Inc.* editor in chief George Gendron, who had assigned the Zingerman's article and helped guide me through the research; Leigh Buchanan, who'd edited the piece; and George's successor, John Koten, who'd put it on the cover with a particularly catchy cover line—not to mention Ari Weinzweig, Paul Saginaw, and their colleagues at Zingerman's, including Maggie Bayless, Dave Carson, Frank Carollo, Amy Emberling, Holly Firmin, Mo Frechette, Stas' Kazmierski, Ron Maurer, Todd Wickstrom, and Lynn Yates. Subsequently both Ari and George played crucial roles in helping me think through the themes of the book and identify companies I should look at. George, in particular, came through (as he always has) with those incisive observations at crucial moments that are the mark of a great editor. In addition, I received much valuable support and advice from Jack Stack, CEO of SRC Holdings Corp. (formerly Springfield ReManufacturing Corp.), my mentor and sometime coauthor, as well as numerous other friends, relatives, and colleagues, including Peter Carpenter, John Case, Susan Donovan, John Ellis the elder, John R. Ellis the younger, Richard Fried, Gary Heil, Michael Hopkins, Joe Knight, Joel Kotkin, Sara Noble, John O'Neil, Bill Palmer, and Greg Wittstock.

Norm Brodsky, another mentor and sometime coauthor, contributed on several different levels. He suggested companies to look at; he helped flesh out themes; he gave me important feedback at various stages of the process; and his company, CitiStorage, turned out to be a prime example of a small giant, something I didn't realize when I started. Among those who helped me realize it were his colleagues at CitiStorage, including Brad Clinton, Peter Gunderson, Mike Harper, Bruce Howard, Manny Jimenez Sam Kaplan, Noelle Keating, Patty Lightfoot, Patti Kanner Post, Louis Weiner, and last—but far from least—Elaine Brodsky.

The first person I actually interviewed for the book was Gary Erickson of Clif Bar Inc., who immediately turned the tables on me, asking me a series of questions that helped get me on the right track from the start. He was able to do it because he was in the midst of writing his own book, *Raising the Bar*, which addressed many of the same issues I would wind up grappling with. Dean Mayer and Leslie Henrichsen were of great help as well, serving early on as guides through the wonderful world of Clif Bar.

As it turned out, the Erickson interview was just the beginning of one of the most stimulating, uplifting, thoroughly enjoyable reporting episodes of my career. Never have I had the opportunity to hang out with so many interesting people at so many fascinating companies, one right after the other. If you've already read the book, you know what I'm talking about, and you can easily imagine why the experience was exhilarating. Here I would simply like to give credit to the people who helped make the reporting phase so much fun:

- at Anchor Brewing in San Francisco: John Dannerbeck, Fritz Maytag, and Linda Rowe
- at ECCO in Boise, Idaho: Karen Campbell, Rob Corrigan, Michelle Howard, Todd Mansfield, Bob Ohlson, Mike Pironi, Mike Scoll, Chris Thompson, Jim Thompson, Richard Vinson, and Ed Zimmer

- at Hammerhead Productions in Studio City, California: Thad Beier, Dan Chuba, and Jamie Dixon
- at New Hope Contracting in Dorchester, Massachusetts: Chris Howell, Rob Moreno, Chris Painten, Gene Pettiford, Danny Power, Peter Power, and Steve Quinn
- at O. C. Tanner Co. in Salt Lake City: Adrian Gostick, Kent Murdock, Gary Peterson, and Shauna Raso
- at Reell Precision Manufacturing in St. Paul, Minnesota: Bob Carlson, Jim Grubs, George Moroz, Joy Moroz, Bob Wahlstedt, and Steve Wikstrom
- at Rhythm & Hues Studio in Los Angeles: R. Scot Byrd and John Hughes
- at Righteous Babe Records and LFS Touring in Buffalo: Susan Alzner, Mary Begley, Ani DiFranco, Ron Ehmke, Scot Fisher, Sean Giblin, Brian Grunert, Karen Hayes, Phil Karatz, Heidi Kunkel, Sarah Otto, Jessie Schnell, Steve Schrems, and Susan Tanner
- at Selima Inc. in Miami Beach: Selima Stavola
- at The Goltz Group in Chicago: Jay Goltz, Luan Le, and Dale Zeimen
- at TriNet in San Leandro, California: Martin Babinec and Maureen Kleven
- at Union Square Hospitality Group in New York City: Haley Carroll, Jenny Zinman Dirksen, and Danny Meyer
- at W. L. Butler Construction Inc. in Redwood City, California: Michelle Arani, Bill Butler, and Frank York

They weren't alone, either. In the course of my research, I had the opportunity to interview many other great people who graciously shared their time and wisdom with me, including Jim Ansara of Shawmut Design & Construction in Boston; Chris Brown of Bull Moose Music in Portland, Maine; Ed Cardoni of Hallwalls in Buffalo; Robert Catlin of Signature Mortgage in Canton, Ohio; Gary Cristall of Gary Cristall Artist Management in Vancouver, British Columbia; Joe DiPasquale of Planet Love in Buffalo; Paul Eichen of Rokenbok Toy Company in Solana Beach, California; Don Esmond of the Buffalo News; Jim Fleming of Fleming & Associates in Ann Arbor, Michigan; Susan Frazier of Goldenrod Music in

Lansing, Michigan; Laurie Fuchs of Ladyslipper Music in Durham, North Carolina; Virginia Giordano of Giordano Productions in New York City; Danny Goldberg of Artemis Records in New York City; Neil Golding and Brian Silver of Keystone Auto Glass in Toledo, Ohio; Bruce Goode of Works Corp. in Boise, Idaho; Tom Gramegna of Bergen County Camera in Westwood, New Jersey; Darcy Greder of Illinois Wesleyan University in Bloomington, Illinois; Tracy Mann of MG Limited in New York City; Nion McEvoy and Susan Coyle of Chronicle Books in San Francisco; Debbie Mekker of ESP Inc. in Amherst, New York; Robert S. Moore of Solid Earth Geographics in Huntsville, Alabama; Michael Rosenberg of Koch Entertainment Distribution in Port Washington, New York; Jack Schuller of Festival Distribution in Vancouver, British Columbia; Marlin Shelley of Cirris Systems Corp. in Salt Lake City; Carl Singmaster of Manifest Discs and Tapes in Columbia, South Carolina; Barry Steinberg of Direct Tire in Watertown, Massachusetts; and Pat Thompson of Thorner Press in Buffalo.

I also benefited from the work of David Gumpert, who had done a fascinating interview with Fritz Maytag for the *Harvard Business Review,* and who alerted me to the interview that *Inc.*'s founder, Bernie Goldhirsh, had done with *Family Business Quarterly* a year before he died. Bruce Feiler wrote a terrific article in *Gourmet* about Union Square Hospitality Group that brought to life the experience of enlightened hospitality. Liz Conlin's article in *Inc.* about University National Bank & Trust was equally illuminating. Don Macaulay, the former publisher of Bernie's first magazine, *Sail,* helped fill in missing pieces in the early history of *Inc.* Jay Burchfield, chairman of Trust Company of the Ozarks in Springfield, Missouri, answered the questions I had about some of the more arcane aspects of the banking industry. Michael Ansara, Tom Ehrenfeld, Brian Feinblum, Steve Marriotti, David Obst, Derek Shearer, and David Laskin all offered encouragement, support, and good advice.

In addition, I am grateful to all of my colleagues at *Inc.*, who bore with me during the two years when I was researching and writing *Small Giants.* I am particularly indebted to Loren Feldman, who was my editor on articles about several of the companies in this book; to John Koten, who offered constant encouragement while making sure I didn't get lazy in my thinking about the small giants; to Brian Kennedy and Tara Mitchell, who applied their considerable talents to helping me get the word out; to Lora Kolodny, who cheered me on; to Blake Taylor, who gave me consistently excellent advice on matters of art and design; and to Travis Ruse, who made me look good. Of course, I will always be indebted to Bernie Goldhirsh, who founded the magazine, and to George Gendron, who first built it into a pillar of the entrepreneurial economy.

Once we got to the publishing phase of the book, I discovered how fortunate I was to be working with the great team at Penguin Portfolio, including Megan Casey, Elizabeth Hazelton, Stephanie Land, Joseph Perez, Nikil Saval, Will Weisser, and Abraham Young. I already knew how fortunate I was to be working with Adrian Zackheim.

Throughout the process, I would have been lost without the steady hand, sharp mind, and undying enthusiasm of Jill Kneerim. If all literary agents were like her, no author would ever feel underappreciated again. She was ably supported by other people at her agency, Kneerim & Williams at Fish & Richardson in Boston, including her assistant, Seana McInerney, and financial manager, Hope Denekamp.

I also owe a special thanks to Jay Groltz of The Goltz Group, who came up with the title of this book, *Small Giants*, and thereby gave us a name for the entire phenomenon.

Finally, I would be remiss if I didn't give full credit to the most important people in my life. I'm referring to Lisa, my wife of thirty-five years; my daughter, Kate, and her husband, Matt Knightly, one of the two entrepreneurs in the family; my son, Jake, and his wife, Maria Janeff Burlingham, the other entrepreneur; and their son, my grandson, Owen, a small giant if ever there was one. They make it both possible and meaningful for me to do what I do.

CONTENTS

INTRODUCTION

Consider this book a field report from the front lines of an emerging force in American business. Quietly and gradually—under the radar, as it were—a new class of great companies has been forming. These companies don't fit comfortably into any of the three categories we normally put businesses in: big, getting big, and small. Some are tiny; others are relatively large. Most are growing, often in unconventional ways, but several have chosen not to grow at all, and a few have made conscious decisions to scale back their operations.

Size and growth rate aside, the companies in this book do have certain characteristics in common. To begin with, they are all utterly determined to be the best at what they do. Most of them have been recognized for excellence by independent bodies inside and outside their industries. Not coincidentally, they have all had the opportunity to raise a lot of capital, grow very fast, do mergers and acquisitions, expand geographically, and generally follow the well-worn route of other successful companies. Yet they have chosen not to focus on revenue growth or geographical expansion, pursuing instead other goals that they consider more important than getting as big as possible, as fast as possible. To make those trade-offs, the companies have had to remain privately owned, with the majority of the stock in the hands of one person, or a small group of like-minded individuals, or—in a couple of cases—the employees.

That's probably why companies like these have not been identified heretofore as business phenomena in their own right. We tend not to spend much time looking at privately owned companies, especially small ones whose stock is closely held. To an extraordinary degree, our view of business—indeed, our whole concept of what business is—has been shaped by publicly owned companies, which actually make up a small percentage of the entire business population. Virtually every mass-market business best seller, from *Iacocca* to *In Search of Excellence* to *Good to Great*, has concentrated on the people in and the practices of large public companies, or companies that aspire to be large and public. So, too, are those companies the focus of most major business magazines and newspapers, not to mention the business shows on television and radio, or the curricula of business schools.

Along the way, we've come to accept as business axioms various ideas that, in fact, apply only to public companies. Consider, for example, the conventional wisdom that businesses must grow or die. That's no doubt true for most public companies. Steady increases in sales, profits, market share, and EBITDA (earnings before interest, taxes, depreciation, and amortization) are demanded and expected by a public company's investors, and decreases—or stagnation—send them running to the exits. But there are thousands of private companies that don't grow much, if at all; and they don't die either. On the contrary, they're often quite healthy.

Then there's the famous dictum of former General Electric CEO Jack Welch that he didn't want to own any business unless it was first or second in market share in its niche. Some observers have questioned whether GE under Welch actually practiced what he preached. The companies owned by GE Capital certainly didn't. Nevertheless, Welch's celebrity and the performance of GE stock during his tenure helped turn his stated policy into a business mantra, although it's hard to see how it makes any sense at all for the vast majority of companies that are neither large nor publicly owned.

And what about the concept of "getting to the next level"? Although people use the phrase in different ways and different contexts, it always has something to do with major increases in sales—surely no one thinks that "the next level" involves having fewer sales—and there's usually a management component as well. That is, you get to the next level when you can handle the demands of running a much bigger company. Because it's the *next* level, the phrase implies that bigger is better. That may or may not be true for public companies, but it's demonstrably untrue for a large number of private ones.

The greatest confusion, however, comes into play around the notion of shareholder value. For public companies, it has a very specific meaning, since they are legally and morally obligated to strive to produce the best possible financial results for their shareholders. That's the deal. If you take other people's money, you're supposed to give them what they want in exchange, and what buyers of publicly traded stocks want is a good return on their investments. The relationship seems so obvious, so logical that we generally assume all businesses must operate the same way. But that assumption ignores another equally obvious truth: What's in the interest of shareholders depends on who the shareholders are.

The shareholders who own the businesses in this book have other, nonfinancial priorities in addition to their financial objectives. Not that they don't want to earn a good return on their investment, but it's not their only goal, or even necessarily their paramount goal. They're also interested in being great at what they do, creating a great place to work, providing great service to customers, having great relationships with their suppliers, making great contributions to the communities they live and work in, and finding great ways to lead their lives. They've learned, moreover, that to excel in all those things, they have to keep ownership and control inside the company and, in many cases, place significant limits on how much and how fast they grow. The wealth they've created, though substantial, has been a byproduct of success in these other areas.

I call them small giants.

❋

So how were these companies identified, and how successful have they really been? The answer depends, in part, on the yardstick you use to measure success. When Jim Collins and his colleagues selected the companies they would include in *Good to Great*, they had very accurate and objective yardsticks, thanks to their decision to limit their inquiry to publicly traded companies. Collins was looking for companies that had gone through a transition allowing them to deliver extraordinary financial returns to shareholders after years of generating good, but not great, returns. All of the information he needed to identify those companies— as well as the companies he would compare them to—was a matter of public record.

When Collins and Jerry Porras did their research for *Built to Last*, they had a somewhat less objective, but nonetheless very credible, method of choosing the companies they would study. They polled the chief executives of *Fortune* 500 industrial companies, *Fortune* 500 service companies, *Inc.* 500 private companies, and *Inc.* 100 public companies, asking each CEO to nominate up to five companies that he or she considered "highly visionary." Not surprisingly, the eighteen companies they wound up with were all very well known, very large public companies that had been studied and written about extensively in the business media for decades.

Let me hasten to add that I do not mean to take anything away from either book. They are both classics, and deservedly so, filled with innumerable insights and lessons of immense value to people in companies of all sizes, public and private alike. But the methodologies used by Collins and his associates highlight the challenges facing anyone who chooses to focus exclusively on closely held private companies.

To begin with, there are no reliable financial yardsticks available. One of the benefits of being private is that you don't have to share your numbers with outsiders other than tax collectors, bankers, and any investors you may have. Many owners of private companies prefer to hold their financial cards as close to the vest as possible. Only a small minority produce audited financial statements, and an even smaller minority open those financials to the general public. In addition, private companies come in more corporate forms than public ones and have more flexibility in deciding what to do with their cash. Depending on the specific form they choose, moreover, they face different tax incentives. If you pay taxes at the corporate level, as C corporations do, you'll probably make spending decisions different from those you'd make if you had an S corporation or a partnership, whose owners pay taxes at the individual rate. As a result, it's extremely difficult, if not impossible, to come up with financial data that's comparable from one private company to another—even if you do have access to all the information you want.

Beyond the numbers, there's the matter of visibility. The vast majority of private companies are not in the public eye. Even those that strive for publicity are seldom well known outside a relatively small circle of people who happen to come into contact with them. A particular company may become more visible if it wins an award, reaches a noteworthy milestone, produces some important innovation, or advertises heavily; but very seldom does any private enterprise receive the scrutiny or achieve the fame of a 3M, an American Express, a Wal-Mart, a Walt Disney Company, a McDonald's, or any of the other large public companies whose names have become household words. And when a private company does get noticed, what attracts attention is almost always its product or its service, not the inner workings of the business. So conducting a poll to determine the most admired private companies would be a futile exercise: There are few, if any, well enough known for average observers to make informed judgments about them.

Which brings me to the companies in this book. In choosing them, I obviously couldn't rely on the methodologies used by Collins and his associates when they chose the businesses to study for their books. I had to come up with my own selection criteria, starting only with a concept and a bunch of questions. I knew what I was looking for: extraordinary, privately owned companies that were willing to forgo revenue or geographic growth, if necessary, in order to achieve other remarkable ends. By "extraordinary," I meant the company had a distinctive vision and mode of operation that clearly set it apart from others in its industry. I had run across a few such companies in my twenty-one years as an editor and writer at *Inc.* magazine, and I suspected that, if I looked hard enough, I could find others like them. But I had no idea how many there were, how difficult they would be to identify, where they would be located, which industries they would be in, or even what exactly they would have in common with one another that would distinguish them from other companies. I was going on intuition and gut instinct as much as rational analysis. I hoped that, as I went along, the people I spoke with would help me clarify what I was looking for.

I began by spreading my net as widely as possible. I asked everybody I knew to recommend companies. I searched the Internet. I looked in magazine and newspaper databases for profiles of businesses that might qualify. As the list of potential candidates grew, I did an initial screening to identify those that seemed most likely to fit my criteria. I then started interviewing with the goal of narrowing the list further and zeroing in on the qualities that made these companies unusual.

Inevitably, there was a subjective element in my decisions about which companies to include. In an attempt to minimize the subjectivity, I added some additional criteria as I went along.

1. I decided to restrict myself to companies started or owned by people who had actually been faced with a decision and made a choice. That is, they had had the opportunity to grow much faster, get much bigger, go public, or become part of a large corporation, and they'd made a conscious decision not to.

2. I decided to focus on companies that were admired and emulated in their own industries. I wanted companies that had the respect of those who might otherwise be their harshest critics, namely, their peers and their competitors.

3. I looked for companies that had been singled out for their extraordinary achievements by other independent observers. It's always nice to have third-party corroboration that a company is, in fact, worthy of special recognition.

Then there was the question of scale. "Big" and "small" are, of course, relative and highly subjective terms. To a person with a home-based business doing $200,000 a year in sales, a company with six employees and annual sales of $2 million is huge. The mainstream media, on the other hand, tend to view any business with less than $300 million in annual sales as small. (I recall an article in *BusinessWeek* that referred to a $104-million company I'd written about as "itty-bitty.") So I had to decide how to think about size. As I went along, I realized that, for my purposes, the relevant measure was not the amount of annual revenues, but rather the number of employees a company had. The companies I was looking for all operated on what you might call human scale, that is, a size at which it's still possible for an individual to be acquainted with everyone else in the organization, still possible for the CEO to meet with new hires, still possible for employees to feel closely connected to the rest of the company. That was not accidental, either. On the contrary, scale played an important role in their approach to business.

The scale criterion obviously eliminated some private companies right off the bat—those on *Forbes*'s annual list of the largest ones, for example, all of which have sales of more than $1 billion per year. But I wasn't sure about the maximum number of employees a company could have and still be considered human scale. I also had to think about whether or not some companies might be too small to be considered part of the phenomenon. In the end, I decided to include a couple of companies that tested the extremes and see what they could teach us.

Besides companies that were too big or too small, my criteria ruled out other types of enterprises that might otherwise have qualified—lifestyle businesses, for instance. By that, I mean companies whose primary purpose is to provide their owners with a comfortable lifestyle outside the business. Those companies can't grow beyond a certain size without undermining their reason for being, which doesn't leave much room for choice. I also passed on franchisees, whose vision comes from someone else, and franchisors, which have chosen to grow by other means. Boutique businesses that target an elite, high-end market of very picky customers didn't make the cut either. For those companies, staying small is central to their business strategy. They have a time-tested way of building a business, but it's not what I was looking for. I wanted companies that had defied the conventional wisdom and blazed their own path. Finally, I steered away from traditional mom-and-pop companies, that is, small businesses built around the goal of providing employment for members of a family. There are some great ones out there, but they aren't extraordinary in the way I mean.

Yet even with those restrictions, I soon began to realize there were many more companies fitting my criteria than I could possibly do justice to in one book. The longer I searched, the more I found. They were in every corner of the country and in almost every industry. (The exceptions were industries in which companies have to achieve certain economies of scale rapidly in order to compete effectively.) There were retailers, wholesalers, manufacturers, service companies, professional service firms, and artisanal businesses. Some of the companies had achieved a modicum of fame, usually because they had a well-known consumer product. Most were famous only to those they worked with or competed against.

Given the number of companies available to choose from, I had the luxury of selecting those that I thought would give the broadest and deepest sense of the phenomenon I wanted to write about. I looked partly for diversity in terms of size, age, location, and type of business; but I also searched for companies led by people who had taken greatest advantage of the freedom they'd been given as a result of their decision to remain private and closely held and to limit growth. That's the real payoff here. When you're hell bent on maximizing growth, or when you bring in a lot of outside capital, or when you take your company public, you have very little freedom. As the head of a public or venture-backed company, you're responsible to outside shareholders, whose interests you must always look out for. As the head of a very fast-growing company, you're a slave to the business, which has tremendous needs. Either way, you're constantly hiring, selling, training, negotiating, hand-holding, cajoling, mollifying, warning, pleading, coaxing, and on and on.

While the experience can be exhilarating, it leaves little time for anything else, least of all thinking about what you really want to do with your business and your life. People who choose to stay private and closely held and to place other goals ahead of growth get two things back in return: control and time. The combination equals freedom—or, more precisely, the opportunity for freedom. I wanted to include those who had made the most creative use of it.

I eventually settled on fourteen businesses, including the two that I felt represented the extremes of the phenomenon. The smallest, Selima Inc., is a two-person fashion design and dressmaking firm in Miami Beach that has been in business for almost sixty years. The largest is O. C. Tanner Co., a seventy-nine-year-old Salt Lake City company with about nineteen hundred employees and annual sales of $350 million that helps customers set up employee recognition programs and makes the service awards used in them. It also produced the gold, silver, and bronze medals for the 2002 Winter Olympics. The fourteen companies are:

- Anchor Brewing, in San Francisco, the original American microbrewery;
- CitiStorage Inc., in Brooklyn, New York, the premier independent records-storage business in the United States;
- Clif Bar Inc. in Berkeley, California, a leading maker of natural and organic energy bars and other nutrition foods;
- ECCO, in Boise, Idaho, the leading manufacturer of backup alarms and amber warning lights for commercial vehicles;
- Hammerhead Productions, in Studio City, California, a supplier of computer-generated special effects to the motion picture industry;
- O. C. Tanner Co., in Salt Lake City, Utah, the preeminent employee recognition and service awards, company;
- Reell Precision Manufacturing, in St. Paul, Minnesota, a designer and manufacturer of motion-control products, such as the hinges used on the covers of laptop computers;

- Rhythm & Hues Studios, in Los Angeles, a producer of computer-generated character animation and visual effects, winner of an Academy Award for *Babe*;
- Righteous Babe Records, in Buffalo, New York, the celebrated record company founded by singer-songwriter Ani DiFranco;
- Selima Inc., in Miami Beach, Florida, which does fashion design and dressmaking for a select clientele;
- The Goltz Group, in Chicago, Illinois, including Artists' Frame Service, probably the country's best-known independently owned framing business;
- Union Square Hospitality Group, in New York, New York, the restaurant company of renowned restaurateur Danny Meyer;
- W. L. Butler Construction, Inc., in Redwood City, California, a general contracting firm specializing in major commercial projects;
- Zingerman's Community of Businesses, in Ann Arbor, Michigan, including the world-famous Zingerman's Delicatessen and seven other food-related companies.

The youngest of the companies is Hammerhead Productions, founded in 1994; and the oldest is O. C. Tanner, founded in 1927. All of them have been around long enough to have experienced the ups and downs of business. Nevertheless, with one exception, all have been consistently profitable—in some cases, extremely profitable. The exception is Rhythm & Hues, whose lack of profitability is partly a result of conscious decisions the company has made about how to spend its cash. (I should note that a few strong candidates for the list declined to participate. Their owners made it clear that they wanted no publicity about their business operations at all.)

As for the leaders of the fourteen companies, they turned out to be a diverse group, with widely divergent backgrounds, personalities, and temperaments; and they'd traveled very different routes before ending up in very similar places. Jay Goltz of The Goltz Group was a natural-born entrepreneur who had been named a business whiz kid, or "biz kid," by *Forbes* magazine when he was still in his twenties, and he'd spent most of his adult years trying to live up to the billing—eagerly pursuing growth until he decided he didn't want that kind of life anymore. Singer-songwriter Ani DiFranco was wooed by numerous major record labels, which saw her star potential early on, but she turned them down and built Righteous Babe instead because she did not want to be part of a giant corporation. Jim Thompson was an erstwhile accountant at Boise Cascade who bought ECCO because it seemed like a nice little manufacturing business with lots of potential—and then suffered two heart attacks that forced him to decide what to do with it. Bill Butler was living in a California commune when he started his construction company, W. L. Butler; and it was in business eighteen years before it had a listed telephone number. Dan Chuba and his three partners all came from large special effects companies and started Hammerhead Productions with the express purpose of keeping it small enough to give them time to pursue other projects on their own. John Hughes and his founding partners came out of one of Hollywood's original motion graphics companies, Robert Abel and Associates, and started Rhythm & Hues with the goal of creating "an environment where people enjoy working and where people are treated fairly, honestly, and with respect." Selima Stavola, an Iraqi Jew, grew up in Baghdad, emigrated to New York with her GI husband after World War II, started designing clothing to help support the family, and found herself being courted by fashion industry executives and investors who saw in her another Christian Dior or Coco Chanel. Norm Brodsky of CitiStorage watched his first company's annual sales go from nothing to $120 million in eight years—and then from $120 million to almost nothing in eight months, as it slid into Chapter 11 and forced him to question how and why he'd become so addicted to fast growth in the first place. Dale Merrick, Bob Wahlstedt, and Lee Johnson, all 3M refugees, launched Reell Precision Manufacturing with the goal of building a business that would promote harmony between their work lives and their family lives—and wound up creating one of the most democratically run companies in the world.

Yet for all the differences in background, the founders and owners of these companies also have similarities, including clarity about and confidence in their decision to put other goals ahead of revenue or geographical growth. "I've made much more money by choosing the right things to say no to than by choosing things to say yes to," said restaurateur Danny Meyer of Union Square Hospitality Group, and he could have been speaking for others. "I measure it by the money I haven't lost and the quality I haven't sacrificed."

As noted above, I went into this project hoping the people I interviewed would help me figure out what it was that set the kind of company I was looking for apart from the crowd. They did, up to a point. It was obvious their companies had something special that many other businesses lacked, and they knew it. So, for that matter, did other people who came in contact with them. Norm Brodsky of CitiStorage told me about a visit he'd received from Richard Reese, chairman and CEO of Iron Mountain, the largest records-storage company in the country with annual revenues of more than $2 billion. Reese had heard Brodsky give a speech at an industry conference and complimented him on it. Brodsky had invited him to come see the company for himself. He had readily accepted.

On the appointed day, Reese arrived at the CitiStorage offices on the Brooklyn side of the East River. For the next four or five hours, Brodsky showed him around the facility and introduced him to the people who worked there. As it happened, Brodsky's wife, Elaine, was teaching a customer-service class to employees that day. She is vice president of human resources and plays a major role in the business. Brodsky asked Reese if he'd like to watch the beginning of the class. The employees were acting out various customer-service situations, and Reese sat watching them, enthralled, until Brodsky indicated they should move on.

At the end of the day, as Reese was getting ready to leave, he said, "This is a great company you have here. I wish we could do these things."

"What do you mean?" Brodsky said.

"I mean the way you run this company," Reese said. "It's great. Walking around here and talking to your people, I get a feeling from them that I'd like to take back into my company, but I know we can never do that."

"I don't understand," Brodsky said. "Why can't you do it?"

"It's just hard to do when you get big," said Reese. "Maybe you could go around my company and duplicate the feeling, but I'm not sure it's possible." Brodsky took that as a high compliment, which he passed along to his staff.

I had the same reaction to all the companies on my list that Reese had to CitiStorage. There was a quality they exuded that was real and recognizable but also frustratingly difficult to define. I could sense it as I walked around the business. I could see it in the contents of the bulletin boards and on the faces of the people. I could hear it in their voices. I could feel it in the way they interacted with one another, with customers, and with total strangers. But I found the "it" awfully hard to put my finger on.

I was reminded of the feeling I'd had in the past when I'd come into contact with hot companies just as they were hitting their stride—Apple Computer, Fidelity Investments, People Express Airlines, Ben & Jerry's, Patagonia, The Body Shop, even *Inc.* magazine. They had a buzz. There was excitement, anticipation, a feeling of movement, a sense of purpose and direction, of going somewhere. That happens, I think, when people find themselves totally in sync with their market, with the world around them, and with each other. Everything just seems to click. Most of the companies I knew had eventually lost that quality. Somehow the companies I was looking at now had managed to retain it.

But what was "it"? Danny Meyer of Union Square Hospitality Group talked about businesses having soul. He believed soul was what made a business great, or even worth doing at all. "A business without soul is not something I'm interested in working at," he said. He suggested that the soul of a business grew out of the relationships a company developed as it went along. "Soul can't exist unless you have active, meaningful dialogue with stakeholders: employees, customers, the community, suppliers, and investors. When you launch a business, your job as the entrepreneur is to say, 'Here's a value proposition that I believe in. Here's where I'm coming from. This is my point of view.' At first, it's a monologue. Gradually it becomes a dialogue and then a real conversation. Like breaking in a baseball glove. You can't will a baseball glove to be broken in; you have to use it. Well, you have to use a new business, too. You have to break it in. If you move on to the next thing too quickly, it will never develop its soul. Look what happens when a new restaurant opens. Everyone rushes in to see it, and it's invariably awkward because it hasn't yet developed soul. That takes time to emerge, and you have to work at it constantly."

The concept of soul helped explain the process, but it was Gary Erickson of Clif Bar who I felt came closest to identifying the quality itself. He had begun thinking about it at a critical moment in the company's history, when he was struggling to figure out what kind of company he wanted Clif Bar to be. At a trade show in the fall of 2000, he had met a well-known marketer of consumer products who had complimented him on the buzz around Clif Bar's booth, pointing to a competitor's booth that was dead by comparison. "They lost their mojo," the guy had said.

The comment had stayed with Erickson following the trade show. Whatever mojo was, some smart people evidently thought that it was important, and that Clif Bar had it. In any case, it was something he needed to pay attention to. From then on, "mojo" became his watchword, and I could understand why. Having once had the honor of introducing the legendary blues man Muddy Waters at a concert—"I got my mojo working but it just won't work on you"—I thought the word seemed just right for the mysterious quality I'd seen in Clif Bar, CitiStorage, Union Square Hospitality, and the other companies I'd looked at.

It was a quality that you could apparently lose by negligence. In his wonderfully engaging book, *Raising the Bar*, Erickson said he thought Clif Bar's mojo was "something about the brand, product, and way of being in the world that was different. I realized that mojo was an elusive quality and needed to be tended carefully." Hoping to sharpen his thinking, he'd given people at Clif Bar a homework assignment. After relating what had happened at the trade show, he had asked each of them to choose a company that had once had mojo and lost it, and then explain why they felt the company had had it and how they believed it had been lost. The assignment had evidently struck a chord with the employees, who turned in dozens of thoughtful responses. They wrote about companies losing their creativity as they grew. About losing the emotional connection with the consumer. About losing authenticity and compromising quality. About becoming "too commercial" and focusing excessively on reducing costs. About ignoring the relationship with the community and failing to retain the culture. About getting too big too fast.

Erickson followed up with other homework assignments, to which employees responded with equal enthusiasm. In particular, he asked them to write down whether they thought Clif Bar had mojo, and why, and how it might be strengthened or squandered. Eventually he collected all the responses in bound notebooks that were prominently displayed in the office. Reading through them, it was clear that

(1) most people thought they knew intuitively what mojo was;
(2) they had a wide variety of ideas about where it came from;
(3) they tended to define mojo in terms of its effects, rather than its causes—or, as one employee put it, "To me mojo means, 'You got that engine running baby and the sky is the limit!'"

So I was almost—but not quite—back where I had started: At least I had a name I could attach to the phenomenon. The question was, what did companies do to generate mojo? Perhaps it was a combination of factors. One way to narrow the possibilities, I decided, was to look at the common threads among the companies I'd already identified as having mojo.

First, I could see that, unlike most entrepreneurs, their founders and leaders had recognized the full range of choices they had about the type of company they could create. They hadn't accepted the standard menu of options as a given. They had allowed themselves to question the usual definitions of success in business and to imagine possibilities other than the ones all of us are familiar with.

Second, the leaders had overcome the enormous pressures on successful companies to take paths they had not chosen and did not necessarily want to follow. The people in charge had remained in control, or had regained control, by doing a lot of soul searching, rejecting a lot of well-intentioned advice, charting their own course, and building the kind of business they wanted to live in, rather than accommodating themselves to a business shaped by outside forces.

Third, each company had an extraordinarily intimate relationship with the local city, town, or county in which it did business—a relationship that went well beyond the usual concept of "giving back." That was part of it, to be sure, and all of these companies were model corporate citizens, but the relationship was very much a two-way street. The community helped mold the character of the business, just as the companies played an important role in the life of the community.

Fourth, they cultivated exceptionally intimate relationships with customers and suppliers, based on personal contact, one-on-one interaction, and mutual commitment to delivering on promises. The leaders themselves took the lead in this regard. They were highly accessible and absolutely committed to retaining the human dimension of the relationships. Customers responded by sending fan mail. Suppliers responded by providing extraordinary service of their own. The effect was to create a sense of community and common purpose between the companies, their suppliers, and their customers—the kind of intimacy that is difficult for large companies to achieve, if only because of their size.

Fifth, the companies also had what struck me as unusually intimate workplaces. They were, in effect, functional little societies that strove to address a broad range of their employees' needs as human beings—creative, emotional, spiritual, and social needs as well as economic ones. Southwest Airlines' Herb Kelleher once observed that his company's famously vibrant culture was built around the principle of "caring for people in the totality of their lives." That's what the companies I was looking at were doing. They were places where employees felt cared for in the totality of their lives, where they were treated in the way that the founders and leaders thought people ought to be treated—with respect, dignity, integrity, fairness, kindness, and generosity. In that sense, the companies seemed to represent the ultimate expression of a business as a social institution.

Sixth, I was impressed by the variety of corporate structures and modes of governance that these companies had come up with. Because they were private and closely held, they had the freedom to develop their own management systems and practices, and several had done so. Zingerman's had created its Community of Businesses, including its own training company, ZingTrain, which taught the Zingerman's way of doing business. Hammerhead Productions had invented an accordion structure, expanding with each new project, contracting when it was finished. Reell Precision Manufacturing had the closest thing to a corporate democracy I had ever seen, complete with two CEOs—and, strangely enough, it worked. Several of the other companies had turned themselves into educational institutions, teaching their employees about finance, service, leadership, and everything else involved in building a successful company.

Finally, I noticed the passion that the leaders brought to what the company did. They loved the subject matter, whether it be music, safety lighting, food, special effects, constant torque hinges, beer, records storage, construction, dining, or fashion. Though they were consummate businesspeople, they were anything but professional managers. Indeed, they were the opposite of professional managers. They had deep emotional attachments to the business, to the people who worked in it, and to its customers and suppliers—the sort of feelings that are the bane of professional management.

This book is organized around those observations. We'll first examine the choice that these companies' founders and owners have made, how they made it, and how they've dealt with the forces pushing them to go in another direction. Then we'll move on to the characteristics these companies share, three of which involve creating a level of intimacy—

with the community, with customers and suppliers, and with employees—that is difficult, if not impossible, to achieve when a business grows too fast, gets too big, or spreads out too much geographically. We'll also look at some of the corporate structures and practices these companies use to achieve their goals. The penultimate chapter focuses on the issue of succession and its twin, sustainability: Can these companies last beyond one generation and, if so, how? In the final chapter, we'll consider how the founders, leaders, and owners of these companies approach business and what that says about the possibilities of business in general.

The first step, however, is the most important. It's the one that Fritz Maytag of Anchor Brewing took back in 1992 when he suddenly recognized what nobody had told him. His company didn't have to keep growing ever bigger and more impersonal. He had a choice.

1

※

Free to Choose

At the Anchor Brewery on Mariposa Street in San Francisco, the air was thick with the sweet aroma of fermenting beer and the buzz of a tour group sampling the finished product in the oak-paneled taproom, but Fritz Maytag was oblivious to it all as he stood in his cluttered office, thumbing through a small, turquoise hardback book that had just arrived in the mail. There was a look of utter joy on his face. Dressed in a light blue shirt and dark blue vest, khaki pants, and scuffed brown shoes, his glasses pushed back on his forehead, he had the aura of a prospector who had just struck gold. The book, he explained, was the latest edition of the Lakeside Classics, a series of first-person narratives of American history—primarily pioneer Western history—that the printer R. R. Donnelley put out once a year at Christmas, "to show the trade what can be done without much money." Maytag had collected all of them back to 1912. He noted that the color of the cover changed every twenty years. "When you see eighty of them on a shelf, one color and then another—oh, killer," he said. "It just knocks me dead."

Maytag may be the great-grandson of the giant appliance company's founder, but he has an unabashed fondness for small, beautiful things, in business as elsewhere. At sixty-five, he could look back on forty years as the owner and CEO of the premier microbrewery in the country and forty-three years as a partner in the famous gourmet cheese company that bore his family name. While he was obviously pleased with both businesses, he admitted there were moments when the future of the brewery, at least, was very much in doubt. In the early 1990s, it had reached a crossroads, and Maytag had been forced to make a choice—the same choice that all successful entrepreneurs are faced with sooner or later, although most don't realize that there even is a choice until it's too late. To his great relief, Maytag had recognized his choice in time and made the one that was right for him. But it had been a close call.

The issue arose in the early 1990s, at what many people would have considered the pinnacle of business success. For some twenty-seven years, Maytag had owned and run Anchor Brewing, a company that traced its ancestry back more than a century to California's Gold Rush days. It had been on the verge of extinction when he had taken the helm, hoping to save the company and its sole product, Anchor Steam Beer. He'd succeeded spectacularly on both counts. In the process, he had launched a revolution in beer making. His were the first nationally recognized microbrews: high-quality, handcrafted beers and ales, made with the finest ingredients available, using traditional recipes and brewing techniques.

But success had turned out to be a mixed blessing. Anchor Steam Beer and the brews that followed—Anchor Porter, Liberty Ale, Old Foghorn, and Christmas Ale—had become so popular by the mid-1970s that Maytag couldn't come close to meeting the demand. From six hundred barrels in 1965 when he came in, production had soared to twelve thousand barrels in 1973, maxing out the brewery's capacity just as its fame was beginning to spread.

Maytag recalled the next few years as pure agony. With customers beating down his wholesalers' doors, he'd had to start rationing beer. Everyone had pleaded with him for more product. The best he could do was to promise that he would allocate his supply as fairly as possible, which hardly satisfied the distributors, restaurant owners, and beer retailers who had to go without. The low point had come on a day that most companies would have celebrated. Anchor's Nevada distributor had called to say he'd been contacted by the general manager of the new MGM Grand Casino in Reno, whose CEO turned out to be a big fan of Anchor Steam and wanted to serve it on tap in every bar in the house. It was an enormous order, and it would have to keep being refilled for an indefinite period of time. "What did you tell him?" Maytag asked.

"Are you crazy?" said the distributor. "I told him yes, of course."

"Well, the answer is no," Maytag said.

"You can't do that to me," said the distributor.

"I'm sorry, but I told you no new draft accounts," said Maytag. "What do you expect me to do? Short everyone else?"

"Well, I'm not going to tell him," said the distributor. "You'll have to come and tell him yourself."

Maytag had had to fly to Reno and explain in person why Anchor couldn't accept the order. The general manager was not happy. Then again neither was Maytag.

To be sure, there had been alternatives. For one thing, Maytag could have hired an out-of-town brewery to do additional brewing for him. That's how many other microbrewers later got started, but he never even considered the possibility. It would have meant sacrificing something so fundamental as to have violated his entire purpose for getting into the business to begin with—namely, the authenticity of the products. Instead he had sweated it out, torn between the urgent pleas of his customers and his own insistence on selling only the highest quality beer he could make.

Maytag never forgot the experience, and, after Anchor Brewing finally moved into its new building in 1979, he had vowed not to let it happen again. There would be no more rationing while he was around. For the next twelve years or so, he hadn't had any trouble living up to that commitment. Meanwhile, the demand for Anchor Brewing's various beers and ales continued to grow, spurred on by the great American food renaissance of the 1980s. By the end of the decade, it began to dawn on Maytag that, like it or not, another capacity crisis might lie ahead. As a precaution, he bought land across the street, thinking he might put up a building there for storage and packaging, creating more room in the brewery for beer making. Then, in 1992, he started looking into the possibility of doing an initial public offering to raise the capital he would need to finance such an expansion.

His idea was to do a so-called direct public offering, wherein a company sells its stock directly to the public, rather than going through an underwriter. A local man named Drew Field had done a few such deals and written a book on the subject. Field was highly critical of the atmosphere around IPOs—the money wasted on dog-and-pony shows, the practice of flipping stocks, the inside deals—not to mention the end result: a company winding up with a bunch of strangers as shareholders. He thought business owners could save themselves time, money, and grief by going the direct offering route.

And Maytag liked the concept. It looked like his salvation. He figured the brewery could handle another 10 to 15 percent in sales before it ran out of capacity. As long as he expanded by then, he could avoid the problems he'd experienced in the 1970s. Besides, the company would eventually have to move up to the next level anyway. It was the natural order of things. Every business has to grow or die, right? So he thought he might as well expand sooner rather than later. To finance the expansion, he would need outside capital. The direct public offering sounded to him like the best way to get it.

Still, something about the plan bothered him, and as he talked to his employees, he began to have second thoughts. Maytag and his three top people spent hours trying to figure out the implications of going public. What would the new investors expect? How would their demands change the business? Why are we in business anyway? What do we enjoy doing? What are our goals in life? They considered the various possible outcomes and realized they all had reservations. They weren't sure they wanted the company to get much bigger. They loved it as it was. They had no particular desire to "take it to the moon," as Maytag put it. If it got too big, moreover, they might have to give up the parts of it they valued most.

"I realized we were doing the IPO out of desperation—because we thought we had to grow," Maytag recalled. "It occurred to me that you could have a small, prestigious, profitable business, and it would be all right. Like a restaurant. Just because it's the best around doesn't mean you have to franchise or even expand. You can stay as you are and have a business that's profitable and rewarding and a source of great pride. So we made a decision not to grow. I was still very nervous about the prospect of having to ration again, but I decided we'd just face it if we had to. This was not going to be a giant company—not on my watch."

He never regretted the decision. Of course, it helped that the capacity crisis didn't materialize. By the early 1990s, the revolution Anchor Brewing had ignited was sweeping the country, and scores of other microbreweries were springing up to meet the demand. Although Maytag sometimes chafed at competitors' tactics, overall he viewed the increased competition with relief. Rather than resist them, he helped fledgling rivals develop their brewing skills. Their presence in the market left him free to build a company that he enjoyed and was proud of, that would give him the sense of accomplishment and fulfillment he sought, and that would allow him to lead the kind of life he wanted.

And, after all, isn't that the purpose of going into business in the first place?

The companies in this book have a message for every person who sets out to build a business, and it's an important one: If the business survives, you will sooner or later have a choice about how far and how fast to grow. No one is going to warn you about it, or prepare you for it, or tell you when the moment arrives. Chances are, your banker, your lawyer, your accountant, or whomever else you turn to for business advice will be encouraging you to grow as fast and as far as you can. The bigger your company becomes, the better their advice looks, and the more business you're going to do with them in the future.

The outside world will be sending you similar signals. We all want to be successful, after all, and our visions of success are inevitably shaped to a large extent by examples in the media, by the spirit of the times, and by the common wisdom about what's possible. If you constantly hear about the need to grow or die, if everybody seems to be trying to get to the next level, if the only companies being celebrated—or even taken seriously—are the biggest, or the fastest-growing, you may never even think to ask about options other than growing your business as much as you can and as quickly as you can.

Nor can you necessarily count on your friends and family—those who really do have your best interests at heart—to point out that you might find more happiness by choosing another path. They're probably not aware of any alternative. Like most people, they assume that getting big is the whole idea. Then if things don't go the way they want, if they don't like what the company is doing to you—or to them—they'll blame the business rather than your choice about what to do with it. For that matter, you, too, will probably blame the business—or your competitors, or the economy, or your employees, or the government, or whatever—if you get in trouble later on; and you may not be completely wrong.

But you won't be completely right either. As the companies in this book demonstrate, there is a choice; and the payoff for choosing the less-traveled path can be huge. It can affect every aspect of your business—from your relationships with the people you work with to the control you have over your time and your destiny, to the impact you have on the world around you, and to the satisfaction and fulfillment you get out of your professional life.

Unfortunately, many people have to pass through a major crisis to recognize the choice they have. Some don't see it until they've already gotten themselves and their companies into serious trouble. Others have to arrive at a critical crossroads—for example, the moment at which their company is about to be sold. That's an event we tend to view as a normal, if sometimes difficult, transition in the life of a business, the culmination of the process of creating shareholder value, at least in the traditional sense. It's only when the ownership changes hands that you get the reward for all the hard work you've done building something that someone else wants to buy. So, for most entrepreneurs, it's a foregone conclusion that their businesses will eventually be sold, if not by them, then by their heirs. Indeed, they think that if the right deal comes along, you're *supposed* to cash out by going public or getting acquired, in the process turning the business over to other people who—you hope—will take good care of it and "get it to the next level."

But some people manage to pull back at the last minute. They have a moment of revelation—often right as they're about to make an irrevocable decision—when they suddenly see they have another option. For Fritz Maytag, that moment came as he was getting ready to take Anchor Brewing public. For Gary Erickson, the moment arrived as he was preparing to sell his $39-million-a-year company, Clif Bar, for $120 million.

It was an April morning in the year 2000, and the deal was all but done. The papers were ready to be signed. The buyer's representatives were waiting. Although Erickson will say only that the acquirer was a midwestern food conglomerate, other sources have identified it as Quaker Oats. In any case, he knew he should have been thrilled. He was getting a fantastic price, and his 50-percent share would set him up for life. Just eight years before, he had been a more or less destitute long-distance cyclist, rock climber, and musician. He'd developed the recipe for his energy bar in his mother's kitchen and named both the product and the company after his father. Now here he was, about to walk away with $60 million. What more could a man ask for! And yet as he stood with his partner, Lisa Thomas, in the company's offices in Berkeley, California, he felt miserable. His hands began to shake, and he had trouble breathing. Realizing he was having a panic attack, he excused himself and went outside for a walk.

Up to that point, Erickson had been convinced that he had no real choice but to sell. His two largest competitors—Power Bar and Balance Bar—had recently been sold to Nestlé and Kraft, respectively. He and Thomas, who was the CEO, were terrified of competing head-to-head against multibillion-dollar conglomerates that had the financial resources to wipe them out overnight. They believed that, by selling to another giant company, they could protect Clif Bar and its employees, since they themselves would remain in control. They believed it, that is, until the buyer informed them toward the end of the contract negotiations that, within a few months, Clif Bar would be moved to the Midwest and placed under new management.

As Erickson walked around the block on that spring morning, he began to weep. He was overcome with remorse for what he was about to do. Then, all at once, a thought popped into his head. The deal wasn't done yet. Nothing had been signed. He could still back out. His gloom lifted immediately. He returned to the office and informed Thomas that he couldn't go through with the sale. She should send the buyers, the bankers, and the lawyers home.

At the time, it looked like either a wonderfully gutsy or an extremely foolhardy move, depending on your viewpoint. Not only was Erickson turning his back on a fortune, but he was proposing that Clif Bar remain independent and continue to operate as a relatively small private company in a marketplace filled with huge conglomerates out to get it. The investment bankers assured him that the company would be crushed in short order. So did the venture capitalists he spoke to. His partner agreed, and the risk of losing everything she'd worked for frightened her. Shortly thereafter, she resigned from the company and insisted that Erickson cash her out. (She could insist because, as a 50-percent owner, she could have shut the company down if her demands weren't met. A less-than-50-percent owner does not have as much leverage.) They eventually settled on a deal whereby he would pay her $65 million over five years. He had $10,000 in his bank account at the time.

Erickson, who took over as CEO, had to begin by rethinking the business and rebuilding its culture, which had been decimated in the buildup to the sale. "Morale was at an all-time low and dysfunction at an all-time high," he recalled, sitting in his Berkeley office. "I had to answer for myself, 'Why am I keeping this company? Why are we in business?' I decided that our reason for being here was to prove you can have a healthy, sustainable company that grows by natural demand and that is profitable."

Somehow he and the people in his company pulled it off. Despite crushing debt, Clif Bar survived. More than survived, it prospered. Over the next five years, the company more than doubled its sales, from $39 million in 1999 (the last full year before the aborted sale) to $92 million in 2004, and it did so without taking on any outside investors or even greatly expanding its workforce.

Given the circumstances, the choices made by Erickson and Maytag were particularly dramatic, but you don't have to be on the verge of going public or getting acquired to find yourself confronted by the same decision that they had to make. You simply have to be successful.

Consider Ari Weinzweig and Paul Saginaw, cofounders of Zingerman's Deli in Ann Arbor, Michigan. They'd launched the store in 1982 with the intention of having it carry the finest artisanal food products and serve the best sandwiches known to man. "We wanted sandwiches so big you needed two hands to hold them and the dressing would roll down your forearms," said Saginaw. "We wanted people to say about other sandwiches, 'This is a great sandwich, but it's not a Zingerman's.'"

Within a decade, they'd accomplished all that and more. Articles extolling the deli's food had appeared in *The New York Times*, *Bon Appétit*, *Eating Well*, and other publications. "In Zingerman's," novelist Jim Harrison raved in *Esquire*, "I get the mighty reassurance that the world can't be totally bad if there's this much good food to eat, the same flowing emotions I get at Fauchon in Paris, Harrod's food department in London, Balducci's or Dean & DeLuca in New York, only at Zingerman's there is a goodwill lacking in the others."

Yet despite their success—or rather, I should say, because of it—the partners soon came face-to-face with the realization that they had a choice to make. Weinzweig can pinpoint the exact moment it reared its head. It was a sultry summer day in 1992, and the lunchtime rush was in full swing. In addition to the usual headaches involved in feeding the hungry multitudes, a cooler had broken down. Weinzweig was racing around, trying to deal with the problems, when Saginaw came hurrying in. "Ari, we got to talk," he said.

"Okay, Paul, but not now," Weinzweig said. "I've got too much going on here."

"No, it's important," Saginaw insisted. "We've got to talk right now. Let's go outside."

Weinzweig reluctantly followed Saginaw out the side door and sat down next to him on a bench. "Okay, what is it?" he asked.

"Ari," Saginaw said, "where are we going to be in ten years?"

"I couldn't believe it," Weinzweig recalled many years later. "I sat there thinking, *I don't have time for this. The cooler is broken. The kitchen staff is stretched thin, and he hauls me out to talk about ten years from now?* But I had to admit, it was a real good question."

It was also the start of a two-year debate that tested the limits of their partnership. Saginaw felt strongly that success had led the company to grow smug and complacent, leaving it vulnerable to competitors who could copy Zingerman's merchandising and chip away at its customer base. The partners had recently settled a lawsuit against one such copycat, and the experience had convinced Saginaw that legal protections were a poor substitute for innovation. The business needed to be shaken up. It needed to build higher barriers to competitors by expanding, improving, and trying different things. In short, Zingerman's needed a new vision for growth, and Saginaw thought that all options should be on the table, including the possibility of opening Zingerman's clones in other cities. That was the most logical way to grow a retail food business. A lot of people had already suggested it and offered to get involved. "We might be stupid not to do it," Saginaw told Weinzweig.

There was just one problem: Weinzweig was dead set against it. "I didn't want to spend my time flying to Kansas City to see some mediocre Zingerman's," he explained. "For me, it was important to be part of something great and unique. You lose the uniqueness when you try to replicate the original. I said to Paul, 'I can't say you're wrong from a business standpoint. If that's what you want, maybe you should do it, but it's not something I want to be associated with. I'll leave.'"

"You have to understand," said Saginaw, "Ari is a guy who studies the history of orange marmalade. He has an emotional attachment to the product. He was afraid the coleslaw would be bad, and his name would be on the door. I said, 'Your name isn't on the door, and I don't care about the coleslaw. We can throw it out. But if you care so much about it, fine. We'll find another way.'"

That other way, however, proved frustratingly elusive. Saginaw and Weinzweig had no interest in pursuing acquisitions or moving to another location, and they knew of no alternative growth strategies for small companies like theirs. So they did a lot of reading, thinking, and talking—meeting regularly to discuss their ideas at a picnic table next to the deli. They wrote vision statements and then rewrote them, soliciting input from people inside and outside the business. By 1994, the outlines of a grand design had emerged.

It was called the Zingerman's Community of Businesses, or ZCoB, for short. Weinzweig and Saginaw envisioned a company comprised of twelve to fifteen separate businesses by 2009. The new businesses would be small and located in the Ann Arbor area. Each would bear the Zingerman's name but would have its own specialty and identity, and all would be designed to enhance the quality of food and service offered to Zingerman's customers while improving the financial performance of ZCoB and its components. There was already a bakery, Zingerman's Bakehouse, as well as the deli. There could also be a training company, a mail order business, a caterer, a creamery, a restaurant or two, a vegetable stand—you name it.

The strategy—if it worked—would allow Zingerman's to avoid the stagnation and atrophy that can beset any company after several years no matter how successful it has been. Weinzweig and Saginaw would be able to grow the business, and to do it in a way that would let them preserve the attributes that had led them to start the company in the first place—close contact with a community, intimacy with customers, team spirit among employees, exceptional quality of food and service. However much Zingerman's grew in the next fifteen years, it would remain a local operation—a collection of small local businesses, each striving to be the best at what they do.

And the strategy did work. Not only did it reinvigorate the company it also reenergized the founders themselves. In 2002, midway through the implementation process, with seven of the businesses up and running,

Weinzweig could say, "We've been in business for twenty years, and I look forward to coming to work even more now than I did in the beginning. I'm having more fun, and I'm more at peace with the realities of life. Success means you're going to have better problems. I'm very happy with the problems I have now."

Not all the entrepreneurs in our sample have been as fortunate as Weinzweig, Saginaw, Maytag, and Erickson. A few required more convincing, especially those who were in the throes of what Norm Brodsky, the founder and CEO of CitiStorage, calls Groundhog Day syndrome. During more than twenty-five years in business, he has noticed how often people fall into certain patterns of behavior that lead them to make the same mistakes over and over, more or less like the lead character in the movie *Groundhog Day*. Brodsky is familiar with the phenomenon not only because he has observed it in other people but also because he had to cure himself of his own Groundhog Day tendencies before he could begin building the kind of business that would give him what he really wanted in life.

He had started his first company, a messenger business, in 1979. It was based in Manhattan, probably the most competitive market in the world for an industry with virtually no barriers to entry. Literally hundreds of messenger companies competed on price for the same customers. Nevertheless, Brodsky managed to carve out a profitable niche for himself, thanks mainly to a customer at an advertising agency who told him she would hire any messenger service that could produce an invoice showing which of the agency's clients should be charged back for each delivery. That sounds like a simple enough request today, but back then most small businesses were still using typewriters and keeping records by hand. Brodsky's competitors said it was impossible to produce such an invoice. He knew better. He'd been one of the first in his industry to buy a computer. With it, he was able to develop the software required, and his sales skyrocketed, landing his company, Perfect Courier, on the *Inc.* 500 list of fastest-growing private companies for three straight years.

Those were the go-go 1980s, the era of junk bonds, corporate raids, hostile takeovers, and the Predators' Ball, and Brodsky wanted to play with the high rollers, which meant going public, ramping up sales, and establishing branches all over the country. His ambition became focused on a single number. "If you'd asked me what I wanted back then, I'd have told you right away, a $100-million company," he recalled. "I couldn't have told you why I wanted it. I never thought about the why. It was just my goal. I was determined to have a $100-million company, and I was willing to do almost anything to get it."

In 1986, Brodsky acquired one of Perfect Courier's competitors that was already publicly traded and merged the two businesses. Under its new corporate name, CitiPostal, the company became one of the fastest-growing public companies in America, but—at $45 million a year in sales—it was still well short of Brodsky's target. Then a friend of his told him that an even larger competitor called Sky Courier, with $75 million a year in sales, was on the block. Although it had some significant problems, Brodsky realized he could buy it and reach his goal in one fell swoop.

He couldn't resist. Against the advice of almost everybody he spoke to, he went ahead and bought Sky Courier—and set in motion a disastrous chain of events. The company turned out to have much worse problems than he'd realized. Brodsky pumped in $5 million from the Perfect Courier branch of CitiPostal, but it wasn't enough. So he put up another $2 million and pledged several million dollars of Perfect Courier's credit to keep Sky Courier alive, thereby tying their fates inextricably together. Not once did he consider cutting his losses by selling or shutting down his latest acquisition. He'd been in tough situations before. He was sure he could handle whatever came along.

"What I didn't take into account was the inevitability of unpredictable events," he said. First there was the stock market crash of October 1987, which took a heavy toll on the financial printers who formed the core of Sky Courier's customer base. Its sales dropped 50 percent almost overnight. Perfect Courier, meanwhile, was getting hit hard by the sudden popularity of fax machines. As more and more people began faxing documents instead of sending them by messenger, the company lost 40 percent of its sales in a few months.

The combination of blows was simply too much. In September 1988, the various entities that made up CitiPostal all filed for protection from creditors under Chapter 11 of the U.S. Bankruptcy Code. When the company finally emerged in 1991, just fifty of its three thousand employees remained, and sales were less than $2.5 million. "Believe me, that's culture shock," said Brodsky. "It took a few years before my head cleared enough for me to figure out what had really happened, and why, and how I could keep it from ever happening again."

Among other things, the experience forced him to think about why he was in business in the first place, what he was really looking for; and it made him aware of the tremendous responsibility he had for his employees. "Before we got in trouble, it was all about getting more sales and building a bigger company," he said. "I didn't think about the effect of my decisions on other people. I was in denial about that right up to the day we filed for bankruptcy.

"Understand, when you're in the middle of a financial crisis, you're surrounded by chaos. Everybody is calling you wanting to know when they're getting paid. Your only concern is keeping your company afloat. When your lawyer says, 'Maybe we should look at Chapter 11,' you say, 'Hell, no. That is not an option. Don't bring it up again.' You simply don't accept that you can't turn things around. So you plunge ahead and get swallowed up in the day-to-day minutiae and sink deeper and deeper. You need to collect your receivables quicker, so you ratchet up the pressure on your customers, who don't like to be pressured. You need to hold on to your cash, so you stall your vendors, who don't like to be stalled. Your employees know something is going on. They're getting calls of their own. But you're isolated. You really don't want to talk to anybody. You're in this downward spiral, and you can't cut costs fast enough. Maybe you last another three or four weeks, but it's complete torture. By the time you realize you may have to look at Chapter 11 after all, there's nothing else to do.

"That's when reality sets in. Suddenly you see what the next step is, and you think, *Oh, my God, look at all these people I have to lay off*. I mean, even though I'd put a ton of money back into the company, even though I'd stopped taking salary and was paying all the expenses out of my pocket, I still had assets that weren't going to be affected. I'd have to cut back on my lifestyle, but I'd be okay. Here were all these other people, thousands of people, who depended on me, and now they're going to be out of work. If you're a decent person, if you have any conscience at all, you have to say, 'How did I screw this up so badly?'"

The answer didn't come to him right away partly because he had so many ready-made excuses. Who could have predicted the stock market crash? Who could have foreseen that the use of fax machines would suddenly take off after twenty years? But Brodsky knew in his heart that external events weren't really to blame, and he eventually forced himself to face up to the truth: He had single-handedly destroyed a solid, profitable business by putting it in harm's way. Without his decision to acquire Sky Courier, and to keep pouring cash into it, CitiPostal would not have been vulnerable to the events that brought it down.

The obvious question was, why had he taken such a chance with the company he'd spent eight years building? "I had to admit that I'd done it because of something in my nature," he said. "I enjoy risk. I like to go to the edge of the cliff and look down. That's the personality trait behind my Groundhog Day syndrome, and it wound up costing a lot of people their jobs, which was an awfully hard lesson. I mean, we had to have armed guards in our offices. We had guys coming up who were extremely angry, and I couldn't blame them. They hadn't had any warning because I couldn't announce our Chapter 11 in advance. So one day they had a job, and the next day they didn't—through absolutely no fault of their own. I can't tell you how hard that was. Today I never ever make a decision that will jeopardize anybody's job, but that's something I had to learn the hard way."

He learned a few other things as well. He learned that he had to control his tendency to act impulsively. Like many entrepreneurs, he hated to spend time deliberating. He loved making snap decisions. Somehow he had to slow himself down. He also realized that he had to start listening better. A lot of people had warned him that he was taking an unreasonable risk in acquiring Sky Courier, but he had brushed them all off. He never even heard what they were saying. So he cultivated a new habit: taking care to understand what other people were trying to tell him before he made up his own mind.

Above all, Brodsky spent time reevaluating what he wanted out of business, and what he wanted out of life. In his mad pursuit of his $100-million mirage, he'd missed the childhood of his eldest daughter. Was he going to miss his younger daughter's childhood as well? Although he and his wife, Elaine, loved to travel, the only traveling he'd done in the 1980s was on business. He'd taken no real vacations for more than twelve years. He'd had precious little family time. He'd let his ambition override all that was most important to him. What he'd lost, he would never get back. But he could make sure he didn't repeat the mistakes in the future.

And what about business? He'd obviously blundered by focusing so intensely on sales, rather than profit. Wasn't it better to have a highly profitable $10-million company than a $100-million company that didn't make any money? Wasn't it better to have a business with a great reputation in its community and its industry—a company known and respected for its fabulous service, its unstinting generosity, and its happy, dedicated workforce rather than its size? He didn't know exactly what type of company that would be, or how he would create it, but he had a pretty good sense of the direction he wanted to go.

And he could thank his bankruptcy for that. "Some people, it takes a huge mistake to really learn from," Brodsky said long after his new company, CitiStorage, had established itself as the premier independent records-storage business in the country. "I think that if I had skated through that and somehow managed to survive without going through Chapter 11, I wouldn't have learned what I did—and I wouldn't have what I have today."

❋

Brodsky's example notwithstanding, it does not always take a crisis to make people aware of the different growth options available to them. Indeed, most owners in our sample didn't go through one before choosing their path, and they never seem to have agonized greatly over decisions to rein in growth when necessary. It's as though they knew instinctively that they had a choice, that they could resist the pressures and the temptations to expand too rapidly or in the wrong direction, and that—unless they did—they would lose what they treasured most about their businesses.

Among other things, they feared putting themselves in a position that would force them to compromise the excellence they strove for. These are people, after all, who are passionate about what they do and dedicated to pushing the boundaries of how well it can be done. Yet the more successful they are in achieving what they want, the more difficult it is for them to stay on course. Because of their success, they find themselves faced with so many opportunities that it takes a conscious effort on their part to keep from heading off in the wrong direction.

Danny Meyer of the Union Square Hospitality Group is a good example. He became a star of the New York restaurant scene at an early age. A native of St. Louis, he'd moved to New York City after college. In 1985, at twenty-seven, he opened Union Square Café, which won critical acclaim from the start, including a coveted three-star rating in *The New York Times*.

Inevitably, people began approaching him about doing another restaurant. Some of the offers were tempting, but he was nervous about overreaching. So he came up with three tough standards that any new place would have to meet. First, it would have to be capable of becoming as extraordinary a restaurant as Union Square Café. Second, it would have to enhance the value of Union Square Café. Third, it would have to bring more balance to his life, not less.

"I was trying to create criteria that would prevent me from doing another one," he said. "Union Square Café was like my great novel. I didn't believe I could write another one, and I had no time for it anyway. I was already working sixteen hours a day."

But eventually he did start a second restaurant, Gramercy Tavern, also located in the Union Square area. He decided to do it in part because he had the opportunity to bring in a great chef who would otherwise have found something else to do. He was also concerned about increasing turnover in the midlevel staff at Union Square Café. He knew good people would keep leaving if he didn't create opportunities for them to expand their horizons within the company. Besides, Meyer himself was ready for a change. "Union Square Café was a great canvas, but I needed a new place to express my creativity," he said. "I didn't think I should alter a successful restaurant just because I was restless. I didn't have to get all of my ideas into one place."

Gramercy Tavern opened in 1994 to high expectations, and it struggled for a while. "It was rough, but I've never done a restaurant opening that wasn't rough," he said. "I view restaurants like wine. I tend to make wines that are awkward at first but fortunately improve with age." That was certainly true in this case. By 1997, Gramercy Tavern was rated the fourth most popular restaurant in New York City by the *Zagat Survey*. (Union Square Café was the most popular.) It held that position the next year, then rose to number three in 1999 and number two in 2000—second only to Union Square Café. The two restaurants remained number one and two in the rankings until 2003, when they switched places. In 2004, they switched back. In 2005, Gramercy Tavern again moved into first place, while Union Square Café came in second.

Meanwhile, the booming economy of the 1990s had changed the restaurant business. Chefs like Wolfgang Puck and Todd English were becoming celebrities, egged on (so to speak) by real estate developers who had discovered that a great restaurant could transform a neighborhood or a mall and drive the growth of hotels, casinos, museums, and other businesses in the area. Sure enough, developers from all over the country began descending on Meyer, hoping to entice him to build a Union Square Café or a Gramercy Tavern in Las Vegas or Los Angeles, or wherever.

Meyer resisted their entreaties, coming up with what he called his five-minute rule. He said he wouldn't start a restaurant in any location that he couldn't walk to in five minutes from his home in Gramercy

Park, three blocks north of Union Square. Aside from wanting to be near his family and not wanting to expand geographically, there was a practical reason for the rule. An important part of a restaurateur's role, he believed, was to have a physical presence in the restaurant, to be a familiar face, to observe and interact with staff and customers while meals were being served. As long as the restaurants were close to one another, he could work lunch at all of them in the same day.

Even the five-minute rule was tested, however. In 2000, Starwood Hotels and Resorts decided to build a W Hotel in Union Square and asked Meyer to do the restaurant. They had two or three meetings to discuss the possibility, but Meyer eventually demurred, noting that W had grown and prospered as a chain because it had a well-defined point of view, "but it's not our point of view." Instead, he expressed his point of view in four other places he opened in the Union Square area from 1998 to 2004. Each had a unique theme and identity. Eleven Madison Park was "a grand restaurant," noted for its spacious art deco dining room and gold-leafed wine bar. Tabla offered a fusion of American and Indian food. Blue Smoke/Jazz Standard served barbecue hearkening back to Meyer's St. Louis roots. The Shake Shack was a classic burger and frozen custard stand in the center of Union Square.

Viewed together, they did indeed seem like the novels of a gifted author. Each had a distinctive plot line and set of characters, defined by the menu, the location, the ambience of the dining room, the wait staff's attire, and the smells and tastes of the food. And yet all the restaurants had a common style as well, characterized by a level of customer service so natural, so warm, and so apparently effortless that patrons didn't experience it as service at all, but rather as the kind of hospitality they might receive if they were guests in the home of a person whom they perhaps didn't know very well but who clearly felt honored by their presence. Meyer called it "enlightened hospitality," and it was the foundation of his company. (We'll have more to say about it in Chapter 5.)

As time went along, moreover, he began to lose some of his aversion to growth, for a variety of reasons. To begin with, he had a management team, a group of partners, and a staff of employees who were capable of handling growth and eager for new challenges. "I'm one of the more reticent ones about growth in the entire team," he said. "I've chosen to surround myself with people who are eager to grow. They're ambitious. If you want to make sure a restaurant remains excellent over a long period of time, you have to hire people with ambition. Not everyone on every team is interested in growing, but the only way to keep a nineteen-year-old restaurant like Union Square Café on its toes is to staff it with people who want to figure out a better way to do everything every day. Over time, you get a critical mass of people like that. Part of my job is to be aware of people's aspirations, and to harness them for the good."

In 2004, he harnessed the ambitions of the entire organization—and fundamentally changed both the company and his role in it—by taking on the immense challenge of opening a new restaurant and two new cafés at the redesigned and renovated Museum of Modern Art (MoMA) on West Fifty-third Street in Manhattan. The restaurant was called The Modern, and it put an end to the five-minute rule. "The only way I could make it there from my home in five minutes would be to hire a car service and have a dedicated traffic lane up Madison Avenue," Meyer said. "We've absolutely crossed the threshold with The Modern because now I cannot be at all places in any one meal service, ever again. So I am clearly transforming myself from a restaurateur into a CEO of a restaurant company."

The Modern was a big step for the company as well, marking the evolution it had gone through over the previous decade. In the early 1990s, Meyer had been urged to open a restaurant at MoMA by one of his regular customers at Union Square Café, a book publisher named Paul Gottlieb, who served on the museum's board. Meyer was tempted. He liked to start restaurants around ideas "born from my own life experience," as he put it, and MoMA fit the bill. His mother had owned an art gallery in St. Louis when he was growing up, and the family had had a membership in the museum. There had always been a MoMA calendar on the wall. But neither Meyer nor the company was ready to do a MoMA restaurant in 1994. By 2004, they were.

In many ways, it was a fundamentally different undertaking from any of the previous restaurants. The cafés introduced an element the company had never dealt with before: a captive audience. "We've tried to develop them with an empathy toward what people might be feeling when they go there," he said a few weeks before the opening. "Every other restaurant has been a stand-alone. Who knows what anybody has been doing before they come in? They could have gotten off an airplane, could have finished a business meeting, could have come from their hotel room, could have walked twenty blocks to get here. But the cafés within the museum are being designed specifically for people who we know have been using the museum. So we're trying to get into the mind-set of what people need after having been in the museum for however long—an hour, two hours, three hours, with kids maybe, from other countries maybe. That's a very different type of experience for us. It changes our understanding of the product people will be in the mood for, as well as the type of service. It's going to have to be quick, because you're already giving yourself a gift by taking time out to go see art. What's the point of eating in a museum? Probably to get you off your feet, eat quickly, and get something in your belly. Our job is to figure out what we can add to the dialogue on those three basic needs."

The project was also different because of its visibility, which increased the pressure and also the opportunities, Meyer said. "There's a much larger context than the restaurant itself. The museum provides the framework for what we're doing. If it was alone on a side street, the restaurant would be the story. Here the story is much larger. It's like riding a very high tide. The restaurant comes along for the ride. It benefits from and has to live up to the spotlight."

With the opening of The Modern, the company's workforce grew to more than a thousand employees, and more growth lay ahead. The management team had come up with a strategy for continuing expansion in the future. Meanwhile, Meyer's thinking about the entire process had changed. "The first thing I always used to look for in a new restaurant was a good idea, and I still do, but nowadays it's also whether or not something fits into our plans for growth," he said. "We're clear on what we're interested in and not interested in. We feel like we've done enough one-off fine-dining restaurants. On the other hand, we created Shake Shack, which shows we're not shying away from having some fun doing smaller things that could potentially be replicated."

One goal of the strategy was to provide opportunities for employees to move around, which served two purposes. First, it gave people room to grow and find new challenges without leaving Union Square Hospitality Group. That, in turn, allowed Meyer not only to retain talent he didn't want to lose but also to use that talent to "get some of the mother yeast into any new project," as he put it. "Blue Smoke opened with a chef who had eight years at Union Square Café, a general manager who'd done the same, a service director with five years at Gramercy Tavern, a pastry chef with three years at Tabla and 11 Madison Park. And on and on. We just believe that if we can start out having a high comfort level with the culture, the thing can become whatever it's going to become and it will be good."

Strategy aside, the change forced Meyer to start thinking about the company in a different way. Up to that point, Union Square Hospitality Group had been a collection of individual restaurants, but, as it became clear what the future might hold, he realized he had to begin focusing on the organization as a whole, and what he wanted it to look like. How centralized should it be, and what exactly should be centralized? And what relationship would employees have to the company? Would the wait staff, say, at Union Square Café identify first with the restaurant or with Union Square Hospitality Group? "That's something we debate internally a lot," he said. "I'm quite comfortable with people having an allegiance first to their restaurant and secondarily to Union Square Hospitality Group. I've never veered from the notion that, to the degree these are great restaurants, we'll be fine. To the degree they feel like cookie-cutter offshoots of a larger entity, who needs it?"

It was an interesting balance to maintain. The restaurants would be recognizably part of Union Square Hospitality Group, and yet completely different from one another. They would have a common culture, but the feeling of each would be distinctive. They were like kids, Meyer said: Each would have its own personality, but you'd never doubt that they were members of the same family. Some of their DNA would be the same, and some different.

There were, he conceded, some issues that had yet to be worked out. "It's critical for everyone to know what few things should be nonnegotiably similar," he said, "but for me it doesn't go too much further than the sense of how people feel treated. Beyond that, I think things should look different, taste different, smell different—which you need to sustain a high level of interest."

So what were the risks? Wasn't it inevitable that something would be lost if the company got too big? Could a large company retain the sense of intimacy with customers? "Well, maybe they won't have it with me personally," Meyer said, "but customers absolutely want that intimacy with the restaurant. I've walked in to three e-mails this morning from people raving about intimate experiences they've had in my restaurants. One was about a maître d', one about a manager, and one about a waiter who had created that experience. The process of taking an order, cooking for people, feeding them, and managing the operation is not the same as running a big corporation. Our people are running a restaurant with a sense of ownership for how well the restaurant works. But there's no question that the single greatest challenge we have is to never ever lose soul in the restaurants. If that happens, I'm not going to be very interested in growing. That's not of any interest to me."

Overall, Meyer is optimistic. He thinks he can pull it off—he can keep adding to the company without losing the soul. Yet he finds himself in that position only because he resisted the pressures to expand in the early years before he was prepared to handle the challenge without sacrificing the soul. By saying no, he kept his options open and preserved his ability to choose how far and how fast to grow.

And therein lies another lesson: If you want to have the choice, you have to fight for it. All successful businesses face enormous pressures to grow, and they come from everywhere—customers, employees, investors, suppliers, competitors—you name it. As we shall see, those forces will make the choice for you if you let them, in which case you will lose the opportunity to chart your own course.

2

---※---

Who's in Charge Here?

When Martin Babinec started his business in 1988, nothing could have been further from his thoughts than the possibility that it would become one of the fastest-growing companies in America or that he would someday be getting it ready to go public or be sold to venture capitalists. Nor would he have been particularly happy to know that both prospects lay ahead. "I wanted a small lifestyle business, independence of corporate bureaucracy, and more control of my business and my life," he says. "That's what I was looking for." Such a business was not in his future, however, and his experience illuminates the pressures to grow faced by all companies, including the fourteen small giants in our sample.

Babinec was thirty-three years old at the time and had spent the previous twelve years as a human resources manager for Navy Exchanges, a $3-billion, government-owned retailer with outlets on U.S. Navy bases all over the world. After being shuttled around from Davisville, Rhode Island, to Seattle, Washington, to Yokosuka, Japan, to Naples, Italy, to Oakland, California, he and his wife, Krista, wanted to settle down and raise a family in San Leandro, just south of Oakland, where they had bought a house. She had recently given birth to their first child.

Babinec, for his part, was sick of the corporate bureaucracy and ready to strike out on his own. He'd been looking into various business opportunities for two years, but none had seemed quite right. Then, at a national conference of human resource managers, he had heard about a new type of business, the professional employer organization (or PEO)—an outsourcing company that handles the HR needs of small-to-midsize businesses, giving them access to expertise, services, and insurance rates that they could not otherwise get. The concept is often called employee leasing. Within two months, he had quit his job and launched his own PEO, TriNet, Inc., on $5,000 in savings.

What followed was the more or less typical roller-coaster ride of a business start-up. It differed from the norm mainly in that it eventually had a happy ending, if not the one Babinec had planned on. Along the way, he contended with the full range of pressures that often cause entrepreneurs to lose control of their companies at an early stage, with the result that decisions about how much and how fast to grow wind up getting made for them. Only by overcoming those pressures can you preserve your ability to choose the kind of company you'll have in the end.

That's an important point. It's far more difficult than most people realize to keep ownership and control inside a privately owned business as it grows, but unless you do you will wind up with a company driven not by your own aspirations but rather by the need to meet growth targets set by outsiders. Even if you succeed in retaining control, moreover, you still have to deal with a variety of forces pushing you to grow whether you want to or not.

In the beginning, it didn't look as though Babinec's business would last long enough for him to have to think about those issues. For two years, he struggled to figure out what he had gotten himself into and how he could keep the company alive. By 1990, he'd apparently reached the end of the line. TriNet had one paid employee and six clients and was all but bankrupt. Babinec had discovered that he knew nothing about sales and marketing and wasn't particularly good at either one. In addition, he faced the enormous, and extremely expensive, task of educating a market that had never heard of PEOs or employee leasing.

Meanwhile, he and his wife were expecting their second child, and they were in debt to the tune of $250,000. He had spent every nickel he had and borrowed every cent he could squeeze out of people he knew. It was, he says, absolutely the lowest point of his life. He remembers sitting at the kitchen table, with tears in his eyes, feeling like an utter failure, telling Krista, "I just don't see any way out."

There was, in fact, one slim possibility left. He could try to raise money from outside investors, but it was the longest of long shots. How do you sell stock in an illiquid, insolvent company? What do you tell people when they ask why the next two years will be any different from the last two?

As it happened, Babinec thought he had an answer to the second question. Up to that point, he had followed the practice of other PEOs, taking every account he could get in hopes of building a large enough customer base to achieve the economies of scale that would allow him to provide benefits like low-cost insurance and still earn a profit. With no money to advertise, however, he needed referrals to bring in new accounts, and referrals were hard to come by when you followed a scatter-gun approach. Customers and potential customers didn't even know one another, let alone talk to one another. The solution, he realized, was to target a particular market segment of companies that did communicate with one another, and not just any market segment, either. He would go after the type of companies that most needed his services and would therefore be willing to pay him a premium—specifically, the fast-growing technology companies that were sprouting up all over nearby Silicon Valley. They were under enormous pressure from their financial backers to develop their technology as quickly as possible. Babinec could help by relieving them of the need to spend any time on HR administration. Best of all, people in the technology world were constantly talking to one another. If TriNet did a good job—and he had no doubt it would—it would start getting the referrals it needed.

It was a counterintuitive plan and a heretical concept in the small world of PEOs. If you needed large numbers of customers to achieve the required economies of scale, why on earth would you adopt a strategy that excluded the majority of potential users, who would be priced out your market? But Babinec was thinking only about survival at that point, and—to survive—he needed a way to sign up as many high-paying customers as he could, as fast as he could. That meant getting referrals.

He couldn't implement the plan, however, unless he had financing, enough to allow him to keep TriNet open a few more months, maybe as much as $100,000. If he was to have any prayer of raising that much money, he'd have to write up a business plan and put together a persuasive, professional-looking presentation for potential investors. He'd have to rent a room where he could make his case. He might have to bring in some outside experts to help. Doing all that would take more of his own time and money, putting his family deeper in debt, and the odds of succeeding weren't particularly good. If he failed, moreover, he and Krista could lose everything, including their house, and find themselves out on the street—homeless, with a two-year-old daughter, a baby on the way, no income, and a recession looming.

Babinec felt that the decision had to be Krista's. He told her that he thought he should probably start looking for a job. She could easily have said, "I think you're right, Martin. You've given it your best shot, and it just hasn't worked out. We need to get on with our lives." In that case, he would have closed up shop and started searching the help-wanted ads. But Krista was the daughter of an entrepreneur who'd been through rough times of his own. She said, "Are you sure you want to give up now? You've put so much into this. You still have an option. Shouldn't you try it?"

And so he did. He immediately went to work on his business plan. He also enlisted his next door neighbor, who owned a business and had a background in accounting, to prepare and present the company's financials. And he persuaded the guru of employee leasing, T. Joe Willey, to fly up to Oakland from San Bernardino, where he was based, and give the industry overview to the potential investors. Babinec himself would explain the new marketing strategy, and TriNet's only employee, Helen Salamanca, would serve as emcee.

On a warm evening in June 1990, about forty potential investors gathered in a back room Babinec had rented at Strizzi's restaurant in San Leandro. They included everyone he knew who might conceivably be interested in buying stock in TriNet. The event went off smoothly enough, considering the state of TriNet's finances. When its balance sheet appeared on the screen in the front of the room, the line for cash read "$30 (Note: figures not in thousands.)" "Looks like you're a little light on cash," commented Jim Hanson, a local CPA. Nevertheless, he was impressed enough with the concept to put up $10,000 and six other people added another $40,000. That $50,000 turned out to be all Babinec needed to reach positive cash flow. "It was the difference between my having this company today and being somebody else's employee," he said, looking back fourteen years later.

But, ironically, the $50,000 was also the first step toward the loss of his independence. The money came with obvious strings attached. The investors had rescued Babinec, and he was now obligated to give them what he'd promised and what they expected, namely, a good return on their investment. That meant growing the company fairly aggressively. At some point, moreover, he'd have to find a way to cash them out.

In the meantime, he focused on implementing his new strategy, and it worked brilliantly. TriNet quickly began to develop a reputation among start-ups in Silicon Valley as a company that could take care of all their HR needs, leaving them free to focus on getting their technology to market as fast as possible, which was the key to their success. Soon venture capitalists took notice and started referring the companies they invested in to TriNet. Babinec himself became a familiar figure on Sand Hill Road in Menlo Park, California, where several of the major venture capital firms were located.

By 1994, TriNet was solidly in the black and growing fast—but not fast enough, Babinec realized. In the previous six years, he'd come to understand the dynamics of employee leasing extremely well, and it was clear to him that he'd gotten into a business in which scale was everything. The bigger a PEO was, the better it could serve its customers, the lower its costs per transaction would be, and the more likely it was to survive the increasingly fierce competition in the industry. You couldn't have a little gem of a professional employer organization. If Babinec wanted to stay in the business, TriNet would have to get big quickly.

That meant two things: First, he would have to raise a huge amount of money to finance the growth. Second, he would have to hire a management team with experience in building businesses and running companies. Without those managers, he probably wouldn't get the money, and he wouldn't have the in-house expertise he needed to be successful. But such people were in enormous demand. They had their pick of employers, who would offer them all kinds of benefits and perks to sign up. In contrast, Babinec had only three recruitment tools at his disposal (two of which were intangible): the challenge of building a major player in the industry; the opportunity to grow with the company; and equity. Of course, the equity would be worthless unless the stock could be sold at some point. So to attract the people, as well as the investors, it would have to be understood that the company was being groomed either to be acquired or to do an initial public offering.

Babinec did eventually succeed in attracting the people and raising the money he needed, although it took some doing. Because of TriNet's reputation in Silicon Valley, he was able to meet with several top venture capitalists, who listened politely to his pitch and then demurred, saying they did not invest in businesses like his. Instead, Babinec raised $250,000 from his original investors, a couple of other people like them, and a few of his executives—with the understanding that he still planned to bring in a much larger investor. The following year, he sold 50.1 percent of TriNet's stock, a controlling interest, to a large European PEO for $3.9 million, whereupon he ratcheted up the company's growth rate several more notches, opening offices all around the country.

By then, Babinec's notion of having a nice, little lifestyle business was a distant memory. More to the point, he had a lot less control of his company and his life than he'd been looking for when he began. Yes, he was the CEO, with all the perks of the office, but he was by no means a free agent. The responsibilities he'd taken on governed how he spent his time, whom he spent his time with, where he went, what he did, and when he did it. Above all, they determined the kind of business he would have. Given the nature of the industry he'd chosen, his need for outside investment, and the expectations of the people he'd hired, he had no choice but to grow his company as fast as possible, get it as big as possible, and then sell it or take it public.

In fairness, I should note that Babinec was not all that dissatisfied with his situation, as different as it was from the one he'd envisioned. He loved the people he worked with and found the challenges of the business invigorating. Although the pressures were intense, he could handle them, and he readily accepted the level of scrutiny and accountability insisted upon by his investors, especially his European partner. True, he and Krista, with three young children, longed to move back east, where their families lived and where they thought the educational system was better than in California, but even that turned out to be possible. In 1999, the family relocated to upstate New York, and Babinec began to divide his time between San Leandro and Little Falls, New York—a grueling commute. Still, he said, it was a lot better than being somebody else's employee.

But the point here is not to celebrate how well things worked out for the Babinecs, as happy as we are about that. Rather it is to take note of the pressures Babinec encountered along the way, the same pressures that other entrepreneurs have to deal with and that can push any company in a direction its founder never intended for it to go.

Obviously, the crucial decision Babinec made was to choose a business that needed an extremely large customer base to compete successfully. You can't build a small giant if you're in an industry where your success depends on how big your company becomes. In that case, the pressure to grow fast will be irresistible, as it was for TriNet, and sooner or later you'll have to look for outside financing, no matter how much capital you start with.

But even if you don't go into a scale-based business—and even if you don't find yourself in straits as desperate as Babinec did in 1990—you're still likely to face enormous pressure to bring in outside investors, simply because of the economics of growth. That's a fact of life that every entrepreneur must confront sooner or later. For Fritz Maytag, the revelation came right around the time that the demand for Anchor Steam Beer was starting to take off. "I had an epiphany," he recalled. "Let's say you're in a capital intensive business, selling a hundred units of something for $100, and you earn $3 after taxes. To grow 10 percent, you need to make ten additional units. If you have to invest $2 for every new unit of growth, you'll need $20 to grow 10 percent. You can't finance that out of after-tax profit. Using all your after-tax profit of $3, you can only pay for one and a half additional units, meaning you can only grow 1½ percent—unless you get the additional capital somewhere else.

"For example, we're in the wine business, and we need more wine. We're selling a thousand cases of wine per year, and it's not enough. Next year, we'll need a hundred more cases to meet the demand. For that, we'll need an extra ton and a half of grapes. You get about three tons per acre of vineyard. So we need half an acre more. Well, it costs $200,000 easy to plant an acre in Napa Valley. Depending on where you are, it might be a little more. But let's say $200,000, meaning we'll need $100,000 to make a hundred more cases. But we're only making $10 a case, which gives us $10,000 in profit per year. Unless we get an additional $90,000 somewhere else, we won't be able to meet next year's demand.

"The point is, your growth is absolutely limited by your capital, or your ability to borrow capital. That was an eye-opening realization for me. They probably teach this on the first day of business school, but I'd never seen it so clearly before. Every unit of growth needs new capital if you're in a capital-intensive business. Just one more case needs capital. Not only that, but it's almost impossible to grow in tiny little units. You can't grow one case at a time, or even a hundred cases at a time. You probably need a minimum of ten acres of vineyard—otherwise you can't justify buying a tractor. So there are these giant steps you have to take.

"Of course, if you're not in a capital-intensive business, it's different, but you still have giant steps. They just have to do with people. Say you hire a new guy. Unless you're just a jerk, you have a moral obligation to keep him on the payroll for six months, even if you discover you don't need him after all or he's not right for you. Six months of salary is a big bite. I've been told by people in software that the capital intensity there is research. You need a big room filled with very expensive people who are thinking hard all the time about what to do next year when your software will be obsolete because Microsoft is coming out with something better.

"This is what forces companies to sell out. They can't finance their own growth. You sell a piece here and a piece there, and pretty soon you don't have the controlling equity anymore. And success just makes things worse. If you have the only widget in town and customers are beating down your doors, you're riding a rocket ship. That's how many people lose their company—because they're too successful."

To be sure, many people don't lose their companies, but you almost always lose a significant portion of your independence when you sell stock to outsiders, even if the business remains privately owned. As a result, it becomes much more difficult to make the kinds of choices that the companies in this book have made. Not that it's impossible to find investors who'll leave you free to grow (or not grow) the company as you see fit, but there's always a bargain of some sort. The outsiders must at least buy into your vision, which will only happen if they get out of the deal what they want.

So it is not surprising that only four of the fourteen small giants in our sample have stockholders who don't work in the business. One of them is Reell Precision Manufacturing, 56 percent of whose stock is owned by the now-retired founders, their children, and their grandchildren. O. C. Tanner has a similar situation, with 35 percent of the voting stock owned by the founder's nephew and his family. Union Square Hospitality Group began with family investors—Danny Meyer's mother, his aunt, and his uncle. He has a more diverse group of outside investors now, but they, too, give him a free hand. "They understand that they're investing in us as we do business," he says. "I've been careful. I pick people who are friends and whose advice I welcome. When I meet with them, it's an opportunity to surround myself with advisers who are a lot smarter than me." Zingerman's also has outside investors in its restaurant, Zingerman's Roadhouse, but the rest of the company is owned internally.

As for the other ten companies, they have taken care—often extreme care—to make sure that all the equity stays inside. Gary Erickson, for one, struggled for two years to take full ownership and control of Clif Bar after he split with his partner, Lisa Thomas, over his decision to reject the $120-million offer for the company. She was leaving, and even before they had talked terms, he knew he would need at least $50 million to buy her 50-percent share. He first tried to find a commercial bank that would lend him the money and got no takers. He then looked into mezzanine financing, which involved borrowing at a much higher interest rate, and was turned down again. Next, he investigated the possibility of bringing in venture capital and walked away when he realized how much stock and control he'd have to relinquish. In the end, he worked out a deal with Thomas that required him to pay her $15 million up front, plus $42 million over the next five years and another $1 million a year under a noncompete agreement. Since he had very little cash of his own at the time, he had to borrow the first $15 million from a bank, paying a whopping 23-percent interest rate. Even then, he and his wife, Kit, had only 67-percent ownership until Thomas got all her money. Fortunately, the company did well enough in the next two years that he was able to refinance his debt and pay her off early.

You might reasonably ask why Erickson didn't simply sell the business and start another company. In his book, he noted that his ex-partner's attorney asked him that very question, and his immediate, visceral reaction was no. He said he refused to consider the option. He later saw other entrepreneurs try that, and they all regretted it. Besides, he added, Clif Bar was where he belonged—"my place in the world."

Be that as it may, you still have to wonder whether it was worth going to all that trouble, spending all that time, paying all that money, and taking on all that risk to make sure that he and Kit were the sole owners of Clif Bar. "Absolutely," Erickson said, sitting in his office at Clif Bar, in Berkeley, California. "I couldn't have done it any other way. Once you bring in outside capital and give equity to outside investors, there's no turning back. I don't regret my decision [to keep the equity inside] for a moment. I would be very unhappy today if I hadn't done it. My wife and I toast once a week how fortunate we've been."

That's a common thread here. Most of the CEOs in our sample share Erickson's conviction that you can't have outside shareholders if you want to build a small giant, and even Danny Meyer agrees that his investors don't belong unless they buy completely into his particular vision and way of doing business. The reason is simple enough. These companies are searching for something indefinable and immeasurable, something that goes beyond the standard definitions of success in business, something that can easily be lost unless it's protected against the homogenizing influences brought to bear on every company. I call that quality mojo. (See the introduction.) If you are not involved in helping to generate mojo, you have nothing to contribute except, perhaps, capital, and the capital comes at too high a price.

That said, most of the CEOs don't think that it's necessary, or even advisable, for 100 percent of the stock to be owned by one person (or one couple). In five of the companies, the founder has brought in key executives as equity partners. In two others, a majority of the equity is owned by an employee stock ownership plan, or ESOP, of which all employees are members. Then there's Zingerman's Community of Businesses, which has its own system, whereby the managing partners of the subsidiaries have stock in their respective entities. (The Roadhouse is an exception.) The majority stake in O. C. Tanner, the oldest company of the group, is owned by a trust.

Whatever their particular ownership structure, all of the companies guard their equity zealously to make sure it remains in the hands of people committed to the same goals. That's more of a challenge for some than for others. If you do acquisitions, for example, you generally want the option of paying with your stock, so as to minimize the need to borrow money or generate additional cash, but then the stock usually winds up in the hands of outsiders. Most of the companies in our sample have no interest in buying other businesses, given the difficulty of merging corporate cultures. The exception is ECCO, the Boise-based, employee-owned manufacturer of backup alarms and vehicle warning systems. Its chairman, Jim Thompson, and its president, Ed Zimmer, realized that—to compete effectively—ECCO needed a presence in Southeast Asia and Europe; and they decided the best way to get one was to purchase existing businesses with which the company already had relationships. They had a core principle, however, that the company would remain "team-member" owned—that is, no outside shareholders. In the end, they used 5 percent of their stock to purchase a business in the United Kingdom, on condition that the two owners become part of the team. When one of them proved unable to adapt to ECCO's collegial, open-book culture, he was fired, and the company bought back his stock.

Even if you manage to keep ownership inside the company, you still have to contend with other forces pushing you in directions you didn't necessarily want to go. In some cases, you may feel pressure from big competitors—or the fear of big competitors—as Erickson and Lisa Thomas of Clif Bar did. Suppliers, too, will urge you to grow as fast as you can, especially if you're one of their distributors: The more you sell, the more they sell. But, ironically, the most intense pressure often comes from two sources that both determine and define your success as a business, namely, your employees and your customers.

It goes without saying that a great company needs to have great people working for it, but you can't attract them, let alone hold on to them, unless they have room to grow. That is, in fact, why many owners wind up putting their companies on a path of aggressive growth, even if they themselves might prefer to rein it in. "I didn't feel I had a choice," said Jim Ansara, the founder and chairman of Shawmut Design and Construction in Boston, which grew so fast that (like TriNet) it made the *Inc.* 500 list of America's fastest-growing private companies for five consecutive years. "I couldn't see any other way to get the people I needed." Today, at $441 million in annual sales and 501 employees, Shawmut is a well-established and highly respected design and construction firm, with clients ranging from Hard Rock Café to Harvard University, but Ansara plays only a small role in its operations. Instead, he divides most of his time between his family, his lobster boat, the numerous charities he supports, and the boards he sits on.

The CEOs of our small giants have all faced, and continue to face, the same issue. One way or another, they have had to keep their best people engaged and challenged or run the risk of losing them. In most cases, the answer has been a kind of controlled growth that has preserved the company's culture while creating new opportunities for employees. Not that other companies don't control their growth. If they didn't, they wouldn't survive. For a conventional business, however, the growth is the goal, and the control is what you need to keep it in hand. With the companies we're looking at, creating opportunities for employees and opening up new possibilities for the business are the goals. Growth is a natural by-product of the company's success in pursuing its central purpose and reason for being, whatever that may be.

Interestingly, while a few of the sample companies have grown in fairly traditional ways—by launching additional product lines, for example—most have done it by spinning off new ventures, often becoming entirely different entities in the process. We saw in the last chapter how Union Square Hospitality Group has evolved from a single restaurant into a company that starts new restaurants around different ideas. Zingerman's Deli did something similar, turning itself from one stand-alone business into the Zingerman's Community of Businesses, consisting of various food-related companies that share a common culture. Righteous Babe Records added a retail business, a music publisher, a real estate developer, a foundation, and a concert venue. Artists' Frame Service morphed into The Goltz Group, including a home and garden store, a wholesale frame business, and an art gallery. The list goes on.

I don't mean to suggest that these companies have done their spinoffs simply to create new career paths for employees. More often than not, the owners and CEOs were also responding to exciting opportunities that they thought both they and their people were ready for, that would strengthen the company in some way, and that would provide them all with the chance to explore new areas of business. But the new ventures had the effect of giving good people an avenue to grow and take on new challenges without having to find employment elsewhere; and that was, in most cases, one of motives for branching out.

It's the market pressure to grow that is the most problematic for any company to deal with. For openers, there's the psychological factor. The pressure is there, after all, because people like your product or service and want a chance either to buy more of it themselves or to make it available to large numbers of customers who don't have access to it now. Either way, the pressure is a powerful indicator of your success. It's a compliment to your business acumen. It's the fulfillment of the dreams you had when you started the company. How can you say no?

In fact, many people can't say no—especially, I've found, entrepreneurs who happen to be men. Even if he knows in his heart of hearts that his company and his people aren't ready to handle the growth, even if he realizes that the growth may transform the company in ways he can't foresee and may not like, he still can't bring himself to turn business away. Once you start down that path, however, it becomes extremely difficult to go back. By the time you realize that the company is too big, that you're out of your depth, that your work is simply not up to the standards you've set for yourself, you've made a lot of commitments—to employees, to customers, to suppliers—that are hard to break. If you decide to change course, people will have to be let go. Contracts will have to be renegotiated. Customers—good customers, the kind you want to keep—will have to be told that you just can't help them. At that point, you find out just how deeply you care about being the best at what you do.

"I never wanted this to be a big company," said Bill Butler, who was twenty-six years old when he started his construction business, W. L. Butler Construction, Inc., on the kitchen table of the Starhill Academy for Anything, one of four communes along Skyline Boulevard in Woodside, California, south of San Francisco. The year was 1975. Although he was living in the commune with his wife and their son, it was not their legal residence. They didn't have one. Nor did they have electricity and indoor plumbing. "It was like *Survivor* on steroids," Butler said, sitting behind his desk in the company's offices in Redwood City, about eight miles from where it started. "I rigged up the first power line by getting a permit for a well. After PG&E set up the meter for the well, I ran a line into the house.

"In the beginning, I built fences and hung doors," he continued. "I just needed to make a living. I had no insurance or property or anything, but I liked doing business, and I liked building, and I liked people." Eventually he bought a piece of property in Woodside where he and his family moved in 1981. The company finally got an office in 1983, though its telephone remained unlisted until 1994. People who liked Butler's work and wanted to hire him had to chase his truck to get the number.

And a lot of people did like his work. By 1989, Butler Inc. was doing $20 million a year in sales and had 129 employees—and the boss felt completely overwhelmed. He was spread thin and so was his company. Licensed in California, Oregon, Washington, Nevada, and Arizona, it had projects going in all those states; and there were more jobs in the pipeline than it could handle. Meanwhile, the company wasn't making money. The quality of its work wasn't as good as Butler thought it should be. There was no corporate infrastructure. Things were out of control.

"It was my fault," Butler said. "That was tough to admit, but I knew I'd screwed up. I'd overpromised, and we'd bitten off more than we could chew. So we sat down and did a lot of soul-searching. We asked what we did well, what kind of work did we get a better return on, what did we need to improve. And then we changed everything."

To begin with, Butler and his senior people—including Frank York, who later became company president—decided to go from "pounding nails," as he puts it, to being a general contractor, managing projects rather than doing all the work. That was the company's greatest strength and the only way it could grow, and improve, without adding bodies. "The number of people was most important to me," Butler said. "I like to know everyone who works here, and I never wanted to have much more than a hundred people. If we'd kept on the way we were going, we'd have had to staff way up. We had one hundred twenty-nine people then; we have one hundred twenty-five now. That's about right."

At the same time, Butler's team changed its entire perspective on the business. "We wanted to raise the bar," he said. "Instead of trying to do it all, we wanted to be the best at a few things. We physically gave up our licenses in other states so we couldn't work there, and we went from taking every job to questioning every job." That meant getting rid of customers, including some who'd been with the company for a long time. The team spent hours analyzing the customer base, noting which jobs were more profitable, discussing which niches Butler should be in and which clients played best to its skill set, projecting how economic trends would affect different industries, and so on. Then came the cuts. "We went from twenty-five clients to ten clients," Butler said. "Mainly we fired the bad ones, including our biggest client"—a giant financial services company—"that accounted for 50 percent of the value of our jobs. The people they had on our projects were demeaning to us. They'd lie and make us look like fools. We told them we didn't want to work with them anymore."

Those were the easy calls, however. In order to keep the company at the size he wanted, Butler also had to say no to good customers, the ones he wanted to continue doing business with. "To me, a good client is a good corporate citizen, honest and good to the community," he said. "Some of these companies don't care about the communities they do business in, and they don't do win-win. I want to work with clients who see us as their partners. I'd rather lose money than lose a good client."

The problem was, Butler Inc. had more good clients than it could service—even after cutting back. Butler said he felt enormous pressure from customers to grow, and still does. In 2002, Target gave Butler Inc. its supplier-of-the-year award, one of only two contractors ever to receive it, and the other one had built the corporate headquarters. Butler was also the smallest vendor ever to be so honored, as well as the one that received the award in the shortest time. How do you say no to a client like Target when it comes asking you to do a store far out of your region? "It's tough. It's very, very tough," Butler said. "You can only say no so often. We've turned down as many projects as we do, and it's always hard. Sometimes we've had to deal with it by recommending competitors, which is extremely tough for an entrepreneur to do, as you can imagine. And they were our best competitors, too, because we wanted the customer to be happy with whatever work they did."

One competitor later told him, "You're my best salesman. I get more business from you than from my own people."

Yet the more business Butler Inc. turned away, the more its reputation grew. Although Butler avoided publicity—he granted a single newspaper interview in twenty-five years, and that one only because the long-haired reporter reminded him of his commune days—the company became legendary in its community for its charitable works and its extraordinary workplace. Meanwhile, more customers than ever were knocking on the company's doors, and Butler couldn't refuse all of them. The company kept growing in spite of itself and in spite of a recession that was brutal on commercial development. Customers saved the few jobs they had for Butler. In 2001, sales hit $125 million. The following year, they rose 40 percent to $175 million. "That was too much," Butler said. "It was a strain on the infrastructure. People were working too hard. Everybody was too stressed out." So, in 2003, he cut back, dropping sales to $155 million; only to have them jump the next year to $205 million, which was too much again. In 2005, he cut back once more, to $195 million. "We really do strive to stay small," he said.

There is one other major source of pressure to grow, though it doesn't seem to affect everyone, or at least not to the same degree. This one comes partly from the social and cultural environments in which we all live and work, and partly from something in the entrepreneurial psyche. Robert Catlin, founder and CEO of Signature Mortgage Corp. in Canton, Ohio, is one person who has struggled with it. He developed a system that allowed his sixteen employees to outperform mortgage companies with three or four times as many people. The company was wildly successful; and friends, colleagues, customers, and utter strangers said they couldn't understand why he didn't do the same thing in other midsize markets around the country. "People tell me all the time, 'You're crazy, pal. You're missing a golden opportunity,'" he said. "I say, 'Hey, I'm doing just fine. I have control. I have freedom. I have family time and travel time. What more can I ask for?'"

The notion that bigger—and more—is better has so pervaded our culture that most people assume all entrepreneurs want to capitalize on every business opportunity, grow their companies as fast as they can, and build the next Microsoft or Citicorp. That widespread assumption, in turn, can become another pressure to grow, especially when considerations of status and prestige come into play. "It's really tough—because it can be an ego thing," said Catlin. "I spend a lot of time soul searching. What is most important to me? What's this all about? What do I want to do with my life? The world says, 'Go. Get bigger. Go. Go.' But I don't see why I should."

Even Ari Weinzweig of Zingerman's felt that pressure when he and his partner, Paul Saginaw, were struggling with the issue of how to grow the company. "Paul is very good at asking questions," he said. "Once that issue was opened up, he started asking the questions that we hadn't asked ourselves for a long time. Like maybe we're missing the boat and should go open delis around the country. It's hard to fight off that pressure to achieve in the way that everybody thinks you should achieve and that they present as being easy to achieve. Of course, they don't know. It's never easy, and it's really a lot of work. But once you open that door, all those questions are out there."

Some entrepreneurs are more susceptible than others to the blandishments of the growth gods. Jay Goltz readily admits that he was one of those people. Now he refers to himself as "a recovering entrepreneuraholic."

He traces the origins of his addiction back to childhood. Sitting in his office next to his art gallery and above his frame store on North Clybourn Avenue in Chicago, he recalled being inspired at an early age by a friend's father, who was an entrepreneur in the framing business. "I saw him starting, failing, starting, failing," he said. "Turned out he was bipolar. But what I got from him was the excitement of business." His own grandfather, father, and uncle owned a neighborhood dime store that

Goltz didn't think had much of a future. So when he was in his junior year of college, studying accounting and thinking about starting a company, it was the framing business that came to mind, not the dime store.

He didn't get much support. His mother just sighed when he told her what he wanted to do. Friends told him, "I think you could do better." His college adviser said, "You won't get anywhere unless you go to graduate school." Only his brother-in-law offered encouragement, saying, "If you don't do it now, you never will."

Despite the negative reactions, Goltz went ahead and launched Artists' Frame Service in 1978, at the age of twenty-two—and the company took off. Pretty soon, he showed up on the radar screen of *Forbes* magazine, which featured him in an article about hot young entrepreneurs it labeled "biz kids." For the next fifteen years or so, he played the part of a rising mogul, growing Artists' Frame Service as fast as he could and launching half a dozen other businesses along the way. He was a man on the move. He would read articles about entrepreneurial stars like Michael Dell or Fred Smith and push himself even harder. He investigated the possibilities of franchising. He considered getting involved in so-called industry roll-ups. He even thought about going public. Although he didn't take any of those routes in the end, he relished the sense of being part of the action. "I was driven, single-minded, focused, independent, and tenacious, which are great qualities for an entrepreneur," he said, "but would you want to be married to that person?"

Maybe not, but you couldn't deny what he'd accomplished. By the time he turned forty, he was becoming a guru of the framing business, and Artists' Frame Service was widely regarded as the industry's gold standard. His home store and his art gallery were thriving as well. He was in demand as a speaker and as a teacher, and he was writing a book of advice to entrepreneurs. In the part of Chicago where he'd built his businesses, people credited him with leading the neighborhood's revival. Somehow, on top of all that, he was still married to the same woman after sixteen years, and they had three healthy children. "It was because of her," he said. "I didn't recognize at the time what my wife had to put up with, but I do now."

Nor did he recognize his own achievements. "Successful entrepreneurs have a demon they have to get rid of," he said, reflecting on his state of mind at the time. "For me, it was having to do as much as I could. I always worried, *Am I missing an opportunity here? Am I leaving money on the table?* How do you turn that off? How do you keep the success bug from turning into the success disease? And it was harder because of the biz kid thing. I'm twenty-something and I get written up in *Forbes*. I turn forty and I'm not so hot anymore. I hear about a guy worth $40 billion, and I think, *How can that be? How much smarter is he than me?*"

As with most addicts, Goltz had to hit rock bottom before he could summon the will to change. It happened in the spring of 1996. He had bought a building on Clybourn where he planned to create an upscale home and garden store, expanding the home store he had started in leased space down the block. The problem was that the building needed drastic renovation, and the work had to be finished in four months because he couldn't afford to miss the spring selling season. In the midst of it all, he ran out of cash. "I went through my entire credit line," he said. "I had nothing left. It was incredibly stressful. I couldn't sleep at night. Our payables got longer, and we had to watch inventory like a hawk. At the same time, my mother had cancer, and my kid was having trouble in school. It was horrible.

"But that was the real beginning of the change," he went on. "It turns out there are three things you need to realize before you can get into recovery from entrepreneuraholism. First, you have to feel the pain. You need the experience of staying awake all night because you're afraid you might lose your house. I was forty-one, out of cash, in an industry I didn't have a handle on. I'd felt stress in the early days, when I was struggling to grow the business, but that was unavoidable. It went with the territory. This was self-imposed. I was going through it because I'd bought the building and decided to get into this business I knew nothing about. Was I out of my mind?

"That led to a second realization: People who build giant companies from scratch are different from you. It's not just brains; it's composition. They have a stomach you don't have. Then finally, it hits you, the third realization: Things are okay. You think, *I can be happy. I can lead a good life, have a great business, make enough money, without going crazy.* And you begin to notice all the unhappy rich people around, with unhappy families. When Donald Trump was asked whether he was a good father, he said, 'I'm a good provider.' That horrified me.

"Anyway, I went into recovery. For years, I'd been pushing, pushing, pushing, and suddenly I realized I could stop. I began to think, *What would you do with all that money if you made it anyway?* That was a revelation."

There was another important component to the change Goltz went through. Like many entrepreneurs who feel driven to grow their companies, he suffered from a major disability, namely, his own blindness to what he had accomplished. He was haunted by a sense of inadequacy, of not measuring up. He would compare himself with the most famous entrepreneurs in the world and wonder what they had that he lacked. He was so focused on his shortcomings that he couldn't see—or give himself credit for—the real contributions he had made to his community and the positive impact he had had on the lives of people around him. It was as though all that counted for nothing if he hadn't achieved what the world considered the pinnacle of success as measured by the size of his company or his personal fortune.

In the end, it was one of his employees, an older African American woman, who opened his eyes. Her name was Lily Booker. She and another woman, Willie Hardwick, were retiring from Artists' Frame Service after eight years with the company. At their retirement party, Lily got up to say a few words. She talked about her introduction to Artists' Frame Service. She'd been with another custom-frame company for ten years, until it closed up shop and moved to Texas. "I was in my fifties," she said, turning to Goltz. "When you hired me, I never thought I'd ever get another job. I just want to thank you for giving me a chance."

Maybe it was the timing. Goltz himself was turning forty that year and beginning to feel his mortality. In any case, her statement jolted him. "When you're growing your company, all you think about is the people you've failed with," he said. "At the time, I was licking my wounds from all the failures. Managers I'd had to fire. Poor kids I was going to save who kept screwing up and getting into trouble. Longtime employees who'd been caught stealing. From Lily's comment, I realized it wasn't all failure. I looked around and saw a lot of people who appreciated their jobs."

He remembered a story he'd once heard about a girl throwing starfish into the ocean. "An old man comes along and says to her, 'Don't bother. There's millions of them out here. You can't save them. What you're doing won't make a difference.' She looks at the starfish in her hand and says, 'It makes a difference to this one.' And she throws it into the ocean. Lily was one of my starfish."

Afterward, he began to notice some of the other starfish in the company. There was the framer who looked for every opportunity to work overtime. It turned out he was sending the money home to his family in Tibet. And there was Luan Le, who had been a captain in the South Vietnamese navy. After the fall of Saigon, he was arrested and sent to prison for more than eight years, moving from one camp to another until his release in 1983. A year later, he took a hundred people in a motor boat from Vietnam to Malaysia, a three-day journey, surviving an attack by pirates from Thailand en route. He eventually made his way to the Philippines, where he learned English, and then to Chicago. Artists' Frame Service hired him through an agency that places Vietnamese and Cambodian refugees. "He's a champion fitter," Goltz said, "and he's one of my starfish."

It is hard to imagine a small giant whose leader does not recognize his, or her, starfish. Indeed, you could argue that a small giant's mojo comes, in part, from an active appreciation of a business's potential to make a positive difference in the lives of the people it comes into contact with. That appreciation is a common characteristic of all the companies in our sample, and it makes possible the intimacy they are able to achieve with employees, customers, suppliers, and the community—an intimacy that is both one of the great rewards and one of the crucial generators of the mojo they exude. It's also an intimacy you can witness firsthand if you want to. You need only visit the cities, towns, and neighborhoods where these companies are located.

3

The Mona Lisa Principle

The Asbury Delaware Methodist Church stands on Delaware Avenue, the main road leading into Buffalo, New York. It's one of the city's many architectural masterpieces, most of which date back to its glory days in the late nineteenth and early twentieth centuries. Today, it is the home of Righteous Babe, the music company founded by singer-songwriter Ani DiFranco. It's also a symbol of hope for the city of Buffalo, and thereon hangs a tale.

Buffalo, which sits at the eastern end of Lake Erie, was once a thriving center of commerce, where grain from the Midwest would arrive by boat and be unloaded, processed, and sent on to New York City—and the rest of the world—via the Erie Canal and the Hudson River. By the early 1900s, it had become the eighth largest city in the United States and one of the most beautiful, with a street plan patterned after Pierre L'Enfant's plan for Washington, D.C.; a park system laid out by Frederick Law Olmstead; and buildings designed by the most famous architects of the day, including H. H. Richardson and Frank Lloyd Wright.

Beginning in about 1950, however, the city's fortunes took a sharp turn for the worse, a decline hastened by both the opening of the St. Lawrence Seaway in 1959 and growing competition from the Sunbelt and beyond. Businesses moved away, and commerce dried up. On late-night television, Buffalo became the butt of jokes about its long, bleak winters and the futility of its professional football team. With no major corporate headquarters and little industry to speak of, the economy went into the doldrums and stayed there. The city government had to depend on subsidies from the state just to maintain basic services.

Then, in the late 1990s, a band of would-be saviors appeared in the form of the Rigas family, whose cable television company, Adelphia Communications, was growing like gangbusters, its reported revenues rocketing from about $473 million in 1997 to almost $1.3 billion in 1999 to more than $3.3 billion in 2001. Although based in nearby Coudersport, the Rigases were devoted Buffalo boosters. In 1998, they bought the local professional hockey team, the Sabres; and, in 2000, they announced plans to build a $125-million operations center in the heart of the city that would bring a thousand new jobs to the downtown area and spur a wave of new development. At last, Buffalo would get the shot in the arm it needed. It seemed almost too good to be true. Unfortunately, it was. On July 24, 2002, the Rigases were indicted for stealing vast sums of money from their company at the expense of investors and creditors. A few months later, Adelphia filed for Chapter 11 and moved its base of operations to Colorado. Out of sympathy, if not pity, Tom Golisano, the founder and CEO of Rochester-based Paychex Inc.—who wasn't even a hockey fan, let alone a Buffalonian—agreed to buy the Sabres and keep the team in Buffalo.

By then, the citizens of Buffalo were used to disappointment. During five decades of watching their city decline, they had developed a certain fatalism about Buffalo's future, as well as a collective inferiority complex. They'd also come to accept that no matter how bad things got, no matter how much people complained, no one—or at least no Buffalonian—would actually step forward and do anything.

And right at that moment, Ani DiFranco and her business partner, Scot Fisher, Righteous Babe's president, stepped forward.

They were both Buffalo natives, and DiFranco was the city's most famous rock star (though not its only one—Buffalo was also home to the

Goo-Goo Dolls). She had hundreds of thousands of fans around the world and had sold millions of her CDs, plus a smaller number by other artists, under the Righteous Babe label. Her decision to go it alone, despite being ardently courted by all the major recording companies, meant that her albums were seldom played on mass-market radio stations. As a result, she wasn't as famous outside her demographic base as some of her peers were—Alanis Morissette, for example, or Sarah McLachlan—but she was a superstar on college campuses across the country and a celebrity in her hometown as well. Local people who'd never heard her music knew who she was. She had done dozens of concerts in the area and, through Righteous Babe, contributed to numerous community causes. When she performed for charity, as she often did, her picture made the front page of the *Buffalo News*. Although Buffalo was a conservative blue-collar town, its citizens embraced DiFranco. So what if she was a self-described bisexual with a large and devoted following among lesbians? So what if she walked around with flowing dreadlocks, a ring in her nose, and a tattoo across her chest? So what if her politics were somewhat to the left of Karl Marx's? She'd grown up in Buffalo, playing her guitar and singing her songs in local clubs, and she'd remained fiercely loyal to the city even after she became a star.

That was the acid test. As everyone realized, DiFranco could have located her business anywhere, but she'd chosen Buffalo over New York or Los Angeles or any of the other cities with modern recording facilities and lots of musicians. What's more, she and Fisher insisted on using local suppliers to make the company's T-shirts and other merchandise, to print its album notes and posters, and to manufacture its cassette tapes and CDs. In the process, DiFranco had played a major role in building at least three local businesses in addition to her own and was directly responsible for creating about 125 jobs in a city with one of the highest unemployment rates in the Northeast.

But it was what she'd done with the church that had made the biggest impression on the city's psyche. For all its beauty and architectural significance, the building was a ruin by the time Righteous Babe got involved. No one had done any maintenance work on it for decades.

With stones falling off one of its steeples into the street below, the church would have been demolished in 1995 had not Fisher, an ardent preservationist, helped raise $50,000 to make emergency repairs. He thought his role was finished at that point, but in 1999, someone from the city had called to say it had acquired the building and didn't know what to do with it. Was Righteous Babe interested? Fisher and DiFranco talked it over and decided to buy the church, restore it, and use it to house the company's headquarters, as well as a new concert venue, a jazz bar, an art gallery, and the offices of the city's leading avant-garde arts organization.

And so it came to pass that in late 2003, as the city's residents were still recovering from the Adelphia debacle, they saw the scaffolding go up around the Asbury Delaware Methodist Church and work begin; and they took heart. "There was definitely a sense of uplift when that happened," said Don Esmond, a columnist for the *Buffalo News*, who had championed the effort to save the church since the mid-1990s. "There was actual progress on something that people had assumed was just going to sit there, boarded up, for God knows how many years. This was not in some corner of the city, either. Delaware Avenue is one of the main thoroughfares downtown. A lot of people drive right by it every day on their way to and from work. They thought it would be the usual stalemate, and so there was definitely a feeling of communal uplift to see it getting done."

Taxi drivers, bartenders, and longtime Buffalonians echoed the sentiment. "What they did with the church was just great," said Pat Thompson, who works for the company that does Righteous Babe's printing. "Having lived in Buffalo most of my life, I can tell you for a fact that nothing gets done here. When we see Ani and Scot go against the flow and do something, we think, *It's about time someone did.*"

When you look closely at our small giants, one characteristic immediately jumps out at you. Like Righteous Babe, they are all so intimately connected to the place where they're located that it's hard to imagine them being anywhere else. Zingerman's is almost synonymous with Ann Arbor, and Anchor Brewing is a San Francisco institution. CitiStorage is Brooklyn to the core. Reell Precision Manufacturing and the Twin Cities go together like, well, a horse and carriage. The same could be said for Clif Bar and Berkeley, ECCO and Boise, O. C. Tanner and Salt Lake City, Hammerhead and Studio City, and on and on. And the influence runs both ways. The companies shape their respective communities, and the communities shape them.

Nor is that relationship a matter of happenstance. Danny Meyer of Union Square Hospitality Group, for one, views the community as a critical factor in deciding where he will open a restaurant, and what type of restaurant it will be. "I don't want to do a new project unless it's special in some way, and that means the context has to be right," he said. "I don't know what's special about the way the *Mona Lisa* is framed, hung, and lit, but I do know that the effect would not be the same if it were framed, hung, and lit in a different museum, in a different city, in a different country." That's one reason he and his colleagues at Union Square Hospitality Group turned down developers who wanted them to open a Union Square Café or a Gramercy Tavern in Las Vegas. "Those restaurants are part of their community, and the community is part of what they are. They wouldn't fit in in Las Vegas, given the transience of the people and the nature of the place. It's the wrong context."

Ari Weinzweig of Zingerman's offered an analogy for the relationship that companies like his have with their respective communities. "You're talking about something like what the French call *terroir*," he said. "It has to do with the way that the soil and climate in a given region contribute to the flavor of the food. That's because the soil's mineral content, the amount of sun and rain it gets, the local vegetation, and so on—all that is different in each region. So let's say you're going to make cheese or wine using the same recipe in two different places. The animals in one place will be grazing on different vegetation from those in the other, and the grape vines will be growing in different soil and getting different amounts of sun and rain. Because the *terroir* is different, the cheese will be different, and the wine will be different, even if you follow the same process for making them. And that's true. You can taste the difference. It's the same with some businesses. Every community has its own character, which is sort of a spiritual *terroir*. If you're really rooted in that community, it's going to have a big impact on the way you are."

Of course, the opposite is also true—with both food and business. When you mass-produce food, you strive to take the *terroir* out. The whole idea is remove any variations due to climate, or soil, or season, much as companies that are spread out geographically strive to reduce variation and develop a common culture. They work hard to make sure people throughout the organization are following the same rules, living up to the same standards, working toward the same goals, reflecting the same values. And there's nothing inherently wrong with that. Weinzweig points to Whole Foods Markets—the national chain of natural-foods grocery stores—as a large company with a strong, vibrant culture and a commitment to being a good corporate citizen, "but they're not really rooted in a community anymore."

The companies in this book are all deeply rooted in their communities, and it shows. Each has a distinctive personality that reflects the local environment, often in ways that may seem superficial or quirky on the surface but that actually play an important role in the business's success. Righteous Babe is a good example. You don't have to spend much time around the company to notice how similar its spirit is to that of the city in which it resides. Buffalo is an underdog, a team that's always coming from behind. For all the jokes about its weather, the city has a kind of civic pride—the pride of outsiders and strivers—and exerts a powerful, if somewhat mysterious, hold on its inhabitants. Those who go away come back, and those who spend a few months there don't leave. "It gets in your blood," said the cabdriver from the airport, in the midst of a sudden snowstorm, trying to explain why his son had returned from California.

"It has a way of sinking its hooks into you," said Brian Grunert, who'd intended to move to the Midwest, where he'd gone to college, but never got around to leaving. He eventually became Righteous Babe's designer.

"It definitely got into my blood," said Ron Ehmke, a native Louisianan, who attended graduate school at the University of Buffalo. He became Righteous Babe's principal writer.

Part of the appeal has to do with the city's faded elegance, lack of congestion, and inexpensive real estate combined with a far lower cost of living than that of any other metropolitan area in the Northeast. But there's more to it than that. "Buffalo is not a small town, but it feels like one," said Ehmke. "People in the arts, for example, all have connections to one another. The arts community may be small compared with some others, but it's one of the least compartmentalized I've ever seen. That's one of the great things about it."

By the same token, Righteous Babe has the feeling of a small, hometown business, despite its national renown and international customer base. Explaining her decision to stick with her own company rather than sign with a major label, DiFranco told *The New York Times* in 1998, "I have to know for myself that there is an alternative to big corporations. I want to live in a world where one can and does choose to go to the local drugstore on the corner—that old chemist who's been there with his wife behind the counter for thirty years—instead of going to the Rite Aid or the Kmart."

Fisher manages the company accordingly, drawing lessons from his previous career painting houses. "As a housepainter, you're in a small community, and your reputation precedes you," he said. "So you'd better do a good job. You'd better be honest, do what you say you're going to do, treat people right, and pay them on time. If you don't, you simply won't last."

Small towns, he believes, impose a kind of accountability that's missing in today's music business, as well as in most other parts of the corporate world. By way of illustration, he told a story about a well-known promoter who produced a concert that DiFranco did with Bob Dylan. They were playing at an outdoor performance space near a major northeastern city. "We found out that the promoter was adding a $5 parking fee to every ticket even though the parking came free with the venue. It was a sneaky way for him to make an extra $25,000 to $50,000 without giving anything to the artists.

"You couldn't get away with that in a small town," Fisher continued. "Nobody would work with you. Your reputation is all you have, and word travels fast. We want to do as little business as possible with those kinds of people, so we've tried to create a small town environment on a national level. The promoters we use would no sooner cheat us than they would cheat their own mothers. Ani and I sometimes joke about how we live in a fantasyland of honest people who treat each other with respect."

And Buffalo has shaped Righteous Babe in other ways. "There were a lot of reasons why this company shouldn't have succeeded, and location was one of them," noted Grunert, the designer. "On the surface, it's a disadvantage to compete in a national market from a city like Buffalo. But Scot and Ani have used its qualities to their advantage. They've benefited from lower overhead, having printing and manufacturing available at very competitive prices, being able to afford a comfortable lifestyle—for both the business and its employees. Righteous Babe has been able to carve out a spot here much more easily than it could have in a larger market."

The company benefited as well from a substantial talent bank of local artists and writers, whom Fisher and DiFranco wanted to support. "Scot thought everything we did should look professional but not slick," said Ehmke. "If that's what you want, it makes perfect sense to hire people who haven't done it before. I hadn't written bios for millions of rock stars. Our designers hadn't done a lot of record albums or music posters. Our radio guy had started out on a local college station. We were all learning as we went along." Although new to their respective fields, they were unquestionably talented. As a result, the albums, catalogs, and marketing materials they produced were fresh and imaginative but hardly amateurish. In 2003, the music industry recognized their work by awarding DiFranco and Grunert the Grammy for best packaging.

Practical benefits aside, Righteous Babe also drew strength from the Buffalo ethos, the sense of being the scrappy outsider and underdog, fighting against the odds. It imbued the company and served as a motivater for everyone, including Fisher. He had been DiFranco's boyfriend before he took over as Righteous Babe's president—they later split up—and he lacked both the experience and the qualifications normally required of someone who wants to be the business manager of a major musician, let alone the head of a record company. Initially there was considerable skepticism as to whether or not he was up to the responsibility. "It took [Ani's agent,] Jim [Fleming,] a couple of years to tell me that the first time I called, he thought, 'Omigod, it's the boyfriend. How many times have we seen this?' " Fisher said. "But I knew where I stood. I knew people didn't respect me. I'm from Buffalo. I'm used to it."

Perhaps there was a sense of having something to prove, or maybe it was the opposite: a comfort level in knowing that expectations were so low he could easily surpass them. Whatever his state of mind, he threw himself into the job and—working closely with DiFranco—proceeded to build a highly respected, diversified music business, including one of the few successful artist-created labels around. A decade later, Righteous Babe was still going strong, while several of the record companies that had courted DiFranco were out of business.

Fisher believed the city had something to do with the company's longevity. "IRS Records wanted to sign Ani, and we went to see them in Los Angeles," he said. "They had this beautiful office. I thought, *Who's paying for this?* I couldn't see anything they had that we really needed. IRS had a phone; we had a phone. IRS had a fax machine; we had a fax machine. They said they could get Ani's music to a larger audience, but we didn't think she needed them to do that. Now IRS is gone, and we're still here. We must have done something right. And I think that staying in Buffalo all this time, working in a modest office, was a factor. It helped us keep things in perspective."

All the companies in this book have similarly symbiotic relationships with the communities in which they've grown up, and the vitality of those connections is part of their mojo. The companies' owners and employees have a strong sense of who they are, and where they belong, and how they're making a difference to their neighbors, friends, and others they touch. In some mysterious way, all that contributes to buzz around the business, the passion people feel for what they're doing.

You see it with Anchor Brewing, which is so woven into the culture and history of San Francisco that it has become something of a tourist attraction in its own right. The company's Web site traces its lineage to the arrival of one Gottlieb Brekle during the Gold Rush days and harkens back to the early days of West Coast beer making, when the traditional local brews were called steam beers for reasons nobody seems to remember (hence, Anchor Steam). Like the city itself, the brewery has survived all manner of natural and man-made catastrophes—earthquakes, fires, war, Prohibition, financial ruin—each time managing to rise again thanks to the intervention of someone willing to fight to keep it alive. When Fritz Maytag, then a young Stanford graduate, bought a majority stake in 1965, he was just the latest in a series of saviors.

Among the many things Maytag brought with him were a keen appreciation of and respect for the special relationship between Anchor Brewing and San Francisco. Today you can feel the pull of the city's past wherever you look in the company—from its traditional brewing techniques to the saloonlike ambience of its taproom to the labels on its products to its location at the foot of Potrero Hill, in the old industrial section south of Market Street, just two blocks from one of its many former locations. After the brewery ran out of room in its former location, Maytag decided to move it there in 1977, taking over an erstwhile coffee roastery. He says it never even crossed his mind to look for space in one of the suburbs, which would have been much cheaper. Leaving San Francisco would have been unfaithful to the company's heritage.

Jay Goltz and Artists' Frame Service have had an even closer relationship with the Near North Side of Chicago, an area whose name has changed along with its fortunes. Back in 1978, when Goltz started his company, the neighborhood was called New Town (as distinct from Old Town). It was a run-down section of decrepit old buildings and empty lots. There was so little happening along North Clybourn Avenue, where the business was located, that local hot-rodders could hold drag races down both lanes on Friday and Saturday nights. "If you saw a guy running down the street back then, he was probably carrying someone's television set," said Goltz. "These days he's just another jogger."

Indeed, North Clybourn is now a bustling center of commerce, lined with upscale stores and restaurants. Its rebirth has spurred the revival of the entire area, currently known as Lincoln Park, boosting real estate values and attracting such national retailers as Whole Foods, Smith & Hawken, and Crate & Barrel. Local merchants and real estate developers credit Goltz with leading the change. His was the first new business in the area. When he started out, empty space on North Clybourn was going for about one dollar per square foot. That's what he paid for the two thousand square feet he rented on the third floor of an old furniture factory where player pianos were once made. Today real estate is pushing forty dollars per square foot, and the major headache is traffic. Anticipating that parking would become a problem, Goltz bought his own parking lot for his customers a few years back. It's across the street from the building that houses his home and garden store, down the block from the framing shop and the art gallery. The ambiance of the stores—employees refer to them collectively as the campus—reflects the vitality of the neighborhood, and vice versa.

CitiStorage has a different relationship with Williamsburg, the section of Brooklyn in which it is located. Like New Town when Goltz arrived, it was a depressed inner-city neighborhood when Norm Brodsky moved his headquarters there from midtown Manhattan in 1994. At the time, he had concerns about street crime and the danger it posed to the company's employees. He also worried that people would leave because of the location, and that it would scare away potential recruits. On the other hand, he felt it was important that he and the other senior managers be based in the warehouse rather than in offices across the East River. Besides, the move would save the company more than $300,000 per year. As a precaution—and to allay fears—he installed a state-of-the-art security system on the premises and set up a van service for employees going to and from the subway.

But the fears turned out to be largely unfounded. While some people left the company because of the move, those who remained were reenergized. Given the scarcity of well-paying jobs in Williamsburg, moreover, recruiting actually became easier. As more people from the area joined the company, Brodsky and his wife, Elaine, a co-owner and vice president of CitiStorage, worked hard to develop close ties to the community. They invited neighborhood people to the parties they held at their waterfront location. They made space available for a local theater group. And they let employees decide whether to continue having an annual holiday party or to spend the money on a local charity. The employees chose the charity, a school for autistic children, for whom they bought, assembled, wrapped, and delivered Christmas presents.

Today CitiStorage is like the rest of Brooklyn—a melting pot of people from many backgrounds, speaking many languages. There's a hardboiled, no-nonsense, "fuggedabowdit" edge to the culture, combined with warmth, generosity of spirit, and the camaraderie of working people making their way in the world. The employees are deeply loyal to and protective of the company, which has given most of them opportunities they've never had before and would never have had without it. They describe Brodsky as "tough but fair," which they consider a compliment. In many ways, he is like them, a street-smart Brooklynite who pulled himself up by his bootstraps, taking a lot of hard knocks in the process but ultimately coming out on top.

Then there's Clif Bar, which was founded by a guy who, in 1990, seemed like the quintessential Berkeley free spirit—unmarried, thirty-three years old, living in a garage with his dog, his skis, his climbing equipment, a bike, and two trumpets of the type he'd been playing since the fifth grade. He drove a bucket-of-bolts 1976 Datsun and owned a wholesale bakery, Kali's Sweets & Savories, with a friend. His passions were bike racing, rock climbing, and improvisational jazz. Those were still his passions fifteen years later, and he was running exactly the type of business you'd expect such a guy to have if he had somehow managed to grow one beyond his wildest dreams. If you visited its building on Fifth Street in the Berkeley flats, you would see numerous signs of the renovations and expansions that had been required over the years. In the main office area, you'd notice first the huge climbing wall, from which dolls—Cookie Monster, Po from Teletubbies, Piglet, Taz—were hanging to mark Clif Bar's progress toward its sales goals. (Another wall was just for climbing.) Elsewhere in the building, you would find a gym, perhaps with a dance aerobics class in progress, and a sign-up sheet for the personal trainers, not to mention a massage room, an in-house hair salon, a meditation tent, a full bike repair shop, and a well-stocked game room.

It all fit right in. A decade and a half after founding Clif Bar, Gary Erickson had changed a bit—he was married with three children, for one thing—but Berkeley was pretty much the same, just more prosperous. That could be said of Clif Bar as well. Everything that had characterized it in its early days was still there, just more of it and better organized. It had formalized its commitment to a sustainable environment, using certified organic ingredients in its products, organic cotton in its T-shirts, recycled paper in its publications, and as little energy as possible in its operations. It supported a multitude of social programs and had a 2080 program for employees, wherein the company donated at least 2080 hours per year—the equivalent of one full-time person—paying employees to do volunteer work in causes they selected themselves. In almost every way, it was a reflection of the city in which it had been born and raised.

So was Reell Precision Manufacturing, located in St. Paul, Minnesota, and steeped in the business culture of the Twin Cities, which has a long history of corporate community involvement. Companies such as Target/Dayton-Hudson, H. B. Fuller, Pillsbury, and General Mills have championed the notion that businesses have a social responsibility to the communities they serve and have put their money behind it—Target to the tune of $2 million per week. Reell's three founders made social responsibility the cornerstone of the business, pledging "to do what is 'right' even when it does not seem to be profitable, expedient, or conventional." The company's highest purpose, they said, was "to make worthy contributions to the common good."

It's a standard that their successors have incorporated into the day-to-day operation of the business. There is an earnest, wholesome, heartfelt idealism about Reell that would no doubt be considered hopelessly naïve in New York, Chicago, or Los Angeles, but that seems right at home in the Twin Cities. Reell's co-workers are encouraged to debate the moral dimensions of business decisions and play a role in resolving conflicts. The company's leaders are active in organizations concerned with bringing a spiritual perspective to the day-to-day running of the business and are frequently asked to speak on the topic by local universities and community groups. Reell itself has received both the Minnesota Business Ethics Award and the American Business Ethics Award. Somehow it's all tied up with the business culture of Minneapolis–St. Paul. "It's had a big influence on us," said co-CEO Bob Carlson.

To be sure, many large, public companies have also been molded by their communities. Wal-Mart is a product of Bentonville, Arkansas, and Hershey's is a product of Hershey, Pennsylvania. For that matter, Target and H. B. Fuller are just as much products of the Twin Cities as Reell. What's different is the intimacy of the connections. A human-scale company in a single location can be part of a community without dominating it. The CEO and other top managers can establish personal relationships with the company's neighbors, with leaders of local nonprofits, with the rest of the business community, and with government officials. There's a focus, an intensity, a depth of commitment that inevitably becomes harder to maintain as the business expands. That's what Weinzweig means by being "rooted." A large company with branches around the country, or around the world, can do all kinds of good works; can be sensitive to the environment and scrupulous in its ethics; can donate tremendous amounts of money to worthy causes; can sponsor dozens of charitable events. What such a company can't do—and, more important, what its people can't do—is interact with a particular community on a level that defines them both and provides a uniquely gratifying experience all around.

No company illustrates the potential for such a relationship better than Zingerman's.

※

Recall that, in the early 1990s, Ari Weinzweig and Paul Saginaw rejected the idea of setting up branches of Zingerman's in other locations in part because they wanted to deepen the company's ties to the Ann Arbor community and preserve its character as an Ann Arbor business. To an outsider, it's immediately obvious that they've succeeded. Like Righteous Babe, Anchor Brewing, and the others, Zingerman's is a quintessentially hometown business, reflecting the distinct culture of Ann Arbor, a midwestern college community with a large number of East Coast transplants. It is said to have the highest readership of *The New York Times* outside New York. Unlike, say, Madison, Wisconsin, or Iowa City, Iowa, it's next door to a major city, giving it a somewhat more cosmopolitan feeling than most other Big Ten towns—or so Ann Arborians believe. "I think we're more mideastern than midwestern," said Weinzweig, who grew up in Chicago, came to Ann Arbor to attend the University of Michigan, and never left.

However you characterize the community, Zingerman's is a mirror of it. "I see it in the casualness with which we interact, but the seriousness with which we take the food," said Weinzweig. "I'm not saying you couldn't have the same thing in another community, but it's not the norm everywhere, and the contrast is very true to Ann Arbor. We'll have people who are world-famous professors in their field standing there in jeans next to a high school student, next to a nine-year-old, and they're all tasting the same goat cheese and discussing it and learning about its history. And there's the whole intellectual approach we take to the food, which has to do with being in a university environment. Almost any food I'm studying, I can call up the university and find somebody who specializes in it.

"That's something we do a lot of—study food. We're interested in learning about it, and so are our customers. If you come to work here and aren't particularly interested in learning, you'll have a really hard time in the culture. We also tend to get employees who are young and idealistic, which is another part of being in Ann Arbor. They're driven more by how much we contribute to the community than by how much we pay out in bonuses. Sure, they want the bonus, and I want them to get the bonus, but people here get more excited about donations than they do about personal gain, which is nice. Of course, that's partly because many of them are younger and don't have families to feed and mortgages to pay."

The other side of that idealism is a tendency to discuss every issue until the cows come home. In 2000, for example, the Compass Group approached Weinzweig and Saginaw about opening a Zingerman's at the newly renovated and expanded Detroit airport. They agreed it was a great business opportunity, as well as a nice addition to Zingerman's Community of Businesses. They would call it Zingerman's Land of 1000 Flavors. To remain true to the principles Weinzweig and Saginaw had laid out in the 1994 vision statement, Zing 2009, there would have to be a managing partner—that is, a co-owner who would be responsible for managing the store, building the culture, adhering to the Zingerman's philosophy, and meeting its standards of quality and service. Saginaw argued that the Compass Group would play that role. Weinzweig and the managing partners of the other businesses were willing to go along with that.

But there was another sticking point. In the course of producing Zing 2009, the cofounders had made a commitment that all the new businesses would be in the Ann Arbor area, even if other opportunities might appear to offer significant financial benefits. Weinzweig and Saginaw had turned down numerous invitations to open spin-offs in the Detroit suburbs and in other midwestern towns precisely because they didn't want to dilute the Ann Arbor connection. The airport was in Detroit, twenty-five miles away. Would it violate the Ann Arbor principle to open a Zingerman's business there?

"We had enormously long discussions about it," said Weinzweig. "Paul and I spent hours with the managing partners, and we had open meetings with the staff to discuss whether or not we could do in that setting what we were doing in Ann Arbor. Like most things, it wasn't black and white. Anyway, Zing 2009 doesn't say Ann Arbor proper. It says the Ann Arbor area, which doesn't rule out Ypsilanti, say. In the end, we decided that the airport was the gateway to Ann Arbor for many people, and it would be a cool thing to greet people and welcome them to Ann Arbor through the airport store. But it was a matter of intense discussion and lots of disagreement before we finally decided to go forward with the plan." The Compass Group had a last-minute change of heart, however. On the morning of September 11, 2001, it announced it was abandoning the project, and so Zingerman's Land of 1000 Flavors never came to be.

On the surface, it seems absurd for people at Zingerman's to spend so much time debating such an issue. How could it possibly matter so much whether or not they opened a place outside the Ann Arbor area? If it was a good opportunity that they could handle and that would enhance the company, what difference did it make where the new store would be located?

To answer those questions, and to understand the concerns of Weinzweig, Saginaw, and their associates, you have to look at the other side of the relationship—what Zingerman's has done for Ann Arbor, and the effect its work has had on the way its people think and feel about the business.

You would have gotten a hint of the company's impact if you'd been in Ann Arbor in the spring of 2002, when Zingerman's was celebrating its twentieth anniversary. Letters of thanks and praise poured in from all over—from customers, public officials, other businesses, distant admirers, and Ann Arbor ex-pats around the world. But there was one tribute that stood out from the rest. It appeared on a long vertical sign on the outside wall of Zingerman's Next Door, the building adjacent to the deli that houses a dining area and a couple of seminar rooms. The sign said:

> From all of us to all of Zingerman's.
> Thank you for feeding, sheltering,
> educating, uplifting, and
> inspiring an entire community.
> Happy birthday to a deli
> that makes a difference.

Below were the logos of thirteen nonprofits from Ann Arbor and Washtenaw County, where the town is located. Then:

> From the many, many, many,
> people you help.
> With all our hearts.

The nonprofits, which had conceived of and paid for the sign, were not exaggerating. Zingerman's has played a role in the life of Ann Arbor that goes far beyond creating jobs, selling food, and boosting the local economy. You could start with Food Gatherers, the nonprofit organization that Zingerman's started in 1988.

Paul Saginaw said he got the idea for it when he was reading a magazine article about professional food photographers in New York who had begun collecting the food that was left over from photo shoots and would otherwise have been thrown out or taken home by staff members. The photographers had leased a van and would take turns driving around to pick up the food, which they would then drop off at the Salvation Army. "I thought, *Wow, that's kind of a brilliant idea,*" Saginaw recalled. The deli also had leftover food that was perfectly wholesome but not quite fresh enough to sell to the public. Instead, the managers would use it for employee meals, or toss it in the garbage. "And we really tried to be as efficient as possible," he said. "I thought, *If we have waste like that, I'll bet other people do, too. We could do here what those photographers in New York are doing.*"

He was aware that a sandwich line supervisor, Lisa deYoung, was planning to leave and apply to law school. Saginaw persuaded her to postpone her plans and work with him on a program to "rescue" and distribute food that would otherwise be thrown out. She could start by researching the need for such a program. He told her he'd pay her the same salary she'd been making in the deli. Meanwhile, he began calling restaurants and food businesses to gauge their interest in the idea. It turned out that they were very interested and that there was a need—

specifically for fresh produce, meat, and dairy products. Three months after reading the article, in November 1988, Saginaw incorporated Food Gatherers as a 501(c)(3) charitable organization, borrowed a van from a catering business called Moveable Feast, and, with deYoung, made the first round of pickups.

Suddenly Saginaw found himself in the world of nonprofits, and though he didn't know much about them, he had ideas about how they should be run. "I wanted to operate Food Gatherers like a business, meaning that it would be fiscally responsible," he said. "I also knew that I didn't want to have to deal with bureaucracy, or meet certain criteria to get money from people. So Ari and I decided that Zingerman's would fund the entire program, at least in the beginning." That meant paying deYoung's salary as executive director, providing office space, and covering administrative expenses—a significant commitment from a fledgling enterprise.

Over the next eighteen years, Food Gatherers grew steadily. In 1997, it took over the local food bank, which was about to lose its national accreditation due to poor management, and began branching out, providing a full range of food products to homeless shelters, detoxification centers, the Salvation Army, and neighborhood feeding programs in low income neighborhoods. In order to avoid competing with those organizations—and to win their trust—Food Gatherers made a point of not directly feeding people in need and charged the agencies only what it cost Food Gatherers itself to buy certain types of products. (The rescued food was free.) As a result, when Saginaw and others had to go out to raise money to expand the operation, they got no resistance from the nonprofits they supplied because they knew the proceeds would eventually come back to them.

And expand Food Gatherers did. In its first year, it rescued and redistributed eighty-six thousand pounds of food. Seventeen years later, it was doing between two and three tons per *day*. By then, it had twelve full-time employees and an annual operating budget of $1 million, of which Zingerman's contributed the largest share, in addition to providing a huge amount of support and numerous in-kind donations.

Food Gatherers was only the beginning. There was also the Washtenaw Housing Alliance, a group of eleven organizations aiming "to end homelessness in our community," to which Zingerman's was a major contributor. And Non-Profit Enterprise at Work, which helped other local nonprofits improve their management, find and train board members, set up Web sites, and the like. And Wild Swan Theater, which aimed to make high-quality children's theater accessible to low-income and disabled children from the area. And Washtenaw Community College, to which Zingerman's contributed scholarships. And the Shelter Association of Washtenaw County, which ran homeless shelters. And on and on and on.

Saginaw led the way, spending up to twenty-five hours a week on nonprofit work and other community activities, in addition to having primary responsibility for developing new business opportunities for Zingerman's and getting the start-ups off the ground. He took on the title of Chief Spiritual Officer—Weinzweig was CEO—and became the main advocate of the community in the company and of the company in the community. It was a role he loved. "Sometimes I feel like I started a for-profit business so I could be involved in nonprofits," he said. "We plow an enormous amount of money back into the social, cultural, and educational vitality of the community, and I believe it would be a very different community if we didn't do it. I get tremendous satisfaction from knowing the difference we've made."

And yet, interestingly, the company has been careful not to use its community work as a marketing tool. "We don't keep it a secret," Saginaw said. "It's a small town. If people go to a lot of fund-raisers and always see our name, they can connect the dots. But we don't market around it, and I don't trust companies that do—that use their charitable work as a blatant marketing ploy. We do it because it's the right thing to do. We do it because it's part of our mission."

There are people on the left and right, in business and out, who might take issue with Saginaw. Some would argue that companies like Zingerman's should, in fact, trumpet their good works as an example to others. They'd say it's right for socially responsible companies to let the world know, through marketing or other means, how businesses can contribute to the common good. Other people would contend that—while Saginaw is free to spend his own time, energy, and money as he likes— he shouldn't be dragging his company into it. The social responsibility of a corporation is to increase its profits, as Milton Friedman once observed, and its resources ought not be diverted to ancillary purposes.

To Saginaw, that whole debate is beside the point. Zingerman's doesn't contribute to the community to make a political statement, and he doesn't regard his company's involvement in the community as an extracurricular activity. On the contrary, it is one of the reasons he and his colleagues are in business to begin with, and one of the principal rewards they get out of it. "We get so many requests," Saginaw said. "Some things are so off the wall, it's funny, but they're just sweet. So you do it. It's a great pleasure to be able to take care of those requests for people. It's a joy. Being in the community like that is a joy. You can't buy joy. It's wonderful."

It's worth saying a few more words here about the issue of social responsibility in business, and the role it plays or doesn't play in creating mojo. While all of the companies in our sample are active in their communities on some level, they differ from the 1990s brand of socially responsible business—like Ben & Jerry's or The Body Shop—in that they tend to be relatively quiet about what they do. Most of their leaders share Saginaw's aversion to using their good works as marketing tools. Some go even further. Fritz Maytag, for one, is a strong supporter of the view that "the business of a business is business," as he puts it, an idea that he attributes to Friedman.

But if you read what Friedman actually wrote on the subject—for example, in *The New York Times Magazine* of September 13, 1970—you will note that he was talking only about publicly owned corporations. He challenged the notion that a corporation, which is an artificial person, can have such responsibilities. Real people may feel they have social responsibilities, he argued, but corporations can't and don't. What's more, the people who run those corporations are employees of the owners—that is, the shareholders—and therefore duty bound to use the corporation's resources to further the shareholders' interests. When executives use the company to promote their own political or social agenda, they are, in effect, taxing the shareholders without their consent.

As Friedman acknowledged, however, that argument does not apply to closely held private companies. "The situation of the individual proprietor is somewhat different," he wrote. "If he acts to reduce the returns of his enterprise in order to exercise his 'social responsibility,' he is spending his own money, not someone else's. If he wishes to spend his money on such purposes, that is his right, and I cannot see that there is any objection to his doing so."

His point was that there's a difference between people spending their own time and money on a cause and a corporation spending somebody else's time and money on it. What the small giants do is consistent with that distinction. Not only do they generally avoid taking initiatives that carry the whiff of ulterior motives but they also follow the rule that—to be a meaningful expression of generosity and support—an act of charity has to be individual, personal, and largely unheralded (though not necessarily secret).

Anchor Brewing is a case in point. "We've tried to do business well and be a good neighbor," said Maytag. "I've had a general tendency not to get involved in doing good, but we have a dual attitude toward this. We adopted a little middle school near us, helping them in many small ways without blowing our horn. We adopted the little city library branch that's near the brewery. I'm a big believer in small neighborhood libraries, which were terribly important to me when I was a boy. We've sponsored a chamber music group. We sponsored some young men who set out to break the record for bicycling across the United States. We sponsor a rowing team on the bay. But all of this is done quietly and without blowing our horn.

"Then we have a program I'm very proud of and like very much. We'll match any employee's charitable contribution two to one. If you live in Santa Cruz, and you're interested in a local group that works to keep the beaches clean, or to expand the city park along the seashore, and you give then $100, I'll write a check for $200. At one point, we had it up to three or four to one. I said, 'I'm going to keep raising the ratio until people start giving.' We came back to two to one a few years ago. It's like a benefit. I sign many checks along this line.

"I just don't know that companies know what to do in terms of 'doing good,' and frankly I'm averse to the guy whose picture is on the social pages with the cocktail in his hand at the opera because his company has given money to it. I think that's somewhat tawdry. But I love the idea of backing our own employees. Occasionally I write a check to an organization that I wouldn't dream of giving money to, but I have an employee who does, and who am I to say he's wrong? Maybe he's right. We have a deep relationship with our employees. In a small company, you have a real team. So if one of my employees decides to back something, we back it too."

It's all very personal, as is the role that Maytag sees the company playing in the community. "One of the things I love," he said, "and we do a great deal of it, and we've done it for many, many years, is that we open the brewery to small, especially private, charitable groups who come and have a social evening at the brewery, sometimes dinner, but often just light snacks and hors d'oeuvres and beer and maybe they have a board meeting or a membership meeting. We tell them that they can't sell tickets, or require a donation as a condition of attending, but they're welcome to use it for a party, say, to thank their supporters. We've done that for forty years. It really goes back to a time when the brewery in Europe—or even in this country, as far as that goes—was a sort of civic center. The brewery was a place you could go and have a meeting. It's a really marvelous old tradition."

It would be a stretch to describe the other companies as civic centers, but their ties to their communities are no less intimate, and the feelings their people have about the relationship are no less intense. "We have a chance to be part of a community in a way you simply don't get if you're in a big company that's spread out all over the place," said Weinzweig. "I'll tell you a story. We have an interesting customer who's been coming in since we opened. He's at the deli three times a week. He's a professor with big achievements in biochemistry, and he just had his seventy-fifth birthday. He told his sons that the only thing he wanted was to have a Zingerman's sandwich named after him. They contacted us. We put together a special sandwich for him, which he helped design, and we had a sign made up for it that we put up in the deli. We were going to bring it out on a Saturday. Friday night, I'm at the Roadhouse working, and his sons are there with his ex-wife, who lives here in Ann Arbor. They're talking about the sandwich, and the role we play in their dad's life. Then I see him on Saturday morning, and he's so excited. Later he sent an e-mail saying how great the sandwich was.

"And this is not a guy with no life. He's a very successful person, world famous in his field, which has nothing to do with designing sandwiches. That's a good example of *terroir* because people like that are present in a significant way in this community, and we can have that kind of connection with him—because we're here. We wouldn't have it if we weren't here, and we wouldn't be here if we'd done the usual thing as far as growing goes."

That level of intimacy is typical of the companies in this book, and the story illustrates another point as well. For many of these companies, the relationships they have with their communities overlap the relationships they have with their customers, and also with their employees. In those, too, intimacy plays a critical role.

4

Ties That Bind

Marilyn McDevitt Rubin, a columnist for the Pittsburgh *Post-Gazette*, already knew something about Union Square Hospitality Group when she and four friends went to lunch one day at Tabla, the fourth of Danny Meyer's restaurants, which is known for its creative use of Indian herbs and spices with American food. She had eaten at three others—Union Square Café, Gramercy Tavern, and Eleven Madison Park—and found the food delicious and the service impeccable; and she expected that Tabla would offer a similar experience. But impeccable service is not what Meyer strives for. Instead, his restaurants aim to provide what he calls enlightened hospitality. Rubin began to learn what that meant when, shortly after placing her order at Tabla, she turned suddenly in her chair and slammed into a server holding a tray of glasses filled with water that he was about to put on the table.

"I sat watching, transfixed, as the tray tipped, the water leaped from the glasses and, in seeming slow motion, the glasses tumbled over the side," Rubin later wrote in her column. "The crash came like a cannon shot. While diners remained calm, too polite to turn and stare, restaurant staff ran in from all directions. Mops and buckets, dustpans and sweepers appeared. Several people came at me with napkins to pat away the water that had spilled down my front and back. . . . It took several minutes for the tempest to die down, but soon the table was reset, flutes appeared and a very fine private label champagne was poured as a gift from the house to soothe us over our rough beginning."

At any restaurant, such a response would have qualified as excellent service, and Rubin was quite satisfied with it. But there was more. First, Meyer himself showed up to offer his help. "It was my fault," Rubin said.

"I'm sure it wasn't your fault," he replied. Rubin knew it had been entirely her fault, but she realized that Meyer was trying to relieve her of any residual feelings of guilt she might have, lest they detract from her dining experience. They didn't. She reported that she and her friends had an outstanding luncheon: "Treated to every kindness, we were happy. . . ."

As they were getting their coats, the unlucky server who'd been holding the tray with the water glasses emerged from the kitchen and came over to apologize for his clumsiness. "I assured him, as sincerely as I could, that I was the one responsible," Rubin wrote. "But like the man who had hired him, and who had recognized in him the quality of caring required [to work in a Danny Meyer restaurant], the waiter refused me the blame and graciously assumed it for himself."

And that was the message Rubin conveyed to her newspaper's almost one million readers.

Business is business, and mistakes happen no matter how great a company you have, as Danny Meyer is well aware. "If someone finds a small screw in their risotto, they're going to tell everybody they know," he once observed to *Gourmet* magazine. "I can't change that. But what I can do is make sure that when they tell the story they go on to say, 'But do you know how the restaurant handled that?'"

That is, of course, why extraordinary customer service has always made such good business sense, no matter what you have to do to provide it. From eye-popping service come industry legends, rave reviews in the media, and fabulous word of mouth, which is the most effective marketing tool a company can have. Meyer's version of service, however, is a little different from the norm and springs from another source. "What I've learned," he said, "is that I have an intense, nearly neurotic interest in seeing people have a good time." Enlightened hospitality is his name for the process of making sure they do.

In Search of Excellence, coauthor Tom Peters once noted that great companies tend to be founded by people with "not totally stupid obsessions" around which they build their businesses. That's exactly what Meyer has done with enlightened hospitality. He doesn't deny the importance of traditional customer service, but he regards it as a set of technical skills. In a restaurant, he says, service involves such practices as taking the order promptly; having the food arrive while it's still hot; and, yes, cleaning up quickly when a tray of water glasses spills. You can teach people to do all those things, and to do them well. Enlightened hospitality, on the other hand, is an emotional skill involving the ability to make customers feel that you're on their side. That's the mantra of Meyer's restaurant staff: Let them know you're on their side. "It's as simple as that," he says.

Simple it may be, but easy it is not. There are clear limits to Meyer's ability to teach enlightened hospitality. Yes, he can give examples of it in action. He can talk about the waiter who sees customers having trouble deciding between two desserts—and brings the second one free. Or the manager who offers to return by messenger or Federal Express the handbag that the customer has left behind, rather than simply holding it for her until she comes to get it. Or the maitre d' who puts a rose on Table 27 for Mr. and Mrs. Knightly, knowing they always sit there on their anniversary because that's where he proposed to her. Beyond that, Meyer can provide staff members with a computer system that will help them remember such details and others—which customer is a regular, or which one wants the ice from the martini shaker in a separate glass on the side, or which one sounded particularly disagreeable on the phone. (There's an AA next to his name, standing for "appreciates attention.") What Meyer can't do is instill the capacity for empathy in people who don't have it. He can't make them sensitive to the way their actions affect other people. He can't give them the desire to bend over backward to ensure that customers leave feeling they've just had a spectacular dining experience because they've been "treated to every kindness," not just because they've received good service. And he can't teach them to care as much as he does about making sure each customer has a good time. So he hires for those qualities and skills, the human skills; he trains for the others.

And he has consistently gotten what he wants. In fact, he was providing enlightened hospitality before he even knew what it was. The revelation came in 1995, during the difficult period when he was trying to get his second restaurant, Gramercy Tavern, up and running. Things were going so badly that he was afraid he might go bankrupt, as his father had—twice—when Meyer was growing up. Desperate for help, he hired a consultant, who pointed out a paradox. Although the diners in the *Zagat Survey* had ranked the Union Square Café tenth for food, eleventh for service, and out of the money altogether for décor, they had also voted it the third most popular restaurant in the entire city. Evidently there was some other factor at work. The other factor, Meyer and his associates decided, was hospitality, which they then tried to define. In the end, they agreed that it came from their commitment to five core values: caring for each other; caring for guests; caring for the community; caring for suppliers; and caring for investors and profitability—in descending order of importance.

Armed with this fresh insight, Meyer and his team were able to turn Gramercy Tavern around and build it into one of the city's most popular restaurants, second only to Union Square Café. Since then, the five core values have remained the company's firm foundation. "Every gesture, every act in a Danny Meyer restaurant is designed to fulfill these corny-sounding tenets, which make working there akin to joining a cult or the world's jolliest company softball team," wrote *Gourmet*'s Bruce Feiler, who did a three-week stint as a maitre d' at Union Square Café before writing his article. "They also make the job intensely and unexpectedly personal."

※

"Personal" is, indeed, the key word here. Great customer service involves demonstrating to customers that you value their business and will go the extra mile to keep it. Enlightened hospitality means showing them that you care about them personally. You don't want them just to be satisfied; you want them to be happy. It's a step beyond service, and it requires the company to develop an emotional connection with customers through individual, one-on-one, person-to-person contacts.

You don't have to be in the restaurant business to connect with customers in that way. The other companies in this book don't call it enlightened hospitality, but they do much the same thing. It is a key element of their mojo, and the one most visible to the outside world.

Take Clif Bar, for example. Its entire marketing strategy is geared toward connecting directly with consumers at the grassroots level. Although it does some traditional advertising, its competitors spend as much as ten times more than Clif Bar in that arena. Instead, it devotes 75 percent of its marketing budget, as well as the lion's share of its employees' time, to sponsoring and producing between one thousand and two thousand local, regional, and national events around the country every year, many of which are organized, run, and staffed by Clif Bar's own people. It also supports more than one thousand amateur and professional athletes—its ambassadors to the world of cyclists, climbers, and other sportspeople who made up its original customer base. Through the competitions its athletes take part in, the events its employees put on, and the other projects it sponsors—such as the LunaFest women's film festival—Clif Bar has direct, face-to-face contact every week with thousands of people who use its products. From those consumers, it gets honest feedback and new ideas. The consumers, in turn, develop a personal relationship with the people and the company they're buying from.

And that's the whole point. Remember the exercise I mentioned in the introduction, wherein Erickson and his employees first identified companies that had once had mojo and lost it and then tried to figure out how that had happened? The group concluded that, among other things, the companies "forgot about the emotional connection with the consumer . . . and concentrated on the process of business." They stopped being the type of business to which customers feel an intimate connection—the type they identify with and want to be associated with because they share the company's values; or because they perceive it to be authentic, true to itself, the real McCoy; or because they know they can always count on it to come through; or just because they think it's cool. Clif Bar developed its marketing strategy accordingly. Whereas traditional marketing—heavy advertising, lots of retail promotions, high-profile sponsorships—aims to build sales of a product as fast and as much as possible, Erickson focused on another goal: maintaining the emotional connection with consumers, and the mojo that comes with it. The sales, he believed, would follow, and they did.

To be sure, the techniques used by Union Square Hospitality and Clif Bar won't work everywhere. A company has to develop its own methods of establishing intimate customer relationships, based on its particular circumstances, the nature of its business, and the types of customers it has. CitiStorage, for example, provides records-storage services mainly to organizations—law firms, accounting firms, hospitals, government agencies, and the like—rather than individuals. Most of the people it deals with are not owners or top executives, but office managers and other midlevel employees who have specific responsibility for handling the organization's files. CitiStorage's principal owner and CEO, Norm Brodsky, wants them to feel the same personal connection with his company that Gary Erickson wants Clif Bar's consumers to feel with his, and CitiStorage works hard to create it. Brodsky's wife, Elaine, who has a major role in the business, sends personal, handwritten letters to new customers, welcoming them to the company, inviting them to contact either her or her husband directly if there's anything they wish to discuss in the future, and explaining how the two of them can be reached. Brodsky himself meets with all prospective customers. He used to have follow-up meetings with customers at least once a year until they became too numerous to allow it. He still sees as many as he can, and he invites them to company events, including the annual Fourth of July party at the CitiStorage facility on the Brooklyn side of the East

River, from which they have a front row seat for the Macy's fireworks display. Some customers are also honored by having aisles in the warehouse named after their company, always with great fanfare.

But what's most unusual is the role that CitiStorage's four hundred employees play in the relationship. The majority come from the inner city, and many have never before held a stable job offering benefits and opportunities for advancement. Like the other small giants, CitiStorage strives to have an intimate workplace (more about that in Chapter 5) and uses every technique its managers can think of—or can borrow from other companies—not only to create an atmosphere in which employees feel valued and respected but also to make it possible for them to have fun at work. It runs an ongoing game, for example, that pays a bonus to everyone in the company whenever the number of stored boxes reaches a new level. As the box count approaches a major milestone, the company starts another game in which employees try to guess the date that the target will be reached, with a prize for the winner. The company also sponsors some games just for fun (which department can grow the largest Amaryllis) and for health (who can lose the most weight). On top of that, CitiStorage offers generous benefits, including health insurance, a 401(k) program to which it contributes $1.30 for every dollar an employee invests, and an education program that reimburses employees for any outside classes they take as long as they maintain a B average or better.

And the company misses no opportunity to show how much it cares about the people who work there—in good times and bad. After the 9/11 destruction of the World Trade Center, Elaine Brodsky brought in grief counselors to help people overcome the trauma of having watched it unfold from the CitiStorage premises across the East River. Later, Norm Brodsky staged a companywide basketball tournament as a way to lift their spirits. (It worked.) A professional masseuse comes monthly to give massages to employees. They can also buy discounted movie tickets, partially subsidized by the company, and go to home games of New York's professional basketball and baseball teams using the season passes that CitiStorage buys to give out in recognition of exceptional performance. And that's just for starters.

The result is a warm, upbeat, closely knit corporate culture that also happens to be very appealing to prospective customers, as Brodsky began to notice at one point. When he took them on tours of the company, he would stop in the area of the warehouse where CitiStorage puts up huge signs to track progress on its box game. The visitors would ask questions, and he'd explain the company's philosophy and policies. They would smile and shake their heads and say, "Gee, can I get an application to work here?" One new customer sent a letter saying he had decided to store his five thousand boxes at CitiStorage in hopes that they would raise the box count to the next level and the employees could receive their bonus checks.

But it was Elaine Brodsky who saw the opportunity to have employees play an even greater role in building ties with customers. She made the case that CitiStorage should provide customer service training to all of its full-time salaried employees—not just the customer service reps, but to everyone. Although the investment was significant—$10,000 for a trainer, plus the employees' time to attend the three-day course—and her husband was skeptical of the benefits, he went along with the plan. The employees responded so enthusiastically to the program that Elaine decided to continue it after the initial course, holding regular monthly sessions on customer service. She used them to drive home the point that everyone could affect how customers felt about the company. "When you see Norman or someone else giving people a tour, those are usually prospective customers," she said. "We want to make them feel welcome. That means smiling and saying hello."

The effects of the training were even greater than she had expected and could be seen both inside and outside the business. Relationships between departments improved as people began to understand better what role each of them played, what challenges their co-workers faced, and how important it was that they all work together. In the process, they started providing more feedback to one another. When customers called in with praise, the telephone representatives made sure that the warehouse workers heard about it. When there were complaints or special requests, employees were able to coordinate among themselves to do what had to be done.

Norm Brodsky noticed the results almost immediately. People who called him asked if he'd hired new operators. The number of compliments about service soared. In the six months following the start of the program, CitiStorage received more comments, calls, and letters of praise than it had had in the previous fourteen years. One episode in particular demonstrated the impact that employees—even those not directly involved in customer service—could have on customers.

It happened one afternoon when the company president, Louis Weiner, returned to the executive offices with a prospective customer he had just shown around the facility. The prospect was to meet with Brodsky at the end of the tour. As they were sitting in his office, Brodsky asked the man if he was considering other vendors. "Yes, two," he said and mentioned the names of CitiStorage's major competitors.

"Did you see any differences between them and us?" Brodsky asked.

"Yes, I did," the prospect said. "Every one of your employees was smiling, and they all said hello. I've never seen anything quite like it. They must really be happy."

"I hope so," Brodsky said. "Thank you for noticing."

"Because of that, in fact, I've decided to give you the business," the prospect said.

Brodsky was completely taken aback. Sales were never closed on the spot. After the tour, prospects liked to mull over the decision, talk to other people, and give an answer in a couple of days. But Brodsky kept his surprise to himself. "That's great," he said. "I think you've made the right choice."

They chatted until the prospect had to leave, whereupon Brodsky immediately went searching for his wife. "You won't believe what just happened," he said and told her the story. She could hardly contain herself. Without hesitating, she got on the public address system and shared the news with the rest of the company.

※

Intimate customer relationships also figure prominently in the mojo of the manufacturers in this book, but the challenge they face is different from—and, in some ways, more complex than—the one confronting retail businesses and service companies. It requires organizing the entire company around tailoring products to customers' individual needs. In some circles, that's known as adopting a "value discipline."

The concept of value disciplines was popularized by consultants Michael Treacy and Fred Wiersema in their 1995 bestseller, *The Discipline of Market Leaders*, which was the expanded version of an earlier article they'd written in the *Harvard Business Review*. They argued that, to be really successful, a company had to focus on providing one of three types of value to its customers: the best price, the best product, or the best overall solution. Each type of value called for a completely different kind of organization, culture, and mind-set, so you would inevitably get in trouble if you tried to excel at more than one. To have the best price, for example, you needed to focus on being "operationally effective," doing one thing extremely well, day in and day out, thereby keeping your own costs as low as possible. Having the best products called for a whole different focus—on innovation, rather than efficiency—which meant staying several steps ahead of customers, coming up with a product they would need before they knew they needed it, and being driven more by the possibilities of technology than by the current demands of the market. Then again, if you wanted to provide the best overall solution, you took yet another course, becoming "customer intimate," that is, developing products flexible enough to serve a wide variety of customer needs and working closely and collaboratively with customers to give them what they wanted. To do that and still earn a profit, you had to structure the whole company around the customer-intimate discipline. Not that you wouldn't strive to be as efficient and innovative as possible, but you would always do so with an eye toward enhancing your ability to deliver products and services that would help you meet the unique needs of individual customers in a cost-effective manner.

Now, every small giant is customer intimate, but it's a bit more difficult for manufacturers than for others to create the intimacy, and they
have to be a bit more deliberate about it, if only because it requires
them to rethink so many aspects of their business, from the number of
engineers they hire to the organization of work on the shop floor. A case
in point is ECCO, the Boise-based backup alarm and amber warning
light company.

ECCO, originally Electronic Controls Company, was born in 1972
as the direct result of a decision by the federal Occupational Safety and
Health Administration (OSHA) to require backup alarms on certain
types of vehicles. At the time, there was another Boise company making
the alarms, Peterson Rebuilding and Exchange Co. (PRECO), which
had until recently been owned by its two founders, Carl and Ed Peterson, who were brothers. When they'd decided to go their separate ways,
Ed had taken the business, while Carl had held on to the building. At
the time, he'd had no intention of going into backup alarms, but—with
the surprise decision by OSHA—he'd experienced an abrupt change of
heart and started his own backup alarm company, ECCO, leading to
years of litigation, rivers of bad blood, and decades of bitter competition
between the crosstown rivals.

It was hardly an ideal set of circumstances in which to build a company, and—despite a long-term contract with Hewlett-Packard to manufacture parts for disk drives, in addition to making backup alarms for
other customers—ECCO was still struggling by the time Jim Thompson
came along in 1984. Trained in finance, he was looking for a business to
acquire and saw ECCO as "a company with great prospects and terrible
finances," not to mention a broken corporate culture. With the proceeds
from the sale of his stock in an employee stock ownership plan (ESOP)
at a food service company he'd worked for, Thompson bought a 50-
percent stake in ECCO. In 1985, he and two friends acquired the remaining shares. In 1988, they set up their own ESOP.

The company, burdened with a mountain of debt, continued to
struggle under its new ownership. "For the first few years, I was just
thinking about how to get customers to pay, and how to get product

shipped," Thompson recalled. "It was a matter of getting through the day." And not just the work day, either: he and his partner, Ed Zimmer, who was also his brother-in-law and ECCO's aftermarket sales manager, would bring home circuit boards that they would get other members of the family to help solder. Thompson's son, Chris, says only half jokingly that he didn't get dinner until he'd finished his batch.

It was a stressful period, particularly for Thompson, a hard-driving, type-A entrepreneur with a gruff manner, a take-charge leadership style, and a strong belief in employee ownership. Eventually, however, the company began to turn around, helped along by the close personal relationships Thompson and Zimmer developed with their customers, the distributors and vehicle makers that ECCO supplied. "We'd both had those types of relationships with customers when we'd worked for other companies, and we valued them highly," Thompson said. "We thought we could apply the same attitude here with good results. But there was no grand design. We weren't thinking about it strategically." Mainly, the customer orientation reflected the owners' belief, reinforced by the books and tapes of Tom Peters, that staying close to customers was the right thing to do.

By the early 1990s, ECCO had begun to prosper. Its share of the U.S. market for backup alarms had risen from less than 5 percent in 1984 to about 33 percent in 1993. That year, its sales reached $9.5 million, up from $640,000 in 1984—and Thompson had his first heart attack. It was serious enough that it forced him to recognize the need to make significant changes in his life. He asked Zimmer to take over the presidency of the company and gave him a month to decide. A week later, Zimmer came back with an offer to become general manager instead. "Then you can return if I screw up," he said.

"If you screw up, I'm selling the company," Thompson replied. "You have twenty-three days to make up your mind." With some trepidation, Zimmer agreed to take the helm.

With the change in leadership came a change in style, and the beginning of ECCO's transformation from a customer-friendly company into a customer-intimate one. To help with the transition at the top,

Zimmer brought in a behavioral scientist from Boise State University, Roy Glen, who later continued to work with Thompson, Zimmer, and the senior managers on strategic planning, facilitating the three-day off-site meetings they began holding once a year. Along the way, Glen introduced them to the ideas of Treacy and Wiersema. The managers had no trouble deciding which of the three value disciplines they wanted to pursue, but reorganizing the company around the concept of customer intimacy proved to be a bigger, and longer-term, challenge than any of them realized at the time.

Essentially, it meant reinventing a successful business. Judging by the numbers, the company was in great shape. In 1994, it had pretax profit of $550,000 (an increase of 1,000 percent over the year before) on sales of $12.4 million (up 31 percent from 1993). Meanwhile, ECCO—which had moved into vehicle warning lights by then, a natural complement to backup alarms—was rapidly acquiring a reputation for the quality of its products. That year, it became the first U.S. company with fewer than one hundred employees, and the first manufacturer of emergency warning products anywhere in the world, to be awarded ISO-9001 certification. The company also had excellent relations with its customers, including the top hundred distributors in the country.

But becoming customer intimate involved more than getting close to customers and selling them good products. The goal was to develop the ability to provide customers with products that could serve a multiplicity of their needs, and to do it at a lower cost than anyone else in the market. That required, to begin with, some changes in the management team. Within the first four months after Zimmer took over, seven of the nine senior managers either moved into different positions or left the company. In addition, ECCO had to revamp its product-development systems, reorganize its engineering department, recruit a new engineering staff, make significant investments in both hardware and software, hire salespeople with experience in selling such products, train current employees to make and market them, develop new mechanisms of internal communication and coordination between departments—in other words, change just about everything. And because the company did not want outside investors and was reluctant to take on additional debt, it had to finance the whole thing using its own, internally generated cash flow.

It took years and a few costly mistakes to make the change. The company learned the hard way, for example, that it shouldn't spend a lot of time and money developing new products for new customers. They wouldn't buy from a supplier they didn't know if it had no track record in the business, even though the products might appear to be exactly what they needed. Nor did ECCO have much success selling new products to existing customers unless it had already demonstrated its competence in the channel. When it devised an ingenious system for simplifying the wiring on buses, it couldn't persuade the bus manufacturers that bought its backup alarms to go for it. ECCO simply didn't have enough credibility in that area.

But those were not so much setbacks as learning experiences, and as time went along, ECCO became the model of a customer-intimate manufacturer. It could offer customers a choice of six hundred different configurations of backup alarms, rather than the usual thirty or forty, because each one could be easily altered to fit the different needs of different vehicles. The same was true of emergency lights. There might be thirty variations of a specific type of light, but two lenses would fit all thirty. A single replaceable flash tube would fit in fifty lights. A multi-voltage circuit board could recognize how many volts it was dealing with, and any given light could produce a variety of different flashes depending on how its wires were attached.

To create such products, ECCO needed a first-rate engineering staff, and it got one. In 1994, it had had just two engineers, neither of whom was a certified PE (professional engineer). Ten years later, the company had eighteen engineers, all of whom were PEs. Thompson—who was retired from operations by then although he still served as board chairman—remarked that there were more engineers in 2004 than he'd had people when he was running the company. And they were well-equipped engineers, with state-of-the-art tools for both designing products and getting customers intimately involved in the process. One software program, which the engineers dubbed The Vault, allowed customers to access designs via the Internet. Thus an engineer at ECCO could make a change and put it in The Vault, where the customer could look at it and call back with modifications. Customers took to the system immediately. Engineers at Caterpillar, a major customer and the largest user of backup alarms in the world, were constantly accessing The Vault, calling back five minutes after a new design went in.

For all that, ECCO was still spending only 5 percent of its revenues on engineering, as compared to 3 percent a decade earlier. That was possible because of the dramatic increase in productivity that accompanied the changes. In 1994, the company had had $70,000 in sales per employee. By 2004, the figure had more than doubled to $156,000 in sales per employee. At the same time, technological advances allowed the company to respond more quickly to customers needs, and to do it at a dramatically lower cost. The lead time on machine tools, for example, dropped from twenty-six weeks to eight weeks, while the cost of a new tool plunged from $70,000 or more to about $12,000.

ECCO took full advantage of the new technology. As a result, it had the lowest costs of the companies in its industry that aspired to be customer intimate; that is, the ones making lights and alarms that could be reconfigured for use in a broad range of products. It was also one of the most innovative. Eighty percent of its revenue in 2004 came from products that hadn't existed eight years before—40 percent from brand-new products and 40 percent from products that had been improved. At any given time, moreover, the company had twenty product-development projects going, each of which could yield thirty or forty new part numbers (as the different configurations were known). In 2002 and 2003 alone, the development teams came up with 850 new part numbers, worth $9 million in revenue.

For the people at ECCO, customer intimacy was a passion. "I was in three or four dozen companies that used Solid Works," said Todd Mansfield, referring to the advanced computer-aided design program he used to sell, which allowed engineers to do in seconds what had once taken days. "ECCO was tops. They got it way better than anyone else. They knew what they had and what they could do with it." He was so impressed that he switched sides and went to work at ECCO.

Customers are not the only outsiders with whom the companies in this book have intimate relationships. There are also the suppliers that make it possible for them to achieve the levels of excellence they aspire to. The Zingerman's Community of Businesses, for one, is a showcase for its suppliers. It uses the deli, the ZCoB newsletters, and the numerous tastings it does to bring customers into contact with the people and the businesses from which it buys its food. Fortunately, many of those people and businesses have interesting stories for the ZCoB staff to tell. There are Ben and Blair Ripple, who own a farm in Bali, Indonesia, and supply Zingerman's with Balinese Sea Salt and Long Pepper, a spice that has been largely unavailable in Europe and the Americas for four or five hundred years, as Weinzweig reported in one of his weekly e-mail newsletters. Cindy and David Major supply Zingerman's with Vermont Shepherd cheese, made from the milk of their own sheep using a recipe adapted from that of the Ossau sheep cheese makers of southwestern France—and customers can compare the two at the deli. The deli's wild rice comes from the Ojibwa tribe of Minnesota, which harvests it from lakes where it actually does grow wild, unlike—the staff points out—the cultivated wild rice sold in supermarkets. And so on.

To be sure, education is a tool that many companies use to build closer relationships with customers. For Weinzweig, however, it's also a means of connecting customers to the sources of their food, and the food suppliers to the food consumers, in a way that's heartfelt and meaningful, reflecting—as it does—the individual passions and interests of everybody in the chain. As a result, the commercial transactions that occur are somewhat less abstract and anonymous than they would normally be. Not that there's anything wrong with anonymous commercial transactions. We wouldn't have much of an economy without them. But somehow making these connections contributes to a company's mojo, perhaps because it touches on emotional, not simply material, needs.

For lack of a better term, we might refer to the process as building a sense of community—that is, a sense of common cause between the company, its employees, its customers, and suppliers. That sense of community rests on three pillars. The first is integrity—the knowledge that the company is what it appears, and claims, to be. It does not project a false image to the world. The second pillar is professionalism—the company does what it says it's going to do. It can be counted on to make good on its commitments. The third pillar is the one we've been discussing—the direct, human connection, the effect of which is to create an emotional bond, based on mutual caring.

Companies that succeed in developing such a sense of community with their customers and suppliers find themselves in possession of one of the most powerful business tools in the world. No company has done more in that regard than Righteous Babe. Indeed, it elicits a level of devotion seldom seen in any business.

It's evident in the loyalty of Righteous Babe's customers—Ani DiFranco's fans—which is legendary in the industry. Some of them serve as field representatives for the company, spearheading the local promotion for DiFranco's concerts. (They get tickets for their efforts, instead of cash.) Others write in volunteering to help "spread the word" and are sent posters they can put up on college campuses or around town. When Internet file sharing became a problem, DiFranco's fans went out of their way to protect the company, patrolling the Internet and reporting on Web sites that tried to sell her recordings in competition with Righteous Babe. And long before the company moved into the renovated church, people would come from as far away as Australia and Switzerland, not to see DiFranco perform but to visit Righteous Babe's thoroughly nondescript headquarters in downtown Buffalo. "I'm standing here in total awe," wrote one visitor from Los Angeles in the guest book.

"I traveled from Houston to see this," wrote another. "It's amazing to be here."

The company, for its part, is deeply respectful of the special relationship it has with its customers. When they write in—and thousands of them do—staff members respond with individual, handwritten notes, signed by the employee. Every e-mail is answered by someone hired for that express purpose. Customers who call the 800 number (1-800-OnHerOwn) can talk directly to staff members, because—unlike other record companies—Righteous Babe doesn't outsource the function.

"It's not enough for us to be good to customers," said company president Scot Fisher. "We want our relationships with them to be personal and real, not contrived. We handwrite the letters and answer the phones ourselves because we want to be sure that people who write in or call in are dealing with someone who cares."

That can sometimes lead to tricky situations. One young fan became so depressed after missing a DiFranco concert that he cut his wrists, swallowed a bunch of pills, and dialed the 800 number. A staff member answered and passed the call along to Fisher, who stayed on the telephone for forty minutes until he could ascertain that the young man had help nearby. Before hanging up, the caller expressed his thanks, saying, "I knew you would be there. I just knew it."

"He knew that someone would answer, and it wouldn't be a call center in Indianapolis," Fisher said. "It's gratifying to know that people feel they can count on us like that, but it's also scary to realize the kind of reputation we have. We have to be so careful."

The respect for the relationship carries over to the more traditional aspects of the company's marketing. When Fisher and DiFranco decided to put out a catalog from which fans could order things like Righteous Babe T-shirts, refrigerator magnets, and posters, in addition to CDs and tapes, they brought Ron Ehmke in to write the copy. "Scot was very clear about what he didn't want the catalog to be," he recalled. "He said, 'Think about the fans at home. They've been getting funky postcards, and then suddenly they get this full-color catalog with all this stuff to buy. It's got to be about something more. It can't be about cramming merchandise down people's throats.'"

Fisher came up with the idea of including a letter, called the "Hey

Folks" letter, that would update recipients on goings-on in the Righteous Babe world. Ehmke worked hard to develop the right voice for it. "We wanted it to be very down to earth," he said, "sort of my version of Ani's writing voice," although her name would not be on it. Drafts were scrutinized by Fisher and DiFranco, who would sometimes make major changes. "It was a long process of trying to learn the do's and don'ts of getting the voice down. That applied to press releases, communications with fans, everything."

They were as careful about tone as about voice, and about language as about tone. Certain words they strived to avoid. For example, they always referred to "opening artists" rather than "opening acts," and "customers" or "friends" rather than "fans," because DiFranco wanted to discourage a cult of personality. (By the same token, she would have nothing to do with organizing a fan club, and she wouldn't allow her face to appear on T-shirts.) "We used to joke about the forbidden words," said Ehmke. "We were feeling our way. I remember one press release Ani looked at, and her only comment was, 'Be more funny.' There was strong opposition to hype. We had philosophical debates about how you do promotion if you don't believe in marketing and merchandising art but look at it as a necessary evil."

Designer Brian Grunert, a veteran of the Buffalo advertising community, didn't have those qualms about marketing, but he was struck by the way the company went about it. "There really was no conscious effort to sell Ani or Righteous Babe, more than to just present them," he said. "They weren't trying to trick people into buying a record. The idea was to make something worth buying and then put it out there so that people could be attracted—or not."

All of that contributes to the company's reputation for integrity, which is as strong among its suppliers as its customers. Their loyalty to Righteous Babe is matched only by Righteous Babe's loyalty to them. In 1995, for example, Fisher met with Michael Koch of Koch Entertainment, the leading independent national record distributor. Securing national distribution was critical to Righteous Babe, as it is to any independent label. The problem was that the company already had relationships with other distributors, and Koch insisted on exclusivity. Fisher had no qualms about dropping regional distributors that had come on fairly recently and performed disappointingly, but he didn't want to abandon the two distributors of women's music—Goldenrod and Ladyslipper—that had signed up early and promoted DiFranco when she was largely unknown. "I told Koch that we wanted to continue working with them," Fisher says. "He said that couldn't be done. I said, 'Okay, then we can't do a deal.' I was ready to walk away. But Koch came around."

Or consider Righteous Babe's relationship to its suppliers in the Buffalo area, as well as to the city itself. DiFranco has been using the same company, ESP Inc., to manufacture her cassette tapes and CDs since she did her first demo tape in 1988—when ESP's owners were operating out of their basement. Today it's a forty-person business putting out 140,000 CDs per week for a variety of clients, thanks in no small part to Righteous Babe's steadfast support over the years.

Righteous Babe's printer, Thorner Press, has similarly benefited from the company's loyalty to Buffalo. Pat Thompson, who handles the account for Thorner, says Fisher made it clear from the beginning that he wanted all of Righteous Babe's work to be done in Thorner's Buffalo plant, not in its Canadian facility. Then one day he needed a poster on short notice. Thompson said she could get it done quickly only by printing it in Canada. Fisher agreed, but when she delivered the posters, he took her into his office and shut the door. "He said, 'Pat, don't ever let me do that again. If it can be done in Buffalo, it's got to be done in Buffalo.' I said, 'Yes, sir.'"

Righteous Babe has shown the same kind of loyalty to the promoters who produced concerts for DiFranco from the early days. Darcy Greder, for one, put on her first Ani DiFranco concert in 1992 at Illinois Wesleyan University in Bloomington, Illinois, where she works. About 150 people showed up. Six years later, she was handling concerts of as many as 5,000 people. She still produces DiFranco's shows in central Illinois today. "That's their philosophy," says Greder, whose day job is associate dean of students at Illinois Wesleyan. "Dance with the ones who brought you."

One could argue that such loyalties have held the company back and prevented DiFranco from reaching a larger audience. Certainly they have been maintained at a cost. "We've been offered, and we've turned down, excessive amounts of money to break relationships with our existing promoters and go with someone else," says DiFranco's booking agent Jim Fleming, who has represented her for twelve years. "Money is not the major enticement. Ani, Scot, and I respect and honor people who've been with us from the beginning and done a great job on our behalf. I think that's ultimately good business."

But loyalty alone doesn't explain the way suppliers feel about Righteous Babe. There's also the company's reputation for professionalism, which begins with DiFranco herself. Fisher tells a story about an urgent request she once received in the middle of a tour, asking if she could write a song for a particular scene in My Best Friend's Wedding, starring Julia Roberts and Hugh Grant. It was a Tuesday, and the movie people needed the song by the end of the week. DiFranco agreed to do it and delivered the finished package to the movie studio on Friday, with the song synched to the scene. The movie people were grateful—and impressed.

"That's the way Ani is," Fisher said. "People might not like her music, but no one could ever say she was unprofessional, or careless. I always wanted the office to be as professional as she was. Independent musicians have a reputation of not doing things on time. We're not like that. We pay our bills on time. We deliver the CDs on time. We have a policy of no back orders. If you place an order before 2:00 P.M., it will ship the next day."

The people Righteous Babe does business with are duly appreciative. "They're just terrific to work with," said Virginia Giordano, who has been DiFranco's promoter in New York City since the mid-1990s. "They're hands-on, close to their product, honest, completely professional, concerned, always available to work out problems, not trying to squeeze every nickel out of a situation, just really fair. I couldn't say that about every company I work with."

Independent record store operators are equally enthusiastic. "They're the model of the perfect independent label," said Carl Singmaster, founder and—until recently—owner of Manifest Discs & Tapes, a chain of stores in North and South Carolina. "They always fully support their albums. They know when and where to spend their marketing dollars. They never do anything stupid."

But the most unusual aspect of Righteous Babe's relationships with customers and suppliers has to do with the nature of the connections it makes. It has few, if any, strictly business relationships. It shies away from them, striving instead to relate to customers and suppliers as individuals and friends with whom it shares a common mission. "People really believe in this idea of building an alternative, not just to giant record companies, but to the increasing corporatization of American culture," said Ron Ehmke, the writer. "It's a very genuine thing."

They believe it because DiFranco and Fisher have won their trust. "The values they run the business with are the values that guide their lives," said Darcy Greder, the college dean and concert promoter. "There's this seamless consistency between Ani's words, her music, her art, and the reality of her life. The personal is the political, and vice versa."

It all contributes to that sense of community, which everybody in Righteous Babe's orbit seems to share. Even the more traditional businesspeople among them feel the attraction. "If Righteous Babe ever left, it would be a big blow, but more on an emotional level than a financial level," said Michael Rosenberg, president of Koch Entertainment Distribution. "We're all proud that we're working with Righteous Babe and Ani DiFranco. For us to lose them would have a large emotional impact, especially on the sales and marketing staff."

It's important to note, moreover, that DiFranco herself plays a limited role in all this. Koch's sales and marketing staff members have little contact with either her or Fisher. The connection they feel to the company is based mainly on the relationships they have with label manager Mary Begley, retail manager Susan Tanner, and the other people they deal with at Righteous Babe. "They're just such a pleasure to work with," said Rosenberg.

And that speaks to the little secret behind the relationships that mojo companies have with their suppliers and customers. It's generally not the people at the top of the organization who create the intimate bonds. It's the managers and employees who do the work of the business day in and day out. They are the ones who convey the spirit of the company to the outside world. Accordingly, they are the company's first priority—which, from one perspective, is ironic. For all the extraordinary service and enlightened hospitality that the small giants offer, what really sets them apart is their belief that the customer comes second.

5

※

A Culture of Intimacy

Michelle Howard works at ECCO in Boise, Idaho. If you'd dropped by during the fall of 2003, you might have run into her. At thirty-one, she was already a nine-year veteran of the company. A plump, bright-eyed, effusive young woman, she works in customer service and loves it. "I'm always busy, always learning, always problem solving," she said. "My job is to do whatever it takes to make the customer happy, and there aren't many restrictions on that. Say we have a shipping problem—we didn't send the right amount of something. We can overnight it and get it to the customer before 8:00 A.M. the next morning. Or we can give a credit. Or whatever else we think is best."

Like 140 or so of her fellow employees, Michelle is an owner of ECCO. She is a member of the employee stock ownership plan (ESOP) that controls 58 percent of the company's stock. When I met her, her stake was worth $12,000. More important, she feels like an owner and believes she is treated like one. She has a lot of direct contact with the CEO, Ed Zimmer. Among other things, he holds a regular monthly lunch with all the people who have a birthday that month, and they talk about themselves and the company and whatever else they want to discuss. There's also a companywide meeting each month to go over the financials, as well as a steady flow of financial information between meetings. "Things aren't secret here," Michelle said. "Everything is shared, which makes me feel safe. I know we're not going to get bought out, and I'm not going to lose my job. I hope we never get bought out. I don't want to work for a big corporation. I like ECCO the way it is. I know that if anything terrible happened, ECCO would do whatever it had to do to take care of me and whoever else needed it."

She has reason to feel that way. When she first came to work at ECCO in August 1994, she was twenty-three years old and a single mother with three small children—a daughter who was four, another daughter two, and a son seven months old. Her husband, whom she'd married right after high school, had recently walked out, leaving her alone with the children. With little education and few marketable skills, Michelle had no idea how she would make ends meet. She'd never even had a full-time job. She was getting by on food stamps and had only her equally impoverished mother to turn to for help. "It was scary, awful," she recalled. "It was the worst thing that ever happened to me."

Then she got a break. A friend of her mother's who worked at ECCO told her the company was looking for temporary employees to help get a big order out the door. Michelle applied and was hired. While her mother watched the children, she went to work putting labels on strobe lights. In December, with more and more orders coming in, ECCO made her a full-time, permanent employee.

Although the work was simple and repetitive, Michelle was grateful just to have a job. She spent a couple of more months labeling lights and putting them in boxes for shipping and would gladly have kept doing it, she said, but in February 1995, ECCO's vice president of sales, Dan Mc-Cann, asked her to move into customer service, where she would have to be on the phone, fielding questions, taking orders, and handling problems for customers. "I was reluctant," she said. "It sounded so big and scary. I had no experience. But Dan said, 'I think you can handle it.'"

The job was a challenge, requiring her to become familiar with every backup alarm and warning light that the company produced. She had to know how to install the products and how to take them apart. She also had to master new customer-tracking procedures as they were introduced and learn how to use her computer to find the information she needed. And she had to deal directly with customers, some of whom could be difficult.

While she was getting used to her new position, she continued to struggle at home, without any child support from her ex-husband for the first two and half years. "ECCO knew my situation and did everything it could do to help me," she said. "They let me take advances from my paycheck." She recalls countless little kindnesses from people in the company, especially her supervisor, who had also been through a divorce and was supportive. At one point, Michelle's son became seriously ill with what doctors thought was whooping cough—it turned out to be asthma—and the whole family had to be quarantined for five days. Karen Campbell, ECCO's head of human resources, brought food and flowers to the house. "I really cried," Michelle said.

How did she manage to pull through? "God and ECCO," she said. "Without schooling, I'd never have been able to get where I am if I didn't come here. That's what you can do in this company. I remember, at our Christmas party, there was a girl working in heavy-duty alarms, on the production line, and she was talking about how nice it must be to work in the office. I said, 'I started in labeling. You have the opportunity to move up here.' Now she's the lead person on the line."

Today, Michelle and her children live in a house she bought under a Boise program through which qualified applicants can get mortgages as long as they are able to cover the closing costs. With the assistance of ECCO's human resources department, she borrowed the $2,800 she needed from the 401(k) she had set up through the company. "Before, I always lived in a rented apartment with all three kids in one room," she said. "Now they each have their own room. I never thought that would happen to me—ever." As for the children, they were all in school and doing well. "My eldest daughter is the vice president of her eighth-grade class," Michelle said. "I'm so proud of her."

So she can perhaps be forgiven if she goes a little overboard sometimes in expressing her gratitude. At one of the company's meetings to review the financials and share other news, Michelle listened to a visitor explaining why he had decided to include ECCO in a book he was writing. "Go ECCO!" she shouted. "Someone said to me, 'What a kiss up you are,'" she recalled later that day. "I said, 'What do you mean? Don't you feel that way?' I'm just so grateful to God for blessing me with this job, and the learning, the respect, and the love we get here. ECCO cares about the people who work here, and we care about each other. I can't imagine going anywhere else. I'll stay here as long as they'll have me. I want to help make this company as successful as it can be."

There are libraries of books, reams of articles, and endless videos and tapes on how to create a motivated workforce, but if you want to see examples of businesses that have cracked the code, so to speak, you need look no further than the small giants. Indeed, the relationship between the employees and the company is the entire basis for the mojo they exude. You can't have the second without the first. Unless a significant majority of a company's people love the place where they work; unless they feel valued, appreciated, supported, and empowered; unless they see a future full of opportunities for them to learn and grow—unless, that is, they feel great about what they do, whom they do it with, and where they're going—mojo is simply not in the cards. Why? Because everything else that makes a company extraordinary—a great brand, terrific products or services, fabulous relationships with customers and suppliers, a vital role in the community—depends on those who do the work of the business, day in and day out.

Understand, this is not just about morale. There are plenty of happy employees in companies that don't have mojo, just as you can find some unhappy employees in companies that do. Nor is it just about compensation, perks, and benefits, as important as those may be. There's something else shaping the work environment of the companies in this book—something that promotes a profound sense of belonging, of psychic ownership—and it's a necessary, if not a sufficient, condition for achieving what the companies aspire to. That other factor is, once again, intimacy. By that, I mean a relationship so close employees never doubt that the company, its leaders, and the other people they work with care about them *personally* and will stand by them through thick and thin as long as they hold up their end of the bargain.

Obviously, the ability to create such intimacy has something to do with size. With some noteworthy exceptions, there is generally an inverse correlation between the number of people who work for a company and the strength of their emotional ties to it. Not that you can create a great work environment just by keeping the head count down, nor will you necessarily destroy one if you expand your workforce. But there is a limit to the number of employees a company can have and still maintain those intimate, personal connections. Most people recognize it, though few agree on exactly where it is. That may be because the limit varies from company to company, depending on the nature of the business, the imagination and skill of the managers, and the personal preferences of the leader.

At one end of the spectrum is Anchor Brewing, whose owner and CEO, Fritz Maytag, has consciously strived to keep the number of employees as low as possible. For most of the past twenty years, the head count has hovered around fifty full-time people, plus five or ten part-timers, depending on their availability and the company's needs. He has never felt tempted to hire more. "I've always thought it was more fun and satisfying to have all chiefs and no Indians," he once said in an interview with *Harvard Business Review* (HBR). "That was one of my ideas—to have a small group of people, where everyone knows they're all interrelated and where, as far as possible, everybody is in charge and nobody is looking over anyone's shoulder and there are no time clocks."

It was a management philosophy he'd learned growing up in Newton, Iowa. "That's the way my father raised our family, from the earliest moment. Lots of responsibility. We're counting on you. We trust you. And if you screw up, just tell us about it; don't worry about it. We're not encouraging you to screw up, but for heaven's sake, if you do, don't worry. We're all in this together, and we don't know what we're doing either, so come on and join in. And I always liked the idea of a small number of people. I just don't like what happens in large groups."

He had some experience with people working in large groups. As a young man, he had spent his summers doing various jobs at the Maytag factory in Newton, which employed three thousand people, most of whom were unionized. By then, he had gone through several stages in his feelings about being a Maytag—obliviousness, followed by uncertainty and a vague sense of embarrassment, then reconciliation and pride. "I decided that if you had to have a famous name, it might as well be a good one," he said. "The invention of the washing machine freed women from a lot of drudgery, and my great-grandfather improved it considerably. Under my father, the company became known for the quality and reliability of its products, and I was proud of that."

Working in the factory, however, he also saw some of the problems of large companies. "I realized there was good and bad," he said. "It was shocking to me that grown-ups didn't always like to work. When I bought [Anchor Brewing], I wanted it to be a place where people did want to work. I tried to create an environment where people enjoyed work—an environment that was cooperative, not adversarial."

He believed that the smaller the staff, the better chance he had of creating such an environment. In the early years, he had only four full-time employees. It took all of them—and sometimes a couple of other people—to do the bottling. On bottling days, Maytag would put up a "closed" sign and lock the door, and they would all go to work on the bottling line. Later, as the demand for Anchor's beers grew, he invested in equipment that would allow the company to produce more beer while minimizing the need for additional people. Among other things, Maytag believed that the quality would suffer if the staff got too big. For the same reason, he wanted to have only one shift, five days a week, and designed the brewery accordingly. "I'm sure this directly relates to quality," he told *HBR*. "You can never come in and look at your tools and say, 'Ugh, look what the night shift has done. Where's the hammer? Look, those jerks spilled something.' Here, it's all us. Everybody who works here can go home and say, 'I made the beer.' And when they go to a restaurant somewhere and see a bottle, they know they produced it. And I think that kind of pride tends to improve quality. Real quality control takes place every minute. It has to be done right now, not later. A smaller group tends to be more quality oriented. There's an enthusiasm here, a spirit of being on the leading edge of beers and brewing styles. There's a feeling of creativity. Partly that comes from being small, a little team where we all know what's going on."

Keeping the team small also relieved Maytag of some management chores. New people who weren't working out didn't have to be fired. They would leave of their own accord. They simply couldn't last in a small group of people without the support of their peers. Conversely, those who meshed with the culture were embraced by the group and given more responsibility, with Maytag scarcely having to say a word.

A small team, moreover, could do things together. There were numerous parties and outings, some with spouses and children, and some without. Every fall, Maytag would take a group of employees up to the family farm in northern California, near the Oregon border, where the barley for that year's Christmas Ale was being harvested. There they would ride on the combine and visit the coop where the barley was malted. "If you're going to make rubber tires, you should go to Malaya and see the damn rubber trees," he said. By the same token, he would bring employees with him on annual trips to Europe, where they would spend a couple of weeks visiting small breweries, and he had them take university-level brewing courses. It all served to increase the employees' expertise and build camaraderie, while enhancing their understanding of the differences between poor, decent, and exceptional quality beer. "If they're bottling and the beer isn't foaming properly, they're going to say, 'Gee, I don't want to be like those breweries in Europe that have oxidized beer that we all laughed about,'" said Maytag.

Inevitably, a small, close-knit group of people who like each other and spend a lot of time together begins to feel like a family, and Anchor Brewing's workforce was no exception. "I'm embarrassed by that," Maytag told *HBR*. "I'm proud of it, and I like it, but I'm also reluctant to say that I want to be the daddy to the family." Then again, he had to confess that he took enormous pleasure in watching the relationships between employees evolve. "Some of them get into little business deals together.

We've had several people in the company make investments together or do little projects together. I love it."

Wouldn't he feel the same way if the company were larger? "The atmosphere changes when there are more people," he said. "I don't know how many is too many. . . . I know of companies with two hundred employees where the head knows all their names. I've heard of companies with one thousand people that work. But I'm not very good at names. Fifty is about all I can handle."

There is, in fact, no question that a company's ability to achieve the kind of intimacy we're talking about here depends to some extent on the relationship between the person in charge and the employees. If you have no direct contact with a substantial number of the people depending on you for their livelihood—if you don't know who they are and what they do—it is extremely unlikely they will feel the intense, emotional attachment to the business that we see in close-knit organizations where everybody spends time together, has important experiences together, and knows what's going on in one another's lives. That's not to say there aren't great companies around that inspire tremendous loyalty among their employees, even though most of them are far removed from the CEO. But that loyalty is qualitatively different from the feelings of Michelle Howard toward ECCO and the feelings of Fritz Maytag toward the people at Anchor Brewing—if only because both Howard's and Maytag's feelings are based on numerous, ongoing, one-on-one interactions.

So it's fair to ask at what point a company becomes so big that it's impossible for any single human being to know everyone in the organization. Among the companies in our sample, the O. C. Tanner Company, which now has about nineteen hundred employees, most clearly tests the limits. Inside the company, there's disagreement about whether or not it has already grown past the point at which employees can feel they're part of the family. Some old-timers say that it has, especially since Obert Tanner passed away in 1993. Others, however, argue just the opposite—that his successors have managed to strengthen the bonds following the example set by the founder. What everyone agrees is that Obert Tanner himself did an extraordinary job of creating just the kind of workplace we are talking about, and he did it with more than a thousand employees.

Like most companies, O. C. Tanner started small—in the basement of the house in Salt Lake City where Obert's mother lived. It was 1927, and he was twenty-three years old, a student at the University of Utah, earning money to pay for his education by rising before dawn each morning and going out to start up furnaces in the homes of well-to-do families. His diligence attracted the notice of one customer in particular, who owned a jewelry store in town and offered Tanner a job as a clerk, which he accepted. While working at the store, he got the idea for his own business: selling class rings and pins to graduating high school students.

As with most things Tanner did, there was an element of idealism in his choice. He thought that students should have more than a diploma to mark such an important milestone in their lives. That's more or less the pitch he used as he began offering his merchandise to students throughout northern Utah. The response was positive enough to convince him that he could turn his idea into a viable business, but he was unhappy with the quality of the pins and rings he was getting from his vendors, so he started making his own. Meanwhile, he continued his studies, earning his BA from the University of Utah in 1929, an LLB from Utah in 1936, and an MA from Stanford University in 1937. He served as an instructor in religious studies at Stanford from 1939 to 1944 before becoming a professor of philosophy at the University of Utah in 1945. By then, he had married, had six children, and written the first five of his eleven books—all while he was building his company.

In the early 1940s, Tanner decided to expand into the corporate marketplace. He thought companies might be interested in buying his rings and pins to honor longtime employees. They were, as it turned out, and employee recognition eventually became his primary business. Yet, oddly enough, O. C. Tanner was not generally viewed as a service company, nor did it see itself as one. Rather, it was considered a high-end jewelry manufacturer. It earned its money by making beautiful, customized rings and pins with expensive gemstones and precious metals. The jewelry happened to be used for employee recognition, but it was the product, not the service, that carried the business.

O. C. Tanner, the company, retained that manufacturing mind-set for more than sixty years—and did extraordinarily well. It was ideally positioned in the 1960s, when corporate customers began demanding increasingly valuable awards for the employees whose service they were honoring. Sales zoomed from $2.7 million in 1960 to $86.4 million in 1980, and the workforce grew from a couple of hundred employees to more than a thousand. In the following decade, Tanner expanded its product line to include other high-end accessories—watches, clocks, pens, bracelets, and the like—and improved its service component by coming up with a program that allowed it to take the employee database of one of its big company clients and figure out which awards were needed, and when, according to the customer's specifications. Tanner even set up its own brochure business to publish the written materials that went with the awards—and eventually grew it to $20 million in sales. Meanwhile, after a brief lull in the mid-1980s, company sales as a whole took off again, growing 8 to 10 percent a year, reaching $214.1 million in 1993.

As time went along, however, Obert Tanner himself increasingly turned his attention toward his legacy. In 1974, he stepped down as CEO, turning the job over to his longtime sales vice president Don Ostler, while he became chairman of the board. Although he was seventy years old at the time, he still had plenty of energy, and he wanted to devote more of it to public service, philanthropy, scholarship, and securing the future for his employees.

He had already done a lot in all four areas. In some circles, he was known as "Mr. United Nations" for his work championing the organization in the United States and abroad. He had also played a leading role on numerous commissions and boards, including the White House Conference on Children and Youth, the National Commission of the

Bicentennial Celebration of the United States Constitution, the Utah Symphony Board, and the commission that planned the construction of some of Salt Lake City's major cultural centers.

He had made a name for himself in the realm of philanthropy as well. Obert and his wife, Grace, had endowed the renowned Tanner Lectures of Human Values given annually at the nation's elite universities. They had funded the construction of several theaters, museums, and concert halls. They had given more than forty fountains to communities and institutions. And they had established philosophy library rooms at colleges around the country.

On the academic side, Obert continued his studies of religion and philosophy. He had added a Juris Doctor degree from the University of Utah in 1967 and served as professor of philosophy there from 1945 through his official retirement in 1972, whereupon he was named professor emeritus. For his contributions, he was awarded the National Medal in the Arts by President George H. W. Bush in 1990. He was also made an Honorary Fellow of the British Academy and received Utah's first Award in the Humanities, as well as numerous honorary degrees from various colleges and universities.

But it's hard to believe that Obert Tanner was more beloved for anything he did outside the company than for what he did inside it. Company veterans recall how he used to wander the halls, stopping to talk with employees about their families, their hobbies, their aspirations, or whatever else happened to come up in the course of the conversation. On the walls of the Salt Lake City facility were signs with his sayings. "I wish for each one of you, with all my heart, those satisfactions that add up to a great deal of happiness," read one sign. Another declared: "I sometimes reflect that the essence of O. C. Tanner Company's work, expressed in symbolic terms, is putting a drop of oil on the bearings of the free enterprise system."

There were about seventeen hundred people working at the Salt Lake City headquarters in the early 1990s—it also had a factory in Canada and offices elsewhere in North America—and it is said that Obert knew all of them by name. His ambition was for the company to be the employer of choice wherever it had facilities. He had personally trained Kaye Jorgensen, a personnel clerk who went on to become senior vice president of human resources, with that goal in mind. As a result, the company was on the cutting edge of workplace management practices from flexible schedules and job sharing to occupational health services to the employee recognition programs it was known for to regular employee attitude surveys intended to "ensure the work day is the best part of their day," as Jorgensen put it. Long before "variable pay" became all the rage in corporate compensation circles, O. C. Tanner was paying quality bonuses, efficiency bonuses, and delivery bonuses to the people on the shop floor. At Thanksgiving, Obert himself helped hand out hundred-dollar bills to the entire workforce. Everyone got another $100 on his or her birthday—in addition to profit-sharing checks twice a year. At Christmastime, the company gave out more than $1 million in bonuses. All told, a typical employee would make as much as $2,000 a year over his or her regular salary, which tended to be higher than market rates to begin with.

But Obert Tanner's greatest gift to his employees was contained in the provisions he made for the company after his death. He arranged for his 65-percent interest—the other 35 percent was owned by his nephew and the nephew's family—to be put into a so-called one-hundred-year trust, under the terms of which the company could not be sold, merged, or taken public. Tanner's express purpose was to protect his employees by ensuring that, as long as the trust remained in effect, their jobs would not be subject to the financial priorities of outside shareholders. (By law, the trust could last only as long as the lifetime of any descendants alive at the time of Obert's death, plus twenty-one years.)

The employees, for their part, were as appreciative of Tanner as he was of them. By all accounts, the vast majority felt the close, personal connection to the company, and to Tanner himself, characteristic of small giants. In Salt Lake City, the news of his death in October 1993 hit the headquarters like a lightning bolt. "It was shocking. People were crying," recalled Shauna Raso, an illustrator who had been working at O. C. Tanner for fifteen years. "And he deserved that reaction. He was so passionate about employees. People really liked the little statements of his on the walls. He used to look at the cars in the parking lot and say, 'I feel responsible for everyone out there.' Someone could be sitting at a workstation, putting diamonds on a ring, and he'd sit down next to her and want to know how her family was. I don't think it was paternalism. It was the personal touch. It was one of the ways he got across his ideas and theories."

Ironically, the very intensity of his relationship with employees would later pose a significant challenge to his successors, as we'll see in Chapter 8. Nevertheless, Obert Tanner demonstrated that it's at least possible—if not easy—for a leader to have a direct, one-on-one relationship with all of his or her employees even if they number more than a thousand.

Of course, such personal connections alone do not produce the kind of commitment we see in the small giants. If they did, all small businesses would have it, and they don't. So what exactly can you do to create an environment in which people feel their lives are so intimately tied to the business that, as a matter of personal pride, they do everything they can to help it achieve its aspirations and become the best at what it does?

To begin with, you need to get the basics right. That starts with making sure you have the right people on the bus, as Jim Collins put it in *Good to Great*, referring to the primacy of hiring decisions. Although he was writing about large, public companies, the logic applies equally to small or midsize private ones. If you want a company that cares, you need people who care, and they need to be motivated by more than money. Not that there's anything wrong with money. We all want to get paid well for what we do, but if money is the only reason people come to work, they probably belong on a different bus.

Thus Gary Erickson's first impulse after turning down the $120 million deal for Clif Bar was to go to key people in the organization. "I said, 'I think we have five years left as an independent company. I want to keep it private and see what we can do. What we've got here is just too good to let it go now. Sign on with me, and then we'll figure it out.' Later I read *Good to Great* and realized that's what I'd done—get the right people on the bus. The company became a reflection of my values and their values, which were the same."

In addition to having the right people on board, you need to keep the bus in good running condition. That may seem obvious, but you'd be surprised how many companies with wonderful intentions trip themselves up by having poor internal communications, or bad coordination between departments, or inadequate follow-through on decisions, or any of a thousand other fundamental management issues that can negate all the positive initiatives those companies undertake. I have never encountered angrier and more cynical employees than those I've met in socially responsible companies that have been so focused on saving the world they neglected to do what was necessary to save themselves. Some of them were famous for their mojo early on, but they lost it, in part because they didn't take care of the basics.

That's not to say that the companies in this book don't have management problems of their own, but they have mechanisms for bringing the problems to the surface and working them through. "I think we have the same problems everyone else has," said Ari Weinzweig, speaking about Zingerman's Community of Businesses. "We just hope that we're able to deal with them more constructively than most companies and, I guess, have more fun and be more supportive of one another in doing it. Maybe other companies don't work at it like we do. A lot of times, people will look at companies like ours and say, 'It's all because of their culture.' That isn't accurate. It takes well-designed, appropriate, and values-driven systems and processes to support and create the kind of cultures we're all going after."

Zingerman's has done more than most companies—even other small giants—to formalize its mechanisms for managing the business and handling problems as they arise. That's partly because of a process that began in 1994, when it launched its own training subsidiary, ZingTrain. The impetus for ZingTrain actually came from outside the company, mainly from specialty retailers around the country who admired the culture of Zingerman's and wanted its help in dealing with their own management issues. "Rather than figure out what someone was doing wrong and trying to fix it, we thought we'd show people what worked for us," said Maggie Bayless, ZingTrain's cofounder and original managing partner.

Teaching turned out to be a powerful discipline in its own right. For ZingTrain to start teaching, it first had to develop a language to explain what the company was already doing. At the same time, Weinzweig, Saginaw, and other key managers—who did much of the teaching—felt indirect pressure to become more deliberate and systematic in their management practices. They needed the "well-designed, appropriate, and values-driven systems and processes," not only to run the business and reinforce the culture but also to show other people how it all worked.

ZingTrain began by distilling various practices into easily understandable and teachable concepts and principles. "We already had the 3 Steps to Great Service," said Weinzweig. "We just kept building from there." One by one, additional rules and tools were developed: the 5 Steps to Handling Customer Complaints, the 4 Steps to Order Accuracy, the 3 Steps to Great Finance, the 4 Steps to Productive Resolution of Differences, the 5 Steps to Bottom-Line Change, and on and on.

At a certain point, you have to roll your eyes at the sheer number of them, but when you look closely, you realize that each one contains a nugget of management wisdom while providing a structure for further discussion. To give good service, after all, you really do have to "1. Figure out what the customer wants. 2. Get it for them—accurately, politely, enthusiastically. 3. Go the extra mile." What's more, it's important for employees to know that. "Of course, if you're already great at service, you'll say, 'It's not that simple,' which is true," said Weinzweig, who readily acknowledges that Danny Meyer's enlightened hospitality is on a different plane. "But we can't wait until people get all the subtleties of great service. We need a recipe people can use right away."

As time went along, Weinzweig and his colleagues began applying the same thinking to other aspects of management, including training, leadership, and organizational development. A voracious reader of business books and a prolific writer, Weinzweig turned out long papers on Zingerman's application of concepts like "stewardship" and "entrepreneurial management." He then worked with the ZingTrain people to reduce those concepts to a series of steps, points, definitions, and compacts, thereby turning the ideas into management tools. "What we look for is elegant simplicity," he said. "We want to make each one something that anyone can understand and use."

Through this process, ZingTrain got a steady supply of the material it needed for its seminars, which began filling up fairly regularly. In addition, the curriculum had a huge impact on Zingerman's itself, since its staff members took the courses. Those courses helped open the world of business to them. While people were baking bread, selling gelato, or roasting coffee, they were studying business and management, as well as the history and sociology of food, since that was part of the program. Along the way, the company became a kind of school—the University of Zingerman's, as it was known internally.

The effect was to create a culture that was not only intellectually stimulating but unifying. "All those three-step things really do work," said Amy Emberling, a managing partner at Zingerman's Bakehouse, "but they also gave us a language we could use to talk to each other. Everyone in the different businesses had the same vocabulary, which helped create the culture in the community as a whole."

Perhaps most important, "all those three-step things" ensured that people throughout the company were constantly thinking about the processes of management, about how the company was supposed to work and how business should be conducted. In that environment, there was little danger that problems would be swept under the rug. When a problem developed, it quickly rose to the surface, where it could be addressed. Zingerman's thus minimized the risk that it would trip itself up on the basics, whatever other challenges it might face.

※

But there's more to creating a culture of intimacy than simply avoiding mistakes, and there's more than one path as well. The small giants in our sample have different philosophies and approaches, all of which seem to work, even though some of them appear to be directly contradictory. For example, Bill Butler of W. L. Butler Construction, Inc., the construction company, takes pride in having a workforce full of people who are related to one another. "We're a family company that's owned by one and operated like one," he said. "There are a hundred and twenty-five people here. If we fired all the relatives, we'd have fifty people left. Out of one family, a Mexican family, we hired the father, his son, his two brothers, and his cousin. We encourage nepotism. There are sisters, uncles, aunts, in-laws and outlaws. That's who we are—a family business in the full meaning of the term."

Not so CitiStorage, the records-storage business. Norm Brodsky has a rule *against* hiring members of the same family. "I don't like rules in general, and we have only three," he said. "You can't do drugs. You can't smoke within fifteen feet of the building. And you can't hire relatives or friends of anybody who works here. Some people don't agree with that, but we had three or four really bad incidents that convinced me we had to have it. The danger is that, if you have a problem with one person, you wind up losing the others as well, and it can get pretty ugly. I love the employees we have now. I don't want to take a chance on losing them because we hire a friend or a relative who doesn't work out."

Notwithstanding any disagreements people may have on such matters, there are three broad imperatives that all of the companies pursue in different ways and with different means. From what I have seen, moreover, these imperatives must be a priority if a company wants to create a culture of intimacy and the mojo that goes with it.

The first imperative involves articulating, demonstrating, and imbuing the company with a higher purpose. That purpose may relate to the work that the business does, or the way that the business does it, or the good that comes from doing it, or some combination of the three, but however you frame the higher purpose, it serves the same function. It makes the work people do meaningful; it continually reminds them how their contribution matters and why they should care about giving their best effort.

I'm not talking about having a mission statement here. Some of these companies have mission statements expressing their higher purpose; some don't. What sets the companies apart is the extent to which the higher purpose is woven into the fabric of the business. It has to be a constant presence, a part of the everyday life of the company, that people never lose sight of, let alone forget about, as so often happens with mission statements.

From this perspective, Danny Meyer's enlightened hospitality is not just about giving exceptional customer service. It's also about consistently providing an extraordinary experience that customers can't get anywhere else and that will bring each of them happiness—a higher purpose in itself.

Similarly, ECCO and Reell are not simply trying to improve productivity when they give stock to employees, share financial information with them, and teach them what it means and how to use it. The companies are also making a statement. They're saying that a major goal of the business is to enhance the lives of the people who work there—another higher purpose.

Or when employees find themselves caught up in the culinary education going on at the University of Zingerman's, they're not only getting information they can use on the job. They're also learning about one of the company's higher purposes—to enrich the lives of customers by providing them with great food and connecting them to the people who produce it. For that matter, when Anchor Brewing's employees go on one of their field trips, they're learning about a higher purpose as well: mastering the art of beer making and earning a place among the finest brewers in the world.

And when any of these companies does work in its community, goes to bat for a cause, sponsors a charitable event, saves a neighborhood, takes steps to sustain the environment, or whatever, there's no need to explain higher purpose. It's obvious to everyone: Having a great business is one way of making a better world.

✳

The second imperative for creating a culture of intimacy involves re-minding people in unexpected ways how much the company cares about them. The crucial word there is "unexpected." These days most compa-nies realize how expensive it can be to replace an employee and how critical it is to retain a good one, and they use a variety of tools to let people know they're wanted and appreciated—performance bonuses, special benefits or perks, flexible schedules, recognition awards, parties, promotions, and so on. The companies in our sample use all those tools as well, but with a difference. They go out of their way to make sure the message gets through, either by doing what most companies wouldn't dream of doing or by using one of the standard tools in an unusual way.

Norm Brodsky, for one, has what he calls his knock-your-socks-off policy. When there is an opportunity to reward people, he wants the re-ward to take their breath away, which means doing what they don't ex-pect when they don't expect it. A small example: Brodsky learned at one point that CitiStorage's new executive assistant, Patty Lightfoot, was working a second job, cleaning offices after hours for $75 a week in hopes of saving enough money to go back to school. Although she had been the executive assistant for just three months, she had impressed everybody in the office with her reliability, resourcefulness, and intelli-gence. Normally she wouldn't come up for a raise until she'd been there for six months, but Brodsky saw an opportunity to send her a message. "I talked to the managers and said, 'Listen, if we give her a raise three months from now, it will be nice. If we give it to her now, she'll never forget it.' They agreed," he said.

The next day, he called Patty into his office and told her to have a seat. "I understand that you have a second job you do at night," he said.

"Yes, that's right," she replied tentatively.

"Well, I'm afraid we can't allow that," he said. "We need you to be fresh and well rested when you come here in the morning." She slumped in her chair. "I also understand that this other job pays you $75 a week. We're going to raise your salary by that amount so you won't lose any income."

"Oh, thank you," she said.

"And one other thing," he said. "You should know about a policy we have. Anybody who works here for a year can go to school, and we'll pay for it as long as you earn a B or better." Brodsky said Patty was beaming as she left his office. He had no doubt she knew the company cared about her.

Fritz Maytag has a slightly different philosophy but a similar intent. After paying bonuses at Anchor Brewing for a few years, he found that they were no longer bonuses. By the time people got one, they'd already spent it. Instead of a reward, it was viewed as normal compensation and sent no message at all about the company's appreciation of their contributions. So he decided to stop paying regular bonuses. In a meeting of the company, he explained why. Then, once he was sure people had heard him and understood his reasoning, he quickly paid a bonus—and waited a long time before paying another. "It's a game," he told *HBR*. "I've concluded that the best approach is to pay people well and on a rational basis. And then do things like the barley harvest and the trips to Europe and the courses and the dinners and the ball games and the company van that you can borrow over the weekend if you're moving. Those things form a package that's a little vague but that's clearly there for you to count on. And if your mother-in-law arrives unexpectedly, and you want to tell us that you can't come in, that's fine. And if you're sick, there's no policy about how many days you can get sick and all that sort of thing. The fewer written rules, the better."

Bill Butler has yet another approach, based on the unusually close relationship he has with his employees. For him, that relationship is the major reason he's in business at all. He says he didn't even think of W. L. Butler as a real company until he began to realize the responsibility he had for the people he employed. If he was responsible for them, he wanted to know them, and when it looked as though they might become so numerous he would lose touch with them, he put on the brakes. In 1989, the company had 129 employees; sixteen years later, it had 125 employees. "We stay small because I want to know everyone," he said. "When you don't, you're too big."

Walk with Butler around his company, and he will relate the personal history of every person you meet. There's Miguel, a Mexican immigrant who's been with him eighteen years and who taught him how to hang drywall. "I've been to all his kids' baptisms. Now he's our drywall superintendent. He has a new Corvette, makes close to six figures a year plus benefits, and owns an apartment building. His daughter graduated from Santa Clara University with honors and is applying to med school. He is the American Dream."

There's Jamie, the receptionist. "She's one of our single moms. Two years ago, we had a housing problem. We had single moms living in one room with two kids, and we were losing them because the commute was too far. I bought an apartment building here in town with two-bedroom, two-bathroom units and a swimming pool. It's six blocks from the office. We subsidize the rent. If the kids get sick, they can come to work with their mothers. Jamie has a son with ADD, who comes and does chores. That benefit has no dollar value, but people miss less work and don't worry about their kids."

There's Gina, the CFO. "She's the only member of our leadership team with a college education. She has an AA, a BS, and an MS. She started as a file clerk and answered the phone. Now she's our VP of finance. We paid for her education. I need to have people around me who are brighter than me. She's one of them."

Another one is Frank, the company's president. "He started as a laborer. He worked for a lot of the guys whose boss he is now. He's also the coexecutor of my estate. I've never done a performance review of him, and he's never asked for a raise, but he gets them anyway. I told him he'd be a millionaire when he was forty, and he is."

Then there's Olga. "She worked for a job-training facility that we support. She came here as a receptionist, but her English wasn't really good enough to handle that job, so she moved to file clerk. Now she's one of our top-rated project assistants, working on some of our higher profile projects. You see a lot of that around here—people moving up or moving sideways. We have a huge training budget. We call it Butler University. It's online training. We have 125 people and 125 laptops.

Anybody can have any tool they need. Of the 125 people, 50 are not native born. They're Mexican, Spanish, Indian, Russian—you name it. We had a Portuguese guy who didn't speak English. We tutored him in reading and writing. He went from building maintenance to customer service. With Olga, we took her weakness and made it a strength. She translates for our Spanish-speaking employees who have HR questions. She's been with us eleven years, and owns her own home, and drives a brand new SUV—another American Dream."

He didn't add, because he didn't have to, that all those people know how much the company cares about them.

The third imperative concerns an attribute that, at first glance, you might think companies have little control over, namely, collegiality. I'm referring to feelings that employees have toward one another, the mutual trust and respect they feel, the enjoyment they get out of spending time together, their willingness to work through any conflicts that might arise, their collective pride in what they do, and their collective commitment to doing it well. Those qualities are readily apparent when you're around the people who work in these companies. Your first reaction is liable to be, "What nice people they have here," and you might come away believing that's all there is to it. But the closer you look, the clearer it becomes that the company has played a major role in promoting the collegiality you see.

Consider the employees of LFS Touring, the Righteous Babe subsidiary that handles Ani DiFranco's tours and stages the eighty to hundred concerts she puts on around the world in a typical year. (LFS stands for "little folk singer.") Unless she's traveling with a band, the road crew consists of just ten people, including a tour manager, a lighting designer, a sound engineer and production manager, a monitor engineer and stage manager, a merchandise person, a guitar technician, and a recording engineer. They're together for almost six months of the year, going by bus from city to city for two, three, or four weeks at a time. Most of them have been touring with DiFranco for seven years or more. Some have been around more than a decade. That's unique among touring companies, where people typically stay together for a year or two.

To a person, the employees of LFS Touring describe themselves as a family. "It's not *like* a family. It *is* a family," said Susan Alzner, the tour manager. What she means, of course, is that they're all very, very close, which is somewhat different. As Jay Goltz pointed out, no business is really like a family, nor can it be. "A family is unconditional love," he said. "Business is conditional love." Companies with a family feeling wouldn't have it if the employees weren't good enough at what they do to have earned the trust and confidence of their peers.

But that's not to deny Alzner's main point—that the employees of LFS Touring have strong feelings of love and loyalty toward one another. In fact, the crew is a lot closer than most families. For one thing, there's little, if any, sibling rivalry. "Every one of the people here has a reputation in the industry as being tops in their field, but there are no ego problems, which makes my job a lot easier," said Alzner. "And this is an industry built on ego. We support each other. We share ideas, thoughts, observations. The lighting designer routinely comes to help me. You have no idea how unusual that is."

The other members of the group agree that the collegiality they feel is anything but common in the industry. They have all worked in, or with, road crews for other performers. "What we have here is really rare," said Sean Giblin, the stage manager and monitor engineer, who has toured with bands such as Blues Traveler, Sugar Ray, and Joan Osborne. "I've been on tours where some people actually sabotaged the group. They'd create divisions on purpose. But even without that, it can be hard. When you're on the road, you live in a submarine. You're with the other people twenty-four hours a day. When you get a day off, everybody usually scatters. Here we gather on our days off. We go to the museum. We go out to dinner. That just doesn't happen on most tours."

So why do they get along so well? "The difference is that Ani has no hidden agenda," said Steve Schrems, the production manager, who had been with the company for eight years at the time we spoke. "With some crews, you get the feeling that people are there for the after-show party.

We're all here to do what we love—making great music. That's why Ani is here, too, and she's very loyal to the people who support her."

But while loyalty and a shared purpose are no doubt important, it's also worth noting that LFS Touring is operated like few, if any, other touring companies. For openers, the employees are all on salary, a practice virtually unheard of in the industry. Not only that, but people have health insurance, which is equally rare, not to mention 401(k)s. "I have a lot of jealous friends on the road," said Phil Karatz, the lighting designer, who joined the company in 1998 after three and a half years with Bob Dylan's crew. "Being on salary solved a lot of problems for me. I have a house in Minneapolis that I make payments on. Before I had to keep bouncing back and forth from one tour to another to be sure I had a steady income. Occasionally, I still work for some other people when Ani isn't touring, but not as much."

It was Schrems, the longtime production manager, who originally raised the salary issue. In 1999, he had been married five years, and he and his wife had a baby daughter. Seeking more predictability in his income, he approached Righteous Babe president Scot Fisher about receiving a weekly paycheck throughout the year, rather than getting paid by the tour, as was standard industry practice. Fisher worked with him to come up with a formula and offered the same option to other employees. Some didn't want it at first, but they soon changed their minds and went on salary as well. The effect has been to create a level of stability that allows LFS Touring to have the collegial environment for which it is famous, and which has itself become a magnet for talented people.

"These are the kind of people you want to have around," said Fisher. "Every one of them would take a bullet for Ani. We want them to feel secure. A couple of years ago, we were planning an Australia tour and called it off. People said, 'It's going to be tough to get by without that income.' We said, 'We'll pay you anyway.' If they're turning down work for our sake, we have to take care of them."

The point here is that such policies affect not only the way that people feel about the company but also the relationships among the employees themselves—indeed, the whole texture of life inside the business. That, in turn, speaks to another characteristic of companies with mojo, namely, their leaders' awareness of the little worlds they are creating internally. To be sure, every business is, to some degree, a society in microcosm with its own rules, its own hierarchies, its own standards of right and wrong, but that society is usually viewed as a by-product of something else, rather than a primary focus of the business. Why do companies exist anyway? Not to build their own internal ecosystems but to provide products and services to customers, or to generate returns for shareholders, or maybe to create jobs. The little societies that arise in the process are afterthoughts. They aren't planned. They just happen. To the extent that we recognize them at all, we think of them as part of a company's culture.

But to small giants, culture is not the whole story, although it plays a critical role. "I think of culture as the unwritten constitution," said Fritz Maytag. "Rome had no written constitution, just a common understanding about how people should behave. When that fell apart, the Roman Empire did, too." The leaders of these companies spend an extraordinary amount of time and energy working on the systems and processes that create the culture and shape the community, and they do it with a consciousness of the kind of society they wish to have. In effect, they are attempting to build a better way of life in their own little corner of the globe. They want their businesses to be places where people can lead fulfilling lives, and they see the quest to create such a business as a fulfilling mission in itself.

They can pursue that quest, moreover, because they've made choices that have given them the freedom to experiment, to try new ways of organizing and operating their businesses. As we shall see, some of them have used that freedom in extremely creative ways.

6

Galt's Gulch

When the premier issue of *Reell Stories* appeared in the fall of 2002, it featured an article you wouldn't normally expect to find in a company newsletter. Titled "A Matter of Conscience," the article detailed the inner turmoil an employee named Joe Arnold had experienced over a project he'd been assigned to work on. A design firm had hired Reell Precision Manufacturing to develop a hinge for a point-of-purchase display box to be used in convenience stores and at trade shows. The hinge was supposed to hold the lid open and, at a touch, allow it to float slowly down. As an engineer, Arnold found the project challenging, and he immediately began sketching out ideas. Then he learned who the design firm's client was: a cigarette manufacturer.

Clearly the display box was going to be used to sell cigarettes. Arnold had qualms about being involved in promoting the use of a product that some people would eventually die from. Then again, he was also excited about some of the ideas he'd come up with to provide people at the design firm with an inexpensive hinge that would do exactly what they wanted. He struggled with his dilemma in private for a while until his office mate—who shared his qualms—asked him how he felt about working on the project. Arnold confessed that he was torn.

That evening he asked his wife what she thought. She said, "I don't know much about business, but there's no way in the world I'd do that." In his heart, Arnold agreed with her. They had six children. How would he feel if the display box was used to sell cigarettes to kids? He decided he had to raise the matter with the salesperson in charge of the account, Jon Strom.

As it happened, Strom and his colleagues had been under enormous pressure for the previous year or so, as sales had slumped badly due to a recession that had dealt a big blow to personal computer makers, a significant portion of Reell's customer base. To avoid layoffs, managers had taken a pay cut of 12 percent to 16 percent, and all except the lowest paid employees had seen their wages reduced 7 percent. The entire company was counting on the salespeople to bring in new business that would allow the pay cuts to be rescinded. The contract with the design firm was just the sort of opportunity they'd been looking for. Because the technology would have numerous different applications that could be sold to numerous different companies, it could, in time, turn out to be a significant new source of revenue. In that sense, it was a classic Reell product: The company has grown by solving problems for clients, then using the technology for other applications.

After hearing what Arnold had to say, Strom said he thought the engineer was overreacting. Reell's customer was a design firm, not a tobacco company, and the display box would have many uses in addition to the sale of cigarettes. It happened that a tobacco company's needs were driving the development of the hinge, but the end user could just as easily have been a potato chip company or a candy company. Would anyone have batted an eye, Strom asked, if the display box were being designed to sell Snickers?

Arnold still didn't feel comfortable with the project. No matter what anyone said, his work was going to be used to sell an addictive product that killed people. Unable to resolve the issue themselves, he and Strom took up the issue with other members of the business development group, but they couldn't reach a satisfactory compromise either. At that point, Arnold turned to one of Reell's co-CEOs, Bob Carlson, for advice. Carlson listened to his account of the debate and said, "It'll be interesting to see how you guys figure this out."

Finally, Arnold and Strom agreed to turn the decision over to the three men who headed up the business development group. The leaders asked Arnold whether he felt so strongly about the issue that he would quit if Reell didn't drop the contract. No, Arnold said. In fact, he would continue working on the hinge if they thought it was important. "But over the years, I [have] gone to schools and talked to kids about what I do," he said. "I bring product samples. . . . If I work on this product, I would not be proud of it. In fact, I wouldn't even show it to kids if I felt they could recognize it from a convenience store. And they would." After hearing both sides, the leaders decided that Reell would not do the display box.

The decision left some hard feelings. Although Arnold didn't gloat over his victory, he did kid Strom about it. "Don't push that," Strom said. "It doesn't feel so good." In time, however, the salesman got over it. Although he disagreed with the outcome, he considered the process fair. "I was OK with Joe and myself, as counterparts in a development team, trying to resolve the issue and then bringing it to a larger group, which also couldn't resolve it," he said. "Then we had the ability to throw it up the ladder to our managers and leadership, who made the decision. I felt I was heard in my perspective, and Joe was heard in his. To some extent, that's about all you can ask for."

You might wonder why the project wasn't simply assigned to an engineer who didn't have Arnold's concerns, but that idea was never seriously considered. "I can't even remember anybody suggesting it," said Carlson. "It's not how we handle things around here. I suppose if someone had really wanted to do the display box, we would have had to give it some thought, but it didn't come up."

In any case, Strom, Arnold, and the management team all contend that the episode wasn't really about a hinge, a contract, or even the ethics of promoting the sale of cigarettes. Rather the key issue was trust. Did Strom and Arnold trust each other enough to work together toward a solution? Did they have confidence that both of them were acting in what they thought were the company's best interests? For that matter, did management trust them and their co-workers enough to let them work it out by themselves?

Yet there are undoubtedly those who would question both the process and the outcome. Strom, after all, had made a strong case for accepting the contract, particularly at a time when employees and their families were suffering due to lack of sales. Should one person's qualms have overridden the needs of the entire workforce? Couldn't it also be argued that—by not making the decision themselves—co-CEOs Bob Carlson and Steve Wikstrom weren't so much empowering employees as abdicating their own responsibilities? Isn't it a CEO's job to make the tough calls? What's the point of having even one CEO, let alone two, if he, she, or they are unwilling to tackle such issues?

Carlson and Wikstrom wouldn't disagree with such a definition of their responsibilities. Their job *is* to make tough decisions, they acknowledge, but the tough decision in this case was to trust that the employees would do the right thing for the company, and the CEOs have no problem with the way it all turned out. The company could live without the hinge contract from the design firm. What Reell can't live without are the feelings of ownership that employees have and the responsibility that they take for the welfare of the business. From that perspective, the episode provided a far more effective demonstration of the leaders' commitment to the company's core values than any speeches they might give or mission statements they might write. And in case some people hadn't heard about what happened, or had missed its underlying message, they could read all about it in the company newsletter.

It's been noted that every new business represents an attempt by its founder, or founders, to reorder the world in some way. The great majority of founders do so, however, without giving it much thought; and very few, indeed, think about how far they can go in reordering the world—which is not surprising. Norm Brodsky likes to point out that every entrepreneur's first challenge is to figure out whether or not his, or her, idea can become a viable business—that is, capable of sustaining itself on its own internally generated cash flow. That quest can go on for a long time, even years, provided you don't run out of capital prematurely—in which case the issue of viability becomes moot. If people haven't already thought about how they want their business to look, act, and feel ten years in the future (as they probably should have), they're unlikely to spend much time thinking about it while they're struggling for survival. Should they be fortunate enough to get beyond survival, one of two things usually happens. Either they're so overwhelmed with problems and opportunities that they don't get around to thinking about the bigger picture, or they become so focused on strategy and tactics that they neglect to ask basic questions about the kind of culture and organization they want.

The founders, owners, and CEOs of the companies in this book stand out in part because of the extent to which they have thought about and worked on those questions. Not that they've all come up with the same answers. They have various management philosophies, and their companies have quite different cultures and ways of operating. But together they illustrate the range of possibilities that a closely held, private company has in shaping the world inside its walls. In that sense, each company is its own version of Galt's Gulch in *Atlas Shrugged*—a haven for people who have a common vision of the kind of society in which they want to live and work.

Reell Precision Manufacturing has gone further than most in reordering the world according to the vision of its founders. In the process, it has defied almost every management convention in the book. To get the full picture of how the company works, it helps to have a map and a glossary. (It also helps to get regular updates since the structure keeps evolving.) The organizational chart is a rectangle—or matrix, as they call it—rather than a pyramid. At the center of the matrix are the co-workers, otherwise known as employees. Along the top are the people in charge of the various functional responsibilities, including quality services (called quality control at most other companies), financial services (accounting), I services (IT), and co-worker services (HR). Along the left side of the matrix are the people in charge of the two SBUs (strategic business units) and Reell's European subsidiary. A second band along the top and side indicates which of the two co-CEOs have primary responsibility for each functional unit and SBU, as well as the subsidiary.

In addition to the various departments, there are also internal "working groups," beginning with the co-workers. "Creating and nurturing a work environment that frees co-workers to grow and reach their full potential is the primary purpose of the company," notes one Reell document. Next come the advisers, who would be called supervisors in most companies. An adviser's primary role is "to help [an advisee's] growth within the advisee's existing position." The senior leadership group is known as the cabinet. Its members—the co-CEOs, the SBU heads, and the functional department managers—meet weekly to discuss strategic and tactical issues. Then there's the forum, made up of the vice president of co-worker services and seven randomly selected volunteer co-workers, each of whom represents a different geographical area in the company and serves for three years. That group meets twice a month to address issues of concern to the employees and to monitor how well the company is living up to its Direction Statement (more about that later) in its day-to-day activities.

As in any company, however, the ultimate management authority lies at the top, with the co-CEOs (or the dyad, as they're known) who are accountable, in turn, to Reell's board of directors. The board, for its part, is elected annually by the shareholders, that is, the employee stock ownership plan (ESOP), most of the cabinet members, the three founders, and various members of the founders' families. The shareholders have the ultimate corporate authority. From that perspective, the overall chain of command is not much different from the norm. But how authority is exercised could hardly be more atypical and strongly reflects the values and beliefs on which the company was founded.

The founders were three former employees of 3M, two of whom came together in the 1960s as partners in a manufacturers' rep firm. The firm was called the Dale Merrick Company, after the first of them to take the plunge. Through their work as reps, Merrick and his partner, Bob Wahlstedt, discovered what they thought was an unfilled market niche—making so-called wrap spring clutches for original equipment manufacturers (OEMs). A wrap spring clutch is a mechanical device used to control motion in various types of machinery, from photocopiers to conveyor belts. One of the companies that Merrick and Wahlstedt represented made wrap spring clutches for manufacturers of capital equipment, such as machine tools, which bought them in low volumes and weren't particularly finicky about prices or lead times. OEMs such as 3M or Xerox were another story. To use wrap spring clutches in photocopying machines, for instance, you needed them in large quantities and at a much lower price than a machine tool maker was willing to accept, and they had to be delivered a lot faster than the standard lead times in the industry. The partners saw the OEM market as a tremendous, untapped opportunity for somebody and tried in vain to persuade their client to go after it. They even considered buying the client and reorienting it toward OEMs, but that didn't pan out either.

Then an ill-timed decision got the partners thinking about starting their own manufacturing business. In early 1970, they brought in a third partner from 3M, Lee Johnson, just as the economy was slowing down. With too many people and not enough business, they spent the summer daydreaming together and talked at length about the opportunity in wrap spring clutches. By the fall, they had settled on a plan and a name—or rather a set of initials, RPM, which they figured customers would find easy to remember. Deciding what P and M stood for wasn't hard, but they struggled with the R until Johnson found the word "reell" (pronounced ray-el) in a German dictionary, which defined it as "honest, dependable, or having integrity." They all agreed that the word perfectly described the kind of company they had in mind. In October, Reell Precision Manufacturing was officially born.

Over the next few years, the partners developed not only a successful line of wrap spring clutches but also an unusual way of working together. The three agreed that whenever they decided to act or to change course, the decision had to be unanimous. In practice, that meant that it often took days to reach a decision, simply because of the time required to discuss issues thoroughly and digest one another's opinions. When they still couldn't agree after such deliberation, they would reshape the question and keep talking until they had the unanimity they demanded. Because each of them had veto power, they were all effectively CEOs, even though they later took on different titles (chairman, president, and chief of operations). Collectively they were known as the triad.

Oddly enough, the setup worked. The decisions the triad made usually turned out, in hindsight, to have been good ones. Even more remarkably, the partners maintained close, amicable relationships with one another for the next thirty years, by which point they had all retired from day-to-day operations of the company.

No doubt part of their success had to do with their shared religious beliefs, which were strengthened through their partnership. Although only one of them—Merrick—was a practicing Christian to begin with, the other two had a spiritual awakening in the early years of the company, and their common commitment to their religion shaped every aspect of their approach to business. Aside from studying the Bible, they spent a lot of time listening to Christian audiotapes, which led them to certain critical decisions early on. For openers, they agreed that Reell's primary objective would be to make products of the highest quality. They also established a formal policy placing family responsibilities above business responsibilities, and they committed themselves in writing "to do what is 'right' even when it does not seem to be profitable, expedient, or conventional." All three decisions the founders traced directly back to their Christian beliefs.

Those beliefs also played a key role when they encountered their first major financial crisis. As the economy went into recession in 1975, Reell's only customer, 3M, suddenly announced that it had all the wrap spring clutches it would need for the year. Luckily, the partners had already lined up Xerox, whose orders cushioned the blow, but—with sales down 40 percent from the previous year—the company was clearly overstaffed. After the usual lengthy deliberations, the triad decided not to lay anyone off. Instead, they asked employees to take a 10-percent pay cut, while they themselves reduced their pay by 50 percent. Later in the year, the employee pay cut was increased to 20 percent. As tough as the cuts were, they allowed Reell to get through the period without a layoff, and the practice set an important precedent that had a major effect on the company's evolving culture.

Initially, that culture had an evangelical tinge, as the members of the triad struggled to balance their desire to spread the Gospel with a strong aversion to imposing their views on others. They instituted an optional weekly Bible class that employees could attend on company time, but they asked only that employees support the company's values, not the founders' religious beliefs, and they went out of their way to welcome employees of other faiths, as well as nonbelievers. Nevertheless, Reell inevitably attracted a significant number of born-again employees, and they were not all as sensitive as the partners to others who might not share their beliefs. When it appeared that the Bible-study meetings were actually creating divisions in the company rather than fostering unity and mutual commitment, they were cancelled.

Meanwhile, the business itself was entering a new phase. At the urging of Xerox, the company had begun development of a wrap spring clutch that was activated electrically, rather than mechanically. A working sample was soon delivered to Xerox, but it took the partners five years to come up with one that they felt was good enough to put on the market. The new electric clutch turned out to be worth the wait. Within a year, it became clear that Reell had a hot product with many potential applications that could fuel much faster growth than it had experienced up to that point. The problem was, the partners weren't sure they wanted much faster growth. To resolve the issue, they locked themselves in a room with a facilitator for a whole day and talked the issue through, eventually reaching a consensus. Only by growing the business, they realized, could they create new challenges for employees that would allow them to grow personally without leaving Reell. Soon thereafter they began building a new, larger facility.

The next big change came a few years later and had nothing to do with religion or technology. In its quest for quality, Reell had developed a fairly traditional quality-control program, with inspectors who evaluated every batch of products to leave the plant. As always, the inspection process caused major delays in shipping. Out of frustration more than anything else, someone suggested teaching the people who operated the equipment to do their own quality control. The triad thought that sounded like a good idea and implemented the change. The result: Both efficiency and quality shot up.

That turned out to be the beginning of a fundamental, if unplanned, transformation of the corporate culture. Without really recognizing what they were doing, the founders had built Reell around a command-and-control style of operating. The change in the quality regime was the first step toward an entirely different way of running the business—introducing what others refer to as empowerment, but which people at Reell prefer to call teach-equip-trust, or TET.

It was, said Wahlstedt many years later, a revolution. The change in management style "has shown us that the biggest misconception of American manufacturers is the belief that production workers are not dependable and must be motivated and/or constrained to do quality work," he wrote in the official company history. "We have been amazed by the self-motivation and dedication to quality and productivity that they demonstrate when they are freed to develop and use their full potential."

That revelation was, of course, what lay behind the decision almost twenty years later to let employees decide whether or not to develop the display box for the cigarette company. By then, however, the TET approach had been incorporated into every aspect of Reell's operation and enshrined in various documents outlining the company's management philosophy.

Probably the most important of those documents was the so-called Direction Statement, produced in 1989 at the instigation of a newer member of the management team, Steve Wikstrom. He'd joined Reell as a manufacturing superintendent in 1982 and soon emerged as a potential successor to Dale Merrick, who was getting ready to retire. Wikstrom considered it important to preserve the legacy of the founders but felt that the religious language of the guiding document they'd drawn up, called "Welcome to Reell," seemed to exclude in tone (though not in content) people who were not devout Christians. He proposed renaming it "A Message from the Founders" and creating another statement that would present Reell's guiding principles in more inclusive language.

The drafting of the Direction Statement began a process that continued throughout the next decade—a kind of quasi secularization that preserved the values, management concepts, and ideals developed under the triad and acknowledged their roots but did so without the overtones of evangelism present in earlier documents. The new statement, for example, reaffirmed "the purpose of operating a business based on the practical application of Judeo-Christian values for the mutual benefit of co-workers and their families, customers, shareholders, suppliers and community." It talked about "providing an environment where there is harmony between work and our moral/ethical values and family responsibilities and where everyone is treated justly." It even spoke of being "challenged to work and make decisions consistent with God's purpose for creation according to our individual understanding." But unlike "Welcome to Reell," it did not mention offering employees "an opportunity to integrate Christian life with a career."

As time went along, more and more co-workers were drawn into the discussion about faith and business. When the original Direction Statement was revised in 1992, everyone was invited to participate. In the end, seventeen people worked on the revision, talking at length about the challenge of remaining true to the company's spiritual heritage and foundation without making those of other faiths—or no particular faith—feel like outsiders. Given the growing diversity of the workforce, it was an important discussion to have. Coincidentally, it also put Reell in the forefront of the burgeoning international movement to explore the role of spirituality in work, and of work in spirituality. (The process that the company went through was subsequently written up in a case study by an ethics professor in the nearby Graduate School of Business at the University of St. Thomas.)

In 1998, the company added a second key document on the initiative of Wahlstedt. As much as he liked the Direction Statement, which expressed Reell's values, principles, and priorities, he thought something else was needed—a statement spelling out the fundamental beliefs that underlay the company's entire approach to business. The resulting "Declaration of Belief" illustrated just how ecumenical the company had become. Among other things, it declared: "Because many spiritual traditions speak powerfully regarding the conditions necessary to provide for the common good, foster individual development and respect human dignity, we will encourage each other to draw wisdom from these traditions and from individual expressions of spirituality." (In 2004, the Direction Statement was revised again, becoming even more ecumenical in the process.)

Together, the two documents served as a sort of constitution for the organization, laying out for everyone to see the standards to which Reell would hold itself. In the statements, the company publicly pledged to always do what was right; strive for continuous improvement; help co-workers be all they could be; follow the Golden Rule; "seek inspirational wisdom . . . especially with respect to decisions having far-reaching and unpredictable consequences"; take an action "only when [it] is confirmed unanimously by others concerned"; and meet various specific commitments to co-workers, customers, shareholders, suppliers, and the community. It was a tall order, but Reell was serious about filling it. The company even created the working group mentioned above called the forum, to make sure it was living up to its promises and to recommend corrective action when it fell short.

While all this was going on, Reell was also dealing with the challenges posed by the imminent retirement of the three founders, notably the transfer of ownership and leadership. Those are, of course, the central issues of succession, which we'll be looking at more closely in the next chapter. Suffice it to say here that the founders approached them as they had every other issue they'd confronted. Given their stated principles, moreover, many of the decisions they made were hardly surprising. After all, who else could they sell their stock to, if not their employees and members of their families, and still remain true to their beliefs and values?

But the changing of the guard did raise a new set of governance questions. For example, what role should the board of directors play in the future? How should the directors be selected? Whom should they represent? What were the board's specific responsibilities? In seeking answers to those questions, the company's leaders looked far and wide for inspiration and guidance and—in the process—came across the writings of Robert K. Greenleaf, the former director of management research at AT&T and an iconoclastic thinker about how organizations should work. After retiring from AT&T in 1964, Greenleaf had started the Center for Applied Ethics (later renamed the Robert K. Greenleaf Center) and embarked on a second career as a university lecturer, consultant, and author. Along the way, he had written a series of seminal essays on the theme of "servant leadership," and they continued to resonate long after his death in 1990.

They resonated, not only at Reell, but at Zingerman's, which taught its employees about servant leadership and made it a guiding concept in the management of the Zingerman's businesses. Reell was in a different situation. The company had already implemented many of Greenleaf's management ideas, although it had followed its own route to come up with them and didn't use the language of "servant leadership" to talk about them. Greenleaf's essay on "The Institution as Servant," however, had a major impact on Reell's board, which adopted his approach as the basis for deciding how directors would be chosen and what their responsibilities would be. In particular, Greenleaf rejected the notion that directors should represent different groups of shareholders. He considered that an invitation to divisiveness. The board, he said, should be the driving force behind the company's mission and thus its members should be selected for their ability to fill that role, not to promote the narrow interests of a particular set of owners.

With that in mind, Reell elected a new board of directors in March 2000. Its primary job was to monitor the continuing evolution of Reell's reordered world, including fulfillment of the extraordinary commitments the company had made in its Direction Statement.

Clearly Reell's system has worked for Reell, and the principles it espouses are a lot like those that several other companies in this book have built their cultures around, including Clif Bar, ECCO, O. C. Tanner, Rhythm & Hues, Righteous Babe, Union Square Hospitality Group, and Zingerman's. While all those companies have different cultures and systems of governance, they have quite similar approaches to management and business—approaches that, consciously or not, are very much in sync with the ideas of Robert K. Greenleaf.

But you don't have to believe in servant leadership to create a small giant. Indeed, if you were to mention the concept to the founders and CEOs of some of the companies in our sample, they would roll their eyes. "The question is, are you a social worker or a businessperson?" said Jay Goltz of The Goltz Group. "It's like, you can't be your kids' friend at the expense of being their parent. I had a guy who'd been with me since the beginning. He was messing up. What do I do? How much compassion can I afford? I'm not saying none. But in the course of being compassionate, you can't relinquish your responsibility to be unmerciful when it's necessary.

"You know, life is unfair but merciful. You can do everything right and get a brain tumor. Business is unmerciful but usually pretty fair. People who go broke often bring it on themselves. For a company to succeed, everybody has to do their bit, and you have to insist on it. Like coming to work on time. We have a company policy. If you're late four times in any quarter, we show mercy. The fifth time you're suspended. The sixth time you're out. No excuses, no exceptions. When you're the boss, you make demands on people. We all have to decide where we want to be on the demanding scale. Jack Welch might be a 10. I don't want to be a 10. Maybe an 8. What's the difference? If an employee doesn't work out, a 10 says you don't give him severance pay. An 8 says you do. A 6 won't do anything because he thinks he's empowering people. Bullshit. You have a responsibility to make those calls."

And the idea of not earning a profit because you want to do what's "right"? Don't get him started. "You should feel really worried if you're not profitable," he said. "If you have an established company and you don't have profits, you're doing something wrong. There's a hole somewhere. Profits are not optional in business. If you don't have them, you're dangerously close to going broke. It's not responsible to your employees. They might not have a job. As the guy in charge, it's your duty to make sure you have a profit. We all need a little accountant inside of us, saying, 'Hey, asshole, what are you doing?'"

Yet as hard-nosed as Goltz comes across, the culture of Artists' Frame Service is as intimate—and as vibrant—as that of any of the other companies in our sample, and the business elicits the same kind of loyalty and devotion from employees. Dale Zeimen, for example, is the production manager in the facility where the frames are made, a job Goltz himself held for eight years before deciding he should find a replacement. He initially looked for people with experience, who'd done the job before, who were older and would be better at managing than he was. He retained a consultant to advise him. It didn't help. Every production manager he hired was a disaster. Finally, it dawned on him that he should be looking for a less experienced person whom he could train. Zeimen came in and blossomed under Goltz's tutelage.

Two years later, another company tried to hire Zeimen away, promising him $10,000 a year more than he was making at Artists' Frame Service. Goltz couldn't afford to match that figure, but he wanted to keep Zeimen and offered to give him a raise. Zeimen went to look at the other company. "It was really disorganized, and they didn't treat employees well," he recalled. "I thought about it and came back to Jay. I said, 'You don't have to pay me more. I'm not going anywhere.' I turned down the job and Jay's money, and I've never been sorry I did. I love it here. I hope to be here forever. I want to make sure this remains the best frame company in the world."

So what is it that he and other employees like so much about working for Goltz? "He's a teacher," Zeimen said. "He takes us to trade shows to show us what we aren't. He wants quality. Before I came here, I worked for a company that did mass production of photo frames for companies like Target and Wal-Mart. A 1-percent rejection rate was considered okay. Here quality is everything. And Jay doesn't micromanage. He gives us parameters. I get to work within them the way that I want. When we make mistakes, he calls us on it, but it's a teaching thing, not punitive. And he has all these ideas. We have meetings of the managers of the different companies, and we learn about what the others are doing, and we get pumped. Jay sits there, listening, and starts spewing out ideas. Sometimes he spews so many ideas so fast that you can't get a word in edgewise, but you can say, 'Hey, Jay. Stop. I need to put this point across.'"

Goltz does, in fact, have more ideas than he knows what to do with, and you can find them everywhere you look in the framing facility. The building is part of an old sheep-shearing plant on Webster Street, a mile from Goltz's stores. He bought a 30,000-square-foot piece of the place in 2002, when he realized he couldn't stay in the former furniture factory on North Clybourn he'd been working out of since 1978. The operation is spread out on a single floor, divided into different departments. "It's a division of labor," Goltz said, walking through the plant one winter day. "A ticket is generated. The frame is cut. It's joined in the next place. Then it's touched up. Then it goes to the fitting department. Then the framers go to work. Out of the forty people here, we don't have one who doesn't know how to do everything from start to finish, but they all specialize in some aspect of the process. People go from one operation to the next. We find out what they're best at and let them stay there."

As you walk through the place, you can't help noticing all the signs on the walls. They read like ersatz fortune cookies. "One who sails by on excuses will drown in a sea of mediocrity." "When we take care of customers, we take care of ourselves." "We're only as good as our last frame job." "A happy customer is the best job security you can get." The sayings are from Goltz. "They're all original. I don't plagiarize," he said. "I'm telling people about business. I think it's a big failure of management, not getting people to understand what they're doing here. On one side, you have employees who just know they're getting laid off from the washing machine factory and don't know why. On the other side, you have customers who just know their washing machine doesn't work. I suppose you could say what I do is a kind of indoctrination. Every couple of months I get new employees together and tell them the history of the company, why we're here, what to do if a problem arises. I say, 'Call me on it if I'm full of it, if anything turns out to be different from what I'm telling you."

The more you look, the more sayings you see. "You can spill some milk if you don't kill the cow." "Values don't break. They crumble." "Our biggest competition is mediocrity." "That's me," Goltz said. "I hate mediocrity. Mediocrity is my enemy." He picked up a completed frame and pointed to a blue screw on the back. "Everyone has their own color. It creates pride of ownership. When the wire on a frame falls off and it comes back, we know who did it. The quality improved significantly when we started doing it."

Just off the shop floor is the lunch room, called the Webster Café, where he and Zeimen hold weekly meetings with the entire staff. "Small businesses don't have enough meetings," said Goltz. "I believe everyone in the company should meet at least once a week. You need that direct contact." There's a stack of eight microwave ovens against one wall, alongside three refrigerators and several vending machines. "That's one of my things. If you only have one or two microwaves, people have to sit and wait for their turn. By the time they eat, their break is over. Why do that? Appliances are so cheap now there's no reason not to get enough."

A buzzer went off and a red light flashed in the area where the fitters were working on high benches. A supervisor stepped over to a timer and reset it, then started writing numbers on a white board as people called them out from their work stations: "three Monday;" "one Saturday, one Monday;" "four Saturday;" "one Monday."

"It's how we keep track of daily production," Goltz explained. "They do it every hour on the half hour. They say how many they've done and for what day"—that is, the day the customer is expecting the finished product. "Our goal is to do a hundred a day. Since the board went up, we've never had a 'bad day.' The old managers used to tell me they had 'bad days' all the time. That was the reason they didn't get the work finished. This allows people to see how they're doing and what they've done. It gives them a sense of accomplishment and nips problems in the bud. If a customer needs a frame job by one o'clock, and a meeting runs late, or someone forgot, we catch it right away.

"You need those kinds of systems. Remember Theory X management and Theory Y management? Well, there are Theory X employees and Theory Y employees. I want the Y employees—people who want to put in the extra effort, who want responsibility and job satisfaction. For them, you need to run a tight ship. Like insisting that people show up on time. The good people resent it when other people come in late."

The company wasn't always so tightly managed. Goltz is the first to admit how much he has learned over the years and how hard it was to learn it. "I tell people there are three stages to every business," he said. "The start-up phase, the throw-up phase, and the grow-up phase. I went through ten years of being overwhelmed until I got things under control. I finally figured out that managing isn't just about learning how to motivate people. It's also about learning how not to demotivate them."

He also had to overcome bad advice. "Somebody told me, 'Get a good right-hand guy and overpay him.' That's the typical advice you get about being a boss, and it's wrong. What you should do is build a good organization. But I had to learn that the hard way. I hired a vice president I thought was going to run the company for me. Instead I learned the difference between babysitting and managing."

The vice president lasted seven years at the company, despite increasing signs of trouble as time went along. At one point, Goltz was approached by one of his most trusted managers who said he was thinking about leaving. He didn't like what was happening to the company. The vice president wasn't taking care of the business, he said. People didn't know what was expected of them and weren't being held accountable. Goltz persuaded him to stay.

Then one day Goltz was in the showroom of the frame store and found a coffee cup left behind by an employee. He was furious. It was something he taught people their first day on the job: No coffee cups in the showroom! He'd already talked to the store manager once about coffee cups he'd found lying around a couple of months earlier. A coffee cup in the showroom was a sure sign of sloppiness, of not caring, of creeping mediocrity, and he wouldn't stand for it. He called her into the office and screamed at her.

When he calmed down, he began to think. Why did this happen? How did he wind up in this situation, screaming at young managers about coffee cups? "It took me a couple of weeks to figure it out," Goltz said. "Finally it dawned on me that the VP I'd appointed had introduced a new concept: being laid back. He was babysitting, not managing. He'd created an environment where people weren't concerned with rules and standards. They thought, 'Oh, that's Jay.' I could see it in every division. People weren't being trained. They weren't being groomed. They weren't being led. His approach was, 'Make sure there are no problems; if there is one, I'll help.' If a kid puts a block in his mouth, you take it out. If the stove gets on fire, you put it out. You don't ask, 'Why did this happen? Who did it? What do they need to learn?' He was creating an environment he was comfortable with, not the one I wanted. But it was my fault. I should have been building a management team. I went back to the manager I'd screamed at and apologized. She said, 'I was getting mixed messages from the two of you.'"

Goltz fired the vice president and—with some trepidation—told the managers of the different companies that they would henceforward be reporting to him. "I'd hired the VP because I wanted more time and flexibility, and I was afraid I'd be overwhelmed if I had eight managers reporting to me," he said. But far from being overwhelmed, his life got easier. "All the managers brought their game up a couple of notches. They'd been with me for a while, so it wasn't a huge adjustment for them, but they made me realize that I didn't need a, quote, right-hand guy after all, and that was a revelation."

He didn't need a right-hand guy, he discovered, partly because he had already put systems in place all over the company that would avoid most problems as long as people followed them. He has a knack for developing systems. It's part of his personality. "I like to figure things out," Goltz said. "I like to find solutions. I told my friend Ira, 'I think I'm obsessive.' He laughed and said, 'You didn't know that? When you were ten, you used to time yourself cutting the lawn.' I said, 'What do you mean, used to?'"

The production board was one such system. There was another to avoid framing mistakes. "We have four key rules," Goltz said. "Number one, don't ever let a customer go away without an invoice. Number two, if customers want art trimmed, draw a line in their presence. Number three, don't do any trimming unless there's a line. Number four, document any preexisting damage to the art before the customer leaves. It's all written down. My job is to make sure the managers manage the systems. If they do, 99.7 percent of the time things go well. Out of a thousand jobs, we might have a problem with three of them."

But there was another reason Goltz was able to manage without a right-hand man: He himself had matured as a manager. "I'm proud that when we moved here, I didn't do much," he said. "It was all Dale, Agripino Betancourt, and Ren Battle, who runs wholesale and does purchasing. I was barely here because we were moving three companies at the same time. We have a new truck that we bought for the move. One of our employees, Armando, and his wife were backing it up over there." He pointed toward an indoor loading dock. "He hit a beam, and it came down and crushed the roof of the truck. We were afraid the building would collapse, but it didn't.

"When I arrived, Armando was beside himself. He said, 'I'm so sorry. I'll pay for it.' His wife was freaked out, crying. All I can say is, I'm glad I'm older now. I knew I had to come right out and say it was okay. They'd been putting in fourteen-hour days and now this. You can imagine what they were thinking. *Omigod, we totaled the boss's new truck.* Before, I wouldn't have yelled, but I would have looked disgusted. I've learned that one of my biggest responsibilities is letting people off the hook in situations like that. I told both of them, 'Don't worry. I could have done it myself.' That has a big impact. There were a lot of other employees standing there. They see how you behave. You could be doing bonus plans, holding rallies, having parties to build morale. Then you scream at someone and throw it all away. Did I scream when I was younger? Yes. I didn't understand the role of the boss. I had to learn the difference between a mistake, which I can live with, and haphazard conduct. Backing into a pole is a mistake. A crooked label is careless."

Meanwhile, Goltz's own role in his reordered world was itself being reordered. "I've gone from being 75 percent entrepreneur and 25 percent manager to 75 percent manager and 25 percent entrepreneur," he said. "I really believe that the secret to business can be summed up in two words: 'leverage' and 'control.' I've always been good at the leverage part—growing into new businesses, leveraging the assets we have. Meatpackers used to say that they sold everything but the oink. I sell everything including the oink. Control is another story. It's about knowing what's going on and making sure that what you want to happen actually happens. I still have some control issues that I can work on—pricing issues, delivery charges, training, making sure the salespeople are saying the right things. That's where I focus my attention now. An older customer once told me, the bigger you get, the harder it gets, but it's not true. I have the systems. I've hired better. I have eight key managers who are totally with the program, who are growing, and I'm spending more time with them. These days, I kvell when things are going great. It makes me very happy and proud."

As different as Goltz's world is from Reell's, they have more in common with each other than either has with Hammerhead Productions or Selima Inc. For one thing, both The Goltz Group and Reell Precision Manufacturing pride themselves on the number of long-term employees they have and the low turnover rate among those who join and make the grade. The same, in fact, could be said about almost all the companies in our sample. Hammerhead and Selima are the exceptions: Both were launched and developed with the explicit goal of giving their founders freedom to pursue their individual passions. That meant minimizing the number of permanent, full-time employees they had.

For Selima Stavola, the ideal number was one. Then again, she never really intended to go into business at all. Born Selima Cohen in 1921, she grew up in Baghdad, the daughter of a rich, well-connected, politically prominent, Jewish Iraqi businessman. Her great-grandfather had been the governor of Kurdistan in the Ottoman Empire. During the Second World War, she fell in love with an American GI stationed in Iraq, whom she eventually married, creating a scandal in the upper echelons of Baghdad society. At the end of the war, she and her husband, Tony, moved to Brooklyn, New York, with the intention of returning to Baghdad, but events overtook them. After the founding of Israel, Jews were viewed as potential spies in Iraq. Selima's father was killed. The rest of her family narrowly escaped with little more than the clothes they were wearing.

Back in Brooklyn, meanwhile, Selima had launched a career in fashion design. Although she had no training in the field, she had enormous talent, as the famous Manhattan couturiere Florence Lustig quickly recognized when Selima showed up looking for a job. She was hired and worked in Lustig's company for eight months, whereupon she was lured away by one of the house's wealthy customers who wanted to open a fashion business of her own. Selima signed up on condition that she could leave every day in time to give her baby girl a bath before she went to bed. As the months passed, however, her new boss made increasing demands on her time. There were heated arguments. After a year and a half, she left, vowing that, in the future, she would work only for herself.

And that's what she did for the next fifty-nine years, first in New York City, then in Miami Beach, and never with more than one employee. She made oodles of money and had a select clientele, made up entirely of people she liked. "I can't do anything for somebody I don't like," she said. "If I don't like her, I'm not going to have a huge creative impulse to make her beautiful. So why would I take her as a customer?" Indeed, Selima would frequently turn away potential customers if she didn't approve of the way they acted or the questions they asked. "If they call up on the phone and ask me how much I charge, I say, 'You can't afford me.'" In many cases, she was undoubtedly right.

Her selectivity did nothing but enhance her reputation. Time and again, she was approached by people who argued that she was burying her talent, that she should reach out and take her business "to the next level." Selima rebuffed them all. "When they say, 'We're really going to go places,' that's when I leave," she said. "It's such a lie, all that business, such a lie. The moment it becomes a manufacturing empire with a label, it's not a person. I take pride in my work, *great* pride, and I would never compromise it, certainly not for money. The end result is not the check. It's how beautiful the customers look, how special they look, and how proud I feel. It's the sense of accomplishment. How would I get that if I'm Calvin Klein?"

She was looking for the freedom to do what she wanted, for whom she wanted, when she wanted, and a larger business would have rendered that impossible. "Why did I keep the business limited? First, because I don't want to be beholden to the business. If it's big, it owns you. You don't own it. Once you have other people involved, you have to compromise. I don't want to compromise what I think is right. Second, I don't want the business to be bigger than my family. Third, I really don't want anyone to tell me what to do. If someone doesn't behave, I throw them out. Money has never been important to me. My father said, 'If you're born to money, you'll never think poor.' And I never have." Then again, thanks to the devotion of her customers and her own business savvy, she hasn't had to.

Neither, for that matter, have the four movie industry veterans who started Hammerhead Productions, the visual effects company in Studio City, California. Like Selima, they wanted a business that would allow them to pursue their creative passions. Although they were all experienced professionals whose services were in great demand, they felt constrained at the large visual effects companies. They could make lots of money there, enjoy numerous perks, and exercise considerable power, but they didn't have the flexibility they needed to do the kind of work they most cared about.

Their opportunity arose in 1994. The company they were working for, Pacific Data Images (PDI), based in Sunnyvale, California, was grooming itself for sale—it was eventually acquired by DreamWorks—and decided to close its Los Angeles office. Jamie Dixon and Dan Chuba, who ran the L.A. branch, had the job of telling producers that PDI wouldn't be able to fulfill its contractual obligations but would find other good people to do the work. One producer refused to accept their resignations. "I didn't hire your company," he said. "I hired you. I'll give you the money. You do it."

As it happened, Dixon and Chuba had been musing about going out on their own. They decided to take the producer up on his offer and use his project to launch a business. They brought in as founding partners two other people from PDI with complementary skills and different dreams—Rebecca Marie, a creative director, and Thad Beier, the head of software. What drew them together was the hope that, if successful, they'd be able to do things they'd had to put off because of the demands of their previous jobs. For Dixon, it was the chance to direct his own films. Beier wanted to develop software. Marie was looking for time to paint, and Chuba for time to write screenplays and do animation work.

Over the next eleven years, the four of them built Hammerhead into the leading small visual effects company in Hollywood, while taking care to retain the flexibility they craved. That meant keeping the head count low—just fourteen full-time people, including the partners—and limiting the number and size of the projects they accepted. When they took on a larger one than they themselves could handle, they would hire the additional people they needed on a project basis. After the project was completed, the additional people would move on to other things, and Hammerhead would revert to its original size.

Luck, as usual, played a role in the company's success. Right around the time the partners launched Hammerhead, there were major changes occurring in the industry. For one thing, the cost of equipment was dropping precipitously. "At PDI, it would cost $100,000 to seat an animator—just for equipment, not salary," said Chuba ten years later. "Now the hardware is almost free and better quality. We chuck all of it and start over every six to eight months." In addition, companies were starting to use nonproprietary software, making it possible for independents to enter the market. Perhaps most important, a whole new class of freelance animators was emerging. These were skilled professionals who enjoyed moving from project to project, and they provided Hammerhead with exactly the sort of flexible workforce it needed. Because there were so many of them, and because they had such varied talents, the company could take on a wider range of projects than would otherwise have been possible. That was critical in an industry where technology was changing at lightning speed. If you couldn't work on projects that broadened your capabilities, you wouldn't develop the skills you had to have to remain competitive. Hammerhead could do those projects without becoming a much larger company only because the freelance talent it needed was available.

Aside from flexibility, Hammerhead's founders also wanted a culture that was more open and less hierarchical than those of most larger special effects companies, a culture in which people would work autonomously, without supervision. The founders wanted it for themselves and also because they believed it would help them attract the kind of animators they were looking for. In the beginning, they worked out of an apartment in Burbank, but once the business was established, they found an old hunting lodge in Studio City and moved the company there in 1998. The lodge sat on four acres of forestland atop a hill in the middle of Los Angeles. There were deer and coyotes in the surrounding woods. The place had a swimming pool and a view of the valley, and it became a prime recruiting tool for Hammerhead. Inside, it had the feel of a country club or perhaps an upscale fraternity house. The environment was deliberately informal. For lunch, which was catered, people sat in stuffed chairs around a table in the living room, in front of a fireplace with a shark above the mantel. "We all get together at lunch and talk about the job," said Chuba. "The animators work in two big rooms off the dining room. There are no barriers. Everybody hears everything."

There was also a pool table. Chuba said people used to play pool and go swimming as they waited for the computers to process their work, but they took fewer breaks as technology got faster. In any case, there were no time clocks or supervisors, which some new recruits found disconcerting. "A lot of our people come from abusive companies that have overtime deals," said Chuba. "New people sometimes want the same thing here. We explain that we don't like to work overtime. We think it's better to take a flat fee and work whatever you consider a normal schedule, which is different for different people. Some people come in at 7:30; some don't come in until the afternoon. The partners keep regular hours, because we have families. If somebody insists on getting overtime, we say, 'Okay, but understand that nobody checks hours. We check productivity.' We're on the honor system as far as overtime goes. You have to come to us and explain."

The system worked well on the smaller projects that Hammerhead undertook in its early years, but as the company began to get larger projects that required many more people to complete, it encountered new challenges. In 2003, for example, Universal Pictures hired Hammerhead to do visual effects for a movie called *The Chronicles of Riddick*. It was the most ambitious project the partners had ever undertaken and called for a larger staff than any the company had assembled in the past—thirty people, by initial estimates. Since its lodge on the hill could not accommodate that many bodies, the whole company moved to Universal Studios in nearby Universal City for the duration of the project. There the Hammerhead people worked in small, boxy corporate offices rather than in the big open rooms they were used to. That was unquestionably a sacrifice, but one the partners were willing to make because of the opportunity that the project afforded. They'd be doing cutting-edge work in special effects—the kind of work made famous by the *Lord of the Rings* and *Harry Potter* movies. Aside from the excitement of working on such a project, it would allow them to upgrade both their skills and their equipment, and it would give them the experience and the credibility they would need to land other such jobs in the future.

And they ultimately achieved their goals, although things didn't play out as they'd planned. For openers, they wound up needing more than twice as many people as they'd bargained on—sixty-five instead of thirty. That meant hiring a lot of people very fast, which created a host of unforeseen difficulties. "In the past, we've always been able to be very picky about the people we hire and how we hire them because we needed so few," said Chuba. "Those few would then get trained by the principals of the company. Here we were having to hire a lot of people on a just-in-time basis. You can't be as picky, and you're often disappointed by what you get. People don't live up to their résumés. They're not as productive as you'd hoped, or as the people you've hired in the past.

"You're also hiring people who aren't familiar with the way you like to work. They're used to how things are done in large companies. They want to be told exactly what to do and how to do it. That's what they're used to. They don't enjoy having the freedom we like. As a result, we had to add more levels of management, which we were reluctant to do, and so we didn't do it as quickly as we should have, which created morale problems. In the process, we lost our culture. We couldn't use the sort of open architecture that we enjoy and that has worked so well for us in the past.

"We also lost some of the talent of our permanent staff because we had to promote them to management positions where they could oversee things. They were good at that, but they weren't on the machines. That was a blow. We wound up having to hire two or three new people for every one of our permanent people who moved up. Later, we had to have our people go back and work shots again, because there were some particularly tricky things to do and we knew they would come through."

In the end, however, they overcame the obstacles and delivered all they had promised, as well as some additional work that other subcontractors were unable to finish. "The plane was flying pretty low to the ground there for a while," said Chuba. "We had to take pieces out and put new pieces in. Our priorities on new equipment changed from looking for the best price to going for the fastest speed. It was stressful, for sure. I don't know that we ever doubted our ability to pull it off, but it was a lot harder than we thought it was going to be. But once the machine clicked in, it went great."

The project lasted a few weeks longer than they had expected. As soon as it was finished, Hammerhead shrank back to its pre-*Riddick* size, fourteen people, and returned to its home on the hill. Looking back, the partners could rattle off a number of significant achievements. First, they'd increased their technical expertise and kept up with the breathtaking rate of technological change in the industry. Second, they had vastly improved the quality of their equipment without taking on any additional debt, since the cost of the new gear came out of their budget on the project. That gear would serve them well for at least another year. Third, they'd learned a great deal about working on large projects and gained considerable confidence along the way. They'd encountered business problems they'd never faced before and come up with creative solutions to them. Afterward, they had a much better idea about when to outsource work to other companies and when to keep it in-house. In the future, that would enhance their ability to manage their temporary expansions.

Most important, they'd made some big mistakes that had taught them important lessons, and those lessons, they believed, would allow them to operate far more efficiently the next time they took on a large job, as they fully intended to do. "We still want to succeed in creating the kind of work environment that we find is the most successful and efficient, that gives people positive feelings and allows them to be the most creative," said Chuba. "One thing we know now is that we need to hire key people a little earlier and immerse them in the way we want to work. We're also trying to get a better feel of the real estate market and see what kind of space is available, so that we won't have the physical barriers we had to deal with this time. If we do a few things like that, we think we can be more efficient, earn more money, and do a better job of making it work in the Hammerhead style."

Hammerhead did, in fact, make money on the *Riddick* project, although not as much as it usually earns. It is a highly profitable business in an industry where successful companies, in a good year, have net margins of

10 percent and where breakeven is considered acceptable. On most jobs, Chuba said, Hammerhead makes "a hefty multiple of 10 percent." Unlike the larger companies, moreover, it doesn't lose much money between projects. "In a big company, you typically get the perfect job and staff up," said Jamie Dixon, Hammerhead's president. "You have a lot of people working—on some projects maybe as many as two hundred people, doing four hundred or five hundred shots. Then the project ends, and you stop getting paid, but you still have all these mouths to feed. It may take two months before the next job starts."

Hammerhead was able to avoid falling into that pattern. As a start-up, it could only get small jobs in the beginning—which turned out to be a blessing. Those jobs invariably had the highest margins. For Hammerhead, the margins were even higher, since the partners often did the work themselves, knowing that the additional money they earned would go toward funding their extracurricular endeavors. For the same reason, the quality was exceptional, enhancing the company's reputation and opening the door to other, more lucrative projects. By keeping the size of the permanent staff down and shrinking back to the core group after each project, the company was also able to minimize the losses between jobs. As a result, it had no trouble generating plenty of cash—so much, in fact, that the rest of the industry couldn't help taking notice. Before long, other small companies began springing up, trying to duplicate Hammerhead's success.

To be sure, there was still strong demand for the services of the larger visual effects companies. Companies like Hammerhead weren't capable of handling the biggest animation projects, which required the work of hundreds of people. At least one of the large companies, however, is every bit as impressive as Hammerhead—Rhythm & Hues in Los Angeles, whose work making animals talk in the movie *Babe* was recognized with an Academy Award. Its other credits range from *Terminator II* and *The Nutty Professor* to *The Lion, the Witch, and the Wardrobe* and *Superman Returns*. It is an extraordinary company, by any measure. Indeed, it exhibits all the same characteristics as the other companies in this book—all, that is, except for one: It earns little, if any, a profit from year to year. "This is a money-losing business," said founder and president John Hughes on a December day in late 2003. "In this business, breakeven is the upper limit. It's hard to keep a company going, and there are a lot of failures. Only one of the competitors we had when we started is still alive, independent, and doing the kind of work we do: Industrial Light & Magic."

The company occupies a modern, open, airy building that Hughes and his partners moved into in 1995. The building is next door to the hangars that once housed Howard Hughes's Spruce Goose and that now serve as motion picture stages. On its corridor walls are drawings that bring to life the history of animation. There are animator sketches of all the Disney characters, from the early Mickey Mouse to the later Peter Pan, as well as various Warner Brothers stars, including Elmer Fudd, Bugs Bunny, and Daffy Duck. You turn one corner, and you run into drawings of characters from *Fantasia*. You turn another, and there are dancers by cartoonist Jules Feiffer, or clay animals from *Babe*, or miniature race horses made out of gum wrappers. There's also much evidence of the company's involvement in the community. We passed a large collection of toys, food, and clothing. "We help support a preschool in South L.A.," Hughes explained.

That month, Rhythm & Hues was a busy place. More than 650 people were working throughout the facility, almost twice as many as usual. The company had staffed up because it had a large number of big projects going, including *Garfield* and *Scooby-Doo II*. As a result, the building was bursting at the seams. Wherever you went, you found animators, compositors, programmers, systems people, and others hunched over computers, holding meetings, making sketches, creating clay models, watching dailies, writing on white boards, taking notes in a Linux class, and on and on. Every inch of space was being used for something. People were packed into darkened rooms with row after row of workstations. Even the conference rooms were filled with desks and computers.

Yet despite all the productive activity going on, Hughes was worried. He had no major projects in the pipeline. "We have plenty of work through next May, and then nothing," he said. "When big projects stop, we lose millions of dollars. After sixteen years in business, we're still in survival mode."

Hughes attributes the company's situation to the competitiveness of the industry. The market, he says, sets his prices, putting constant pressure on margins. It's also true, however, that he has chosen to spend money on his employees that would normally go into profit. He is passionate, for example, on the subject of health care. He considers it an abomination that the United States does not have universal health care and says that he would provide medical insurance for everyone in Los Angeles if he could. Instead, he offers his workforce what he believes are the best health benefits to be found at any business in the country. They cost Rhythm & Hues an average of between $8,000 and $11,000 per person annually, and they're available to any employee who Hughes believes will be around for six months or more. Freelance employees who work off and on for the company retain the benefits for up to three months between jobs. Rhythm & Hues itself covers all medical costs up to $85,000 per person, at which point outside insurance kicks in. The downside is that if the company was ever forced to file for Chapter 11, the employees would have to cover their own medical liabilities, since there is no outside insurer to fall back on.

Hughes decided to become self-insured in the early 1990s when he got fed up with insurance companies questioning employees' claims. He acknowledges that other senior executives are unhappy about all the money being spent on the health care program, though not because they're opposed to it in principle. They just believe that the company can't afford it. In 2002, a tough year, Hughes agreed to institute a "health tax," deducting 1.3 percent of salary for every person covered, up to 3.9 percent for a family, but he has ruled out rolling back benefits or significantly restricting the eligibility requirements. The program, in his view, is an essential element of the business. "It's not about maximizing profit," he said. "For me, it's all about taking care of employees. Not in a paternalistic way. We treat them as adults. Some people here call it 'touchy-feely,' which is a disparaging term. I defend it, as do the other partners. Doing good challenging work is part of touchy-feely. Also doing excellent work. People need to be proud. They have to feel that what they do is worth doing."

The health benefits are just one way the company cares for its people. It also has a 401(k) program into which it puts 10 percent of net profit, "assuming we're profitable," Hughes said. "If it's close, we put some money in anyway." There's an education program as well, under which Rhythm & Hues covers the cost of classes for employees, up to $750 per person per year. The vacation policy is equally generous: a minimum of three weeks for everyone; four weeks after two years; five weeks after five years; and six weeks after ten years. In addition, each employee gets an eight-week sabbatical every five years. So, in a given year, a company veteran might have thirteen or fourteen weeks off altogether, with pay.

Then there are the breakfasts and lunches. At other studios, people tend to go out for their meals, but the vast majority of Rhythm & Hues employees prefer to eat in: The food is better, and it's paid for by the company. At lunch, they crowd into the cafeteria and wait in line to be served. Hughes waits with them. There are no special privileges for executives or VIPs. Everybody eats together at long tables in the cafeteria or—on pleasant days—outside the back door.

The company is almost as egalitarian when it comes to governance. There's an executive committee of fifteen to twenty people, as well as a policy modification (or "poli-mod") committee of ten people, who decide whether new policies are needed or old ones should be revised. "They understand that if they want to change our medical policy, I have a veto," Hughes said. "Of course, I have a veto over any changes, but I don't use it." On the company's computer system, there are three separate discussion tracks—one for official business, one for general chit-chat, and one for politics—ensuring that people have the opportunity to make themselves heard on any topic they care to opine about.

As for financial information, Rhythm & Hues is, like many companies in our sample, open book. Every Friday, the employees get together in the auditorium, where Hughes and other managers update them on bids for television commercials, the status of feature film development, and what's happening with cash flow. Once a quarter, Hughes gives a lesson on the financial statements and goes over the budget. Among other things, he tries to get people to understand the difference between positive cash flow and profit—a crucial distinction in a company that finds it a challenge simply to break even each year. He believes it's important for them to have some idea of what the future holds. "I just think open-book management is more honest," he said. "If our situation becomes precarious, I don't want people to be shocked that there's no money and we have to have layoffs." Despite his best efforts, however, he suspects only a handful of people in the company really understand the financial model that allows Rhythm & Hues to carry on.

At the heart of that model is cash flow, which Hughes watches like a hawk. His skill at managing it explains how Rhythm & Hues has been able to survive for nineteen years. "The cash forecast is key to me," he said. "I don't rely on the income statement. We do a quarterly close, and I use the cash forecast to calculate our needs. I used to have a particular number I tracked: the amount of revenue per technical director"—that is, per digital artist. "We're bigger now, and our cash forecasting is more sophisticated, but we still use revenue per TD [technical director] for budgeting. If the revenues aren't there, we have to lay people off. With 85 percent of our costs in people, we can't cut enough just by being frugal, not even if we slashed health care."

All this raises an intriguing question; namely, can a company have mojo even if it barely scrapes by? Judging by Rhythm & Hues, I'd have to answer yes. I have no doubt, moreover, that the company's employees, customers, suppliers, neighbors, and fellow members of the motion picture industry would heartily agree. The company is universally admired and respected. It has the same type of corporate charisma we see in profitable companies with mojo, as well as the full range of accompanying qualities—the intimacy with employees and customers, the closeness to the community, the passion for excellence, the openness to innovation, the constant searching for new ways to do things better. At the other companies, those qualities have combined to produce great financial returns along with the special magic of mojo. Rhythm & Hues has the magic, if not the money. Of course, the magic won't help if the money runs out. As Jay Goltz observes, a company without profit is dangerously close to not being around at all.

One other element needs to be considered in any discussion of how the founders of these companies create organizations that have such a powerful impact on the people they come in contact with—especially their employees. It's an element that is a little mysterious, very difficult to define, different from company to company, and yet undoubtedly critical to both the culture and the image of the business. I'm talking about the way that people perceive the founders themselves.

That's not something most founders are particularly good at understanding. Some are embarrassed even to discuss it. Others fret about it and try to change it, usually in vain. Yet others shrug their shoulders and say that they can't be responsible for other people's perceptions and don't much care about them anyway.

There are a few founders, however, who have thought about the way they're perceived, analyzed it, and incorporated it into their management philosophy—Fritz Maytag of Anchor Brewing, for example. "I favor a very democratic, open, egalitarian atmosphere combined with a slightly mysterious, quite powerful, benevolent authority—you never know when he might strike, change the rules, get angry, lose his temper," he said in an interview with the *Harvard Business Review*. "I'm reluctant to be too precise about it. There are three or four people here who essentially make up senior management. And I think people sense that it's perfectly okay to go and talk to those people. I think they're a little scared to come and talk to me. . . . I also think that the power is hard to pin down around here. And I like that. I like things to be a little vague and mysterious. Again there's that combination of freedom and toughness. On the one hand, do anything you want. On the other hand, don't go goofing off or fiddling around."

But you can get away with leaving things vague and mysterious only if you make sure you're ultimately in control, which means identifying—

and holding on to—the critical levers of power. In a restaurant, for example, the key person is usually the one who controls the menu. Unless, in a pinch, you can step in and take over from the chef, you're at his or her mercy. In a machining business, that sort of power lies with those who know how to turn a lathe. The machinist, or the foreman, may tell you that something you want to do can't be done. If you can't show him how it can be done, you could find yourself unable to get your ideas implemented.

By the same token, the power position in a brewery is usually held by the brewmaster—the person who controls the brewing process and knows exactly how it's done. Accordingly, Maytag was careful to reserve the title of brewmaster for himself. Other people, he said, could have any title they wanted, as long as it wasn't brewmaster. He had his reasons. "[In] so many small breweries I've seen, the owner or the president is terrified of the brewmaster and of the production and of brewing itself. He doesn't know much about brewing. He comes home from a conference with a bright idea and wants to make an ale or a wheat beer or something. He goes out and talks to Otto, and Otto tyrannizes him" by saying it won't work—we can't do it. "Ultimately if you think he's wrong, the only way to prove it is to say, 'Well, I'm sorry but we can and here is how we're going to do it and I'll show you. Watch me. . . .' If you can't do that, you're in trouble. I've seen many small breweries that I thought could be more creative and successful if the owner knew more about brewing. So I've always thought I would remain the brewmaster, and in that way I could go out there and say, 'Guess what we're going to do now.'"

That, in turn, made it possible for Maytag to preserve the ambiguity he thought was healthy for the company. "Everybody knows who's in charge around here, but there are slightly vague ideas of exactly who's in charge of exactly what," he said. "Of course, what really exists may be quite different from my perceptions. But that's what I'd like to think exists."

When pressed to summarize how that fit into his overall management philosophy, Maytag refused. "Actually, I'm quite uncomfortable talking about all this, pinning it down, because it's all very mysterious," he said. "I think there's a certain amount of magic to all this, and the more you understand it, or think you do, the more you may lose it. Good management in a small company involves a certain freshness and responsiveness and natural feeling that is by definition partly unspoken, unarticulated, undefined."

He is no doubt right about that, and his insight applies especially to companies like those in this book. You can't have real intimacy without a good deal of freshness, responsiveness, and natural feeling. For that matter, it's probably true as well that the bigger the role those spontaneous qualities play in the way the company is managed, the more mojo it is likely to have.

But Maytag's comments also highlight one of the trickier problems faced by these companies. If the founder's mysterious role is as important as he believes, what happens when the founder leaves, or dies? Can companies preserve their mojo through a process of succession? Can they even preserve their independence? If so, how? What does it really take for a company to retain the qualities that have made it so exceptional in the past when the person most responsible for the development of those qualities is no longer around?

Those are questions faced by every business to one degree or another, but they are particularly pressing for small giants, if only because they have so much to lose if the transition of leadership and ownership fails. As it turns out, some companies have been able to pull it off—and some haven't.

7

Pass It On

ad I set out to write this book in, say, 1992, I would have had to give serious thought to including University National Bank & Trust Co. (UNBT) of Palo Alto, California. Although it was publicly owned, it fit the small giant mold in every other particular to a T. Introducing a profile of the bank published in 1991, *Inc.* magazine described it as "a laboratory testing one simple idea—that limited growth offers more opportunities than fast growth does." It was, in fact, such a good example of the phenomenon that I might have been forced to reconsider my decision to exclude public companies from the mix because of their financial obligations to outside investors. Somehow UNBT had attracted shareholders who bought into its philosophy of measured and limited growth, and they were evidently quite satisfied with the return on equity that the company delivered by following such a strategy. Or so it appeared in 1992.

At the time, UNBT had been in business for twelve years. During that period, the bank and its founder, Carl Schmitt, had acquired celebrity status among the legions of people interested in innovative management practices, thanks mainly to Tom Peters and *Growing a Business* author Paul Hawken, who had singled it out in their books and videos for its zany corporate culture, iconoclastic marketing techniques, and extraordinary customer service. UNBT defied every stereotype about banks. Its trademark depicted an alien in a flying saucer crashing through a wall. Originally painted as a mural on the outside of the bank building, the image appeared, among other places, on the credit cards UNBT issued, conveying the message that this was not your ordinary, garden-variety financial institution. "Un-cola banking" was what Schmitt called it, and UNBANK appeared on the license plates of UNBT's trucks. The sides of those trucks were used to make the same point. One, for example, had a caricature of Schmitt in convict clothing, apparently cheating at poker while sitting in prison. On the side of another truck, a senior officer of the bank was shown printing money while two other officers used magnifying glasses to check the quality of the counterfeit bills.

Then there were the ten tons of sweet onions that UNBT shipped in every year from Walla Walla, Washington, where Schmitt and his wife had gone to college. He'd gotten the idea from friends in California, who would ask him to bring home a supply of the town's signature vegetable whenever he went back for a visit. It occurred to him that customers, too, might like to get Walla Walla onions, and so he began importing huge quantities of them each July. UNBT would give them away in ten-pound bags, along with recipes.

In addition to the onions, the bank gave its customers great service, which attracted the attention of Tom Peters, whose office was in Palo Alto. He was particularly impressed with the bank's odd practice of treating customers like friends rather than just revenue generators. "Bounce a check," he wrote in one of his columns, "and the teller will spend five minutes trying to talk you out of letting the bank charge a bounced-check fee: 'You were late getting back from vacation.' 'You just overlooked it.' The unique assumption is that you are of good will and sound mind."

But what most observers missed was the strategy that lay behind the fabulous service and the oddball marketing. They were not just smart tactics, nor were they simply reflections of Schmitt's unique personality and style. Rather they grew out of his reason for starting the business in the first place. As Elizabeth Conlin put it in her *Inc.* article, UNBT had been founded on "the heretical notion that a company's growth has organic, almost preordained, limitations," and that, if you exceeded those limitations and grew too fast, you would undermine your ability to provide excellent customer service, create a great workplace for your employees, and maximize shareholder returns. "We could grow faster, but it would cost us everything," he told her. "In the bureaucracy of growth, you lose your distinctiveness."

Schmitt's belief in the virtues of limiting growth and staying relatively small dated back to his tenure as California superintendent of banks in the 1970s. There he had noticed that smaller banks consistently delivered a higher return on assets than the larger banks did. "It stood out like a sore thumb," he said. The explanation, he suspected, was that—by keeping their overhead low and focusing on a specific market—the small banks were able to operate more efficiently. When they began chasing after growth, they lost their focus, and their efficiency and profitability declined. But a bank with the discipline to maintain its focus, he reasoned, could go on delivering superior returns indefinitely.

It was an intriguing theory, and Schmitt decided to test it himself. He would start a bank that would target a well-defined market—Palo Alto and four nearby communities—and aim to capture a 15-percent market share and no more. He wouldn't force it, either. He would let the market determine how fast he reached the goal. His job would be, first, to develop a culture, a modus operandi, and a set of challenges that would allow him to attract and hold on to the best employees he could find. Then he had to make sure the bank provided a level of service that would bring in customers willing to pay a premium to do business with UNBT. Finally, he had to generate the kind of consistently good financial returns that would keep investors happy and encourage them to be patient.

The plan worked brilliantly, not least because of Schmitt himself. He had a unique combination of entrepreneurial street smarts, the shrewdness of an experienced banker, a lively sense of humor, and a steady hand on the tiller. Those qualities helped him attract the type of employees you would never expect to find in a small bank. He was able to pick off seasoned executives from major competitors like Wells Fargo by offering them competitive salaries and a workplace in which they could actually have fun doing their jobs—perhaps for the first time in their careers. It was a place where people were encouraged to use their judgment and take initiative, and not just the senior managers. Even the tellers were given a free hand. Instead of getting a long list of rules to follow, they were told to trust their instincts in deciding, for example, whether or not to accept a check. "What will kill this company first is a bunch of people running around with their noses stuck in rule books and manuals," he said.

Schmitt saw it as his responsibility to create an enjoyable work environment. It was part of the deal. He couldn't give people fancy titles, he acknowledged, or offer them the prospect of managing a branch. Instead, they'd get a great place to work. He'd pay them well, give them an ownership stake, provide generous benefits, and throw in perks like a fancy cafeteria and various special "Unbank" awards. Above all, they would have fun and the freedom to do their best. The result was almost no turnover, not even among tellers, in an industry where the typical teller turnover rate is about 50 percent.

With customers, Schmitt pursued a strategy designed to produce the kind of returns he needed to keep his investors happy. That involved providing world-class service—right down to free shoe shines in the lobby and postage stamps that could be bought from a teller at cost—but it didn't mean accepting every customer who came through the door. Schmitt turned away people who just wanted to buy, say, one of UNBT's high-yielding certificates of deposit. He was interested only in long-term customers who would do all their banking with UNBT. Toward that end, he insisted that they maintain a checking account with a minimum balance, on the theory that they would then be less likely to shop for bargains elsewhere. In addition, the bank thoroughly investigated the credit history of prospective customers and rejected those who didn't measure up. It was, Schmitt said, his form of quality control.

Once customers were accepted, however, they received a level of service they simply could not get anywhere else. They also enjoyed the security of knowing that the bank would cover for them if they bounced a check or missed a payment or screwed up in some other way. And, of course, they got the bags of onions and the monthly newsletter from Schmitt, not to mention the jokes—like the "safe escape kit," consisting of a screwdriver and a candle in a glass case located inside the vault. Evidently customers loved it: UNBT's customer turnover rate was less than a third of that at other banks in the area.

The results spoke for themselves. In its first twelve years, the value of a share in UNBT rose 500 percent. From the fifth year on, return on equity was 14 percent or higher, and shareholders received 30 percent of the after-tax profits in the form of dividends—5 percent more than the average payout level of other banks its size. In the future, moreover, when the bank hit its goal of 15 percent market share, the dividend payout would go up to 40 percent, as the bank stopped investing in expansion.

Those kinds of numbers made for loyal shareholders. In fact, people who'd invested in UNBT's 1980 IPO still owned 63 percent of the shares eleven years later, and 65 percent of the shareholders were also customers. Schmitt treated them as he treated everyone else—with honesty and humor. One year, for example, he put out an annual report that could be refolded into a model of the bank with the employees waving from the roof. The shareholders were delighted. "Carl is a nut," said George G. Parker, a Stanford business school professor who served on the board. "He's fun to work with . . . He's colorful, buoyant, a real freethinker, which you don't see too much of in this business."

Schmitt was well aware, however, that his gags would take him only so far. He knew that if he didn't consistently deliver return on equity of more than 15 percent, the shareholders might start thinking about selling the company; and there was no shortage of potential buyers, including a number of large banks. He could have given himself a cushion by purchasing so-called brokered deposits. That involves getting money managers with large amounts of cash to buy CDs in units of $100,000 or more (so as to be covered by the Federal Deposit Insurance Corporation), usually offering them a slightly better interest rate in return. The banks can then use the money to expand their loan base. But it's "hot money": It doesn't stay in one place very long. As soon as a better opportunity shows up, the money manager will sell the CDs and put the cash to work somewhere else. Schmitt didn't want those types of deposits. They would dilute his portfolio and undermine its value. The alternative was to boost productivity and efficiency through constant innovation. Although it was the more difficult route, it was also the more rewarding over the long run, and the one Schmitt chose to follow.

He was simply unwilling to pursue growth for its own sake. He believed that, as long as he kept his eye on the ball, growth would take care of itself. It was a matter of logic and principle, and he said he would apply the same approach even if he were in an altogether different business. "It's like you're sailing down a river with many tributaries running off," he told Conlin. "Yes, you pause to consider each tributary and whether it is part of your voyage, but keeping you on course is the knowledge of where you want to be at the end of the trip." A better statement of the growth philosophy of the small giants would be hard to find.

But then fate intervened.

In 1993, Schmitt suffered a mild heart attack. He recovered and returned to his duties at the bank, but he knew he had to think about retiring. Aside from the normal stresses and strains of the job, he was finding it harder and harder to deal with federal regulators who faced pressures of their own following the savings-and-loan debacle of the 1980s and who were taking an increasingly adversarial approach to banks like UNBT. At one point, the Office of the Controller of the Currency (OCC) charged the bank with not making enough loans to low-income neighborhoods, as required by federal law. Schmitt cried foul, noting that the bank had loaned plenty of money to small businesses in low-income East Palo Alto, which the OCC had failed to take into account. He fought the ruling and—after a nine-month battle—got it reversed, but the struggle left scars. "[I]t is now apparent to us that our principal regulator, the OCC, is approaching bank regulation from a 'national' perspective," he wrote to shareholders, ". . . imposing the standard of management bureaucracy that is counterproductive to providing the high level of service that our customers have become accustomed to." The stress was so great that, in 1994, University National Bank & Trust dropped the "National," and became University Bank & Trust, as it switched to a state charter. Nevertheless, the regulatory pressures remained.

Schmitt could read the writing on the wall. He needed to phase himself out of operations and into retirement, which meant lining up a successor—or a buyer. It soon became apparent that the latter would be easier to find than the former. At a board meeting on January 19, 1995, Schmitt reported that—based on his extensive knowledge of the industry, the market, and the bank, as well as efforts he'd made to recruit high-level managers—he was "not confident of UBT's ability to identify a suitable successor." Less than a week later, shareholders gathered in the bank's lobby and voted to approve the sale of UBT to Comerica, the giant bank holding corporation based in Detroit, swapping each of UBT's 1.59 million outstanding shares for 1.75 shares of Comerica. With the latter's stock trading at over $27 a share, the deal as a whole would be worth more than $75 million, of which Schmitt and his family would get about $9.1 million, in addition to his severance and noncompete package, worth another $2.2 million.

Before the vote, Schmitt assured shareholders that Comerica would continue to maintain close ties to the community and provide first-class customer service, but the plain fact was that University Bank & Trust was disappearing into the maw of a giant corporation. It was never again quite the same. Today it is known as Comerica Bank–California University Trust Division in Palo Alto. The only remnants of the old University National Bank & Trust are the bags of Walla Walla sweet onions that the new owners continue to give away every July—more than 300,000 pounds of them in the decade following the completion of the merger—as if the onions held the secret to what made the bank a magical company way back when.

A small giant faces no greater challenge than making its mojo last. That's hard enough to do under the best of circumstances, as history attests. We can all come up with examples of companies we know—not necessarily famous ones—that have had it and lost it through the normal processes of growth and change. But however difficult it may be for a company to hang on to its mojo as it struggles to find its way in a turbulent business environment, it is infinitely more difficult to do so while simultaneously undergoing a transfer of ownership and leadership.

To begin with, it almost always requires the owners to make significant sacrifices. Among other things, they must be willing to accept a lower price for their stock than they could get if they simply sold to the highest bidder. After all, most buyers will look at the company and immediately spot opportunities to increase its profitability. How? By consolidating, centralizing, and cutting out some of the extra things the company does that are not essential to its viability and that don't contribute directly to its bottom line—including many of the practices and activities that go into creating mojo. The more economies a buyer can identify, the greater the cash flow it can project, and the more money it will be willing to spend on the acquisition. A buyer that wants to preserve the company's mojo won't make the cuts and thus won't be able to justify paying as high a price. To be sure, the company might also attract a buyer that wants it for strategic reasons and therefore is willing to pay a premium. But a strategic buyer, which would integrate the business into its operations, is even less likely to preserve whatever it is that makes the company special than one doing the acquisition for strictly financial reasons.

Even if the owners are willing to sell the company for less than they might otherwise receive, there's still the problem of finding buyers with the vision, the passion, and the talent to guide the business while continuing to nurture the qualities that have given it its mojo in the past. Most likely, those people are already working in the company. They understand better than anyone else what it takes to create mojo in that particular business because they've been part of making it happen. But are they capable of doing it on their own? Do they have the necessary leadership skills? Are there resources available to provide them with the support they need? And what about the finances? Is it even possible to arrange a buyout? Is enough cash being generated to cover what would be owed to the previous owner—or to a bank that put up the money to do the deal—without crippling the company?

Sooner or later, every business owner has to confront such questions, and the more successful a company has been in developing mojo, the more difficult those questions are to answer, if only because there is so much more to lose. Given both the complexity and the emotional ramifications of the issues involved, it's no wonder that most owners of private companies put off dealing with succession as long as they can—often until some life-threatening event forces them to face up to their mortality. By then, their options may be limited. Given his fiduciary responsibilities, the amount of money at stake, and the absence of a successor who had been groomed for the job, Carl Schmitt very likely had little choice but to get the best deal he could find for the shareholders of University Bank & Trust, which meant selling to a strategic buyer and hoping for the best.

Unfortunately, the majority of the companies in our sample are not much further along than Schmitt was when it comes to succession planning. Three have been through a process of transferring ownership and leadership from the founders to the next generation, and many of the others have a team in place that could run the company temporarily should the founder die or become incapacitated, but the long-term plan for most of the companies is sketchy at best. "I don't feel the need to get out, but I can't work forever, so I guess I'd better think about it," said Paul Saginaw of Zingerman's. "Currently our exit strategy is to die."

At least one of the founders, Norm Brodsky of CitiStorage, is not particularly concerned about succession. He thinks it's less important whether or not his company outlives him than that it set an example and provide a role model for other businesses to emulate. He hopes that the people who have worked at CitiStorage will take its principles and practices with them wherever they go.

He is an exception, however. When pressed, almost all of the others say that, yes, they would like to see their businesses go on without them, but they haven't figured out how. "We have not done a succession plan," said Danny Meyer of Union Square Hospitality. "Count me amongst the unenlightened when it comes to that."

"It just recently came up a little bit," said Dan Chuba of Hammerhead. "Who knew we'd be around this long?"

"I'm just not sure what to do," said Fritz Maytag of Anchor Brewing, who—at sixty-eight—may have to make some decisions sooner than others. "I think, if the character of the founder is important, a company develops a character of it own. Our company has a personality, and I have a strong feeling to have it continue. I do not have a strong interest in having it be a family business. I have to think more about it. The tax issue is tricky. Is the estate tax killing small businesses? I believe it is."

That point is not lost on Gary Erickson of Clif Bar. In his book, he goes out of his way to remind readers that estate taxes alone can force a business to be sold. If you're the sole owner of a debt-free company worth, say, $30 million, it will go into a trust upon your death, and your estate may owe as much as $15 million in taxes on that single asset (at least as of 2005—the laws are changing). Unless other arrangements have been made, there's only one way the estate will be able to come up with that money: by selling the business. There's also only one way to avoid such a fate: by planning well in advance what will happen to the company when you die. You may, for example, be able to buy life insurance that would cover the taxes due, provided you keep it outside the estate. In any case, you need an experienced estate planner to advise you in such matters.

With the exception of those who've already been through the passing of the torch, Erickson has done more such planning than any other owner in our sample, which is somewhat surprising given his age. He has been working on these issues since he was in his midforties. Maybe his willingness to deal with them has something to do with his hobby of hanging off cliffs and climbing straight up sheer rock faces for hundreds of yards. "I'm very practical about my mortality," he said. "Estate planners tell me that most of their clients don't want to think about dying, and they don't want to think about the company without them. They also struggle with how much to give the kids." Those are all matters that Erickson and his wife, Kit, who is his co-owner, have had to deal with. In his book, he minces no words in saying what he thinks other people should do: "It amazes me how few people have worked on this. I have talked to people who own $700 million companies and have no estate plan. My advice is simple: No matter how big your company is, get counsel and an estate plan as quickly as you can. Take responsibility for the enormous gift that you hope to pass on to the next generation; it's part of the entrepreneur's job."

The process "is very expensive, and it never ends," he added, sitting in his office in late 2004. "You have to keep revising the plan as the company grows and changes. It's really your own desires and needs that will drive the estate plan. The most important thing is to be sure you find the right people to execute it for you."

Of course, estate-planning addresses only one side of the succession issue—making it possible for your chosen successors to keep control of the company when you're gone. That side is certainly important, as the statistics on the survival rates of family businesses attest. Only about 30 percent of them make it through the second generation, and 3 percent to 5 percent through the fourth generation. Those numbers are actually not bad when you compare them to the survival rates of other categories of business, but they do illustrate the challenge of maintaining family ownership of a company over the long term (if that's what you want to do) in the United States, as opposed to, say, France. In the small French village of Sancerre, where I live for part of each year, there are not one but two successful wineries that have been in the same family continuously since 1513. One of them is run by a man named Alphonse Mellot XVIII. His son, who works in the business, is Alphonse Mellot

XIX, or *le dix-neuvième* (the nineteenth). They are a tribute to the durability of primogeniture in Europe. For better or worse—probably better—there is no such tradition in this country.

The other side of succession has to do with the transfer of leadership. By the fall of 2004, Erickson had already turned the job of CEO over to Sheryl O'Loughlin, the former brand chief, who had been with Clif Bar for eight years, including the difficult period around the aborted sale. "We're building the management team," Erickson said. "I'm sure if I went away for six months, the company would be okay. This allows me to work on succession planning. I'm also back in product development, like Bill Gates. And I'm the main spokesperson, which is wearing me out, but I made my own bed. The long-term for me is to be the chair of the company and contribute where I can—not in operations. I play with ideas and throw them into the pot."

The role model for Clif Bar, he said, is Patagonia, the clothing business, whose founder, Yvon Chouinard, and his wife, Malinda, still own the company, though they have long since ceased being involved full-time in operations. (Yvon continues to do research and development of new products in the surfing and fly-fishing lines—a tough life.) Erickson is impressed that, after a quarter century, Patagonia still seems to have its mojo working—which he considers a credit both to them and to their management team. Chouinard told him the company had gone though several CEOs before finding a mix that worked. But as Erickson looked more closely at Patagonia—and at Clif Bar—he became convinced that there was more to it than finding the right CEO, or even the right management team. Just as important was having a clear, well-articulated vision that was ingrained in the day-to-day life of the business. He and Kit eventually came up with five "aspirations" that encompassed their vision for Clif Bar: sustaining the brands, sustaining the business, sustaining the people, sustaining the community, and sustaining the planet. They also developed statistical measurements they could use to determine how well Clif Bar had done on each particular aspiration in any year. It was all part of the succession process, Erickson said. "A company has to move from being entrepreneurcentric to being visioncentric. The goal is that, by the time we're gone, the vision will be secure."

There's one ownership-transfer option that Erickson is still considering, as are many of the other founders in this group: selling a portion of the company to the employees through an employee stock ownership plan (ESOP). The idea would be to give them a piece of the action, partly as a reward for their contributions to the company's past success and partly as an incentive for them to take responsibility for its continued well-being. Thanks to various tax breaks, moreover, founders who sell to an ESOP can often do as well as, or better than, they would if they sold to an outside party—and control stays in the company.

The downside has to do with two sets of liabilities that you take on when you start an ESOP. First, there's the money that the ESOP usually has to borrow to cash out the founders. It gets the stock only as the loan is repaid. That debt can represent a significant burden for the company, sometimes more than it can bear. The second set of liabilities is potentially even more dangerous, mainly because it's frequently overlooked. When contemplating an ESOP, people tend to forget that, if it works as intended, the shares held by all those employee-owners could be worth a lot of money in the future—and eventually the employee-owners will leave and expect to get paid. Unless the company has a plan for cashing them out, it could be forced to look for a buyer, thereby defeating at least one of the purposes for setting up the ESOP—namely, keeping ownership in the hands of the people who work there.

As it happens, two of the companies in our sample—ECCO and Reell Precision Manufacturing—have already had to grapple with the challenges of succession in an ESOP company. Each of them set up an ESOP in the 1980s. By 2004, the one at ECCO was its majority shareholder, with 58 percent of the stock, while the one at Reell was its largest shareholder, with 42 percent of the stock. Meanwhile, both companies had gone through a transfer of leadership and were already looking forward to, and preparing for, the next one.

We have already discussed, in Chapter 5, the leadership change at ECCO, when—following his first heart attack in 1993—Jim Thompson, the principal owner, turned over the job of president and chief operating officer to his partner, and brother-in-law, Ed Zimmer, while retaining the title of CEO for himself. Two years later, Thompson had a second heart attack, this one eventually leading to open-heart surgery, which prompted him to scale back his role even further. "Up to the surgery, I was coming to the weekly meetings of the leadership team and the annual planning meeting," he said, looking back. "It wasn't good for me or them. There were times when I was impatient. I'd complain to the leadership group that we weren't solving obvious problems as fast as we should. We'd identify a quality problem, for example, or a problem with shipping to the wrong location. They weren't difficult to solve. They just needed people's focus. It seemed to me we could solve them more quickly by fiat than by having a committee and reaching consensus. I suppose it's less expensive to let people figure it out for themselves than to send them to school to learn it, but it's hard for me to do. That's why I'm not here in the building. It's too frustrating. Ed and I have different styles. It took me a long time to come to grips with that. Anyway, the company is better off with Ed. It's a major stress out of my life, and he has made a huge contribution to my net worth. The results have been better under him than they were under me. I don't want to screw it up. I'd rather have my net worth be higher than croak in an argument about how to do something."

By 1999, the company was going gangbusters, and Thompson took yet another step back, becoming chairman and director, while giving Zimmer the title of CEO. At the same time, he was beginning to think about an issue that he knew would have enormous ramifications for the company, namely, what to do with his stock. He still owned 51 percent of the outstanding shares, and he was worried about leaving his wife with the weighty responsibility of having to decide what to do with his majority stake after his death. Besides, he might as well sell it while he was healthy enough to enjoy the proceeds. The question was, to whom?

There were plenty of potential buyers around, including a large number of companies—both domestic and foreign—that would have loved to take advantage of ECCO's distribution network and that saw its high-quality, customer-intimate backup alarms and safety lights as a perfect complement to their own product lines. At least seven of them would check in with Zimmer or Thompson on a regular basis, asking, "Are you guys ready yet?"

"No, not yet," they would reply—and then change the subject.

The alternative was for Thompson to sell his stock to the ESOP. With a so-called 1042 rollover (referring to Section 1042 of the Internal Revenue Code), he could defer the capital gains taxes on the proceeds of the sale, provided the ESOP wound up owning more than 30 percent of the company's stock. In fact, he wanted to sell considerably more than that—not all of his stock but enough to make the ESOP the majority shareholder. Because of the tax deferral, an outside offer would have to be 25 percent higher than what the ESOP would pay in order to provide the same economic benefit to Thompson.

And there were other considerations. For one thing, Thompson's son, Chris, had joined ECCO in 1993 after working for five years at an electronics distributor in Seattle. There he had risen from office temp to CFO in three years and became, at twenty four, the youngest member of the company's board by about thirty years. At ECCO, he was widely seen as Zimmer's probable successor, assuming the company remained independent. If another company acquired it, all bets were off. Thompson wanted to give his son a chance to do what he'd done, which argued for selling to the ESOP. Then again, the ESOP would have to borrow about $5.1 million to acquire his stock, and Thompson was concerned about burdening the company with too much debt. He went back and forth, weighing the pros and cons of each option. "I told my dad he could make more money by selling to a strategic buyer," said Chris. "I said, 'Don't decide not do it for my sake.'" Zimmer told Thompson much the same thing.

In the end, he went with the ESOP. "It was a mixture of financial, emotional, and personal reasons," he said. "There was the value of being able to have Chris succeed me and letting him have some of the fun of running an independent entity. I'd always had a personal desire to be independent. I think everybody does. Some people might say, 'I'd rather have the deep pockets. I don't want to have to guarantee all this debt, and then have to borrow more to buy out departing shareholders in the future.' Sometimes I think that—when you load up the ESOP with debt—you set in motion a succession of borrowing and paying it off. I worry that I may have burdened the company for the future, though I tried to avoid burdening it too much by not selling all of my stock. I don't know what I would have done if someone had come along and offered $200 a share instead of $100 a share. But I'm happy with where the company is. I don't need more wealth than I have."

In any such transaction, there's always the risk that unscrupulous owners will take advantage of the company, piling on more debt than it can handle, getting their cash out early, and leaving employees holding the bag. ECCO took care that no such accusation could be ever made about this deal. "We did a ton of due diligence to make sure the ESOP could pay off the loan," said Zimmer. "It was the most comprehensive review we've ever done. Everybody had an attorney. Jim had one as the seller. I had one representing the company. Our CFO, George Forbes, had one representing the ESOP. Then there was the bank." As it turned out, they had little reason to worry. The company was able to absorb the debt payments without any visible impact on its profitability.

The sale had a major impact on ECCO's employees, however. For one thing, it increased the value of everyone's stake in the ESOP, which now had a claim on a much larger percentage of whatever the company was worth. That would eventually translate into a lot more money for people when they cashed out. Before the sale of Thompson's stock to the ESOP, the biggest payout had been $68,000. After the sale, that same ESOP stake would have been worth around $250,000.

Perhaps even more important, the decision by Thompson and Zimmer—who also sold some stock to the ESOP—sent a powerful message to employees, most of whom took it as a sign of their leaders' faith in, and commitment to, both the business and the people. "Jim and Ed could have done a lot better on the open market," said Todd Mansfield, who works in engineering and had joined ECCO in 2001. "When they sold to the ESOP, it was a strong statement. I don't have that much in the ESOP, maybe a few thousand, but it's important. It's highly valued by everyone, and that was a big thing."

Much to the employees' relief, Thompson's decision effectively ruled out the possibility that the company would go on the auction block in the immediate future. No one, however, could guarantee that ECCO would never have to be sold. Looking ahead, Zimmer could see that it would reach another crossroads around 2015. By then, a number of the major players, including Zimmer himself, and a significant contingent of hourly people would be in their early to midsixties. Most, if not all, of them would be thinking about cashing out and retiring. Somehow the company would have to come up with the funds to pay them. "It could be that we figure out how to pay everyone but Chris," Thompson said. "He might have to sell."

That assumes, of course, that Chris will succeed Zimmer when the time comes. Chris, for his part, doesn't take that for granted. "Sure, I'd like to run the company some day," he said. "I want to put myself in a position to be able to do it. I need the necessary skills, and I've taken a lot of different jobs here to develop them. Inside the company, I occasionally hear, 'You wouldn't be in your position if you weren't Jim's son.' I don't take it personally. I don't expect Ed to give me the nod unless I'm ready, and it's right for ECCO."

He is well aware of the challenge he will face if he does become CEO. "I can see a lot of people disappearing in a short period," he said. "If we don't grow enough, we may have to sell. But, you know, it's the same thing that makes the ESOP great. People become motivated to increase the stock value. That creates the liability and also the ability to pay off the liability. We have a lot of opportunities to grow, and our culture is to take advantage of them and reinvest. Some people don't agree with that. They'd rather take the profits than reinvest them, but they stand out like sore thumbs around here. There are also people who see this as their opportunity to get rich. They think, 'When we sell, I'll be wealthy.' And we may be forced to sell at some point. If someone put an offer of $200 a share on the table, we'd have to look at it."

That said, he would not sell the company if he could avoid it. "I like winning," he said. "It's fun to be part of a winning team. I also love the environment here. If you work here, you want to be here. When I drive home at night, I think all the way about what we're doing—the products, how much better we can make them, how much more value we can add, how much more profit we can get from them. I get excited. I want to turn the car around and come back. A lot of that has to do with the people, and being part of an organization that people respect, which goes back to the core values. I grew up with the core values, so they feel right to me. Without the ESOP or the open-book management, I might not be as interested."

Yet, ironically enough, because of his father's decision to sell to the ESOP, Chris himself can't receive any additional shares in the plan. Instead he has so-called performance units, which function like phantom stock and provide no tax advantage. "I'm satisfied with that," he said. "I purchased some stock early. And I have some ESOP stock from before that I can keep until I leave." He also stands to inherit a portion of the 15 percent ownership stake that his father didn't sell but instead put into a family limited partnership for his four children. "It may be an issue when I can't have a tax-free rollover on the performance units, but I plan to make the other stock worth enough that I don't care."

For Reell Precision Manufacturing, the thorniest questions did not have to do with the transfer of ownership, at least not in the beginning. Given the founders' stated beliefs and values, it was completely predictable that they would wind up selling some of their stock to an ESOP and passing some along to their children and grandchildren. In 2005, twenty years after it was set up, the ESOP owned 42 percent of the company's shares, which it had acquired in annual distributions, without taking on significant debt. The other shareholders included the three founders, who still owned 21 percent of the stock; their family members, who owned 35 percent; and various managers, who directly owned the remaining 2 percent (in addition to their ESOP stakes).

What's more, the ESOP had its own "repurchase" fund that could be used to cash out departing members as they left. That, too, had been built up over the years, through Reell's contributions of cash as well as stock. At any given moment, half of the plan's assets were invested in Reell stock and half in mutual funds that could be liquidated to buy out departing ESOP members, whose shares would then be redistributed to the remaining members.

The more difficult challenge was the transfer of leadership from the close-knit triad of the three founders to . . . Well, to what? That was one of the major questions. The issue first arose in the late 1980s, when Dale Merrick was getting ready to retire. As I noted earlier, he had left 3M to start his own manufacturers' rep firm, the Dale Merrick Company, prior to Reell's founding. After Reell was up and running, he had continued to spend most of his time at the rep firm, getting regular updates from the other two founders—Bob Wahlstedt and Lee Johnson—and participating in major decisions. Then, in 1988, he'd sold the Merrick Company and moved to Reell full time. Since he intended to retire two years later, he and his partners had to figure out who would replace him.

The obvious internal candidate was the vice president of manufacturing, Steve Wikstrom, who had been with Reell since 1981, was universally liked and respected, and had played an important role in the company virtually from the day he'd started. But several members of the board weren't sure Wikstrom had all the necessary qualifications for such a key position. So it was decided he would serve a two-year term as the third member of the triad, after which other candidates would be given a shot. That way, the remaining founders would get experience working with several people before they had to make their decision. At the end of Wikstrom's two-year term, however, Wahlstedt and Johnson decided they couldn't do without him, and he was asked to stay on as the third triad member.

By then, Wikstrom was thoroughly committed to the Reell way of doing business, though he'd had some questions about it when he'd started in 1981. He had been twenty-nine at the time, married with two children, and had a secure job with good pay and benefits in a company of 225 employees, a nonprofit that ran sheltered workshops in the Twin Cities. Coming to Reell meant giving up that job for a position in a fourteen-person company, whose future—the founders had warned him—was shaky. They said they'd encountered a major technical problem on a new product they were developing. "We think we have our arms around it," they told him. "We should have it fixed in six months. If not, we'll be out of business."

On top of that, they had given him a rather unusual document, an introduction to the company that, among other things, said it was "committed to follow the will of God" and "to provide its employees with . . . an opportunity to integrate Christian life with a career." Wikstrom, who was not a particularly devout Christian, had quickly read through the statement. "What do you think?" they'd asked.

"There's nothing here I would have a problem with," he'd said. But in the back of his mind, he'd been thinking, "Practically, how does this work?"

Later that evening, he talked things over with his wife. "There are two possibilities here," he said. "It could be a good deal, or the company could be out of business in six months. But I'm twenty-nine years old. I can handle it."

"Is it what you want?" she asked.

"Yes," he said.

"Then do it," she said.

What sold him, he says, was the authenticity of the three founders, the transparency with which the company operated, and its fundamental values and purpose. There didn't appear to be many secrets in the company. When he'd asked about debt, the founders had readily shown him the balance sheet and the income statement. They had also made it clear that their first purpose wasn't the maximizing of shareholder wealth—it was the growth and development of people. "They wanted a business environment that promoted harmony between work life and personal life," Wikstrom said, "and they wanted to give people an opportunity to earn a secure, stable livelihood."

He had not been disappointed. In his first ten years at the company, he'd found that Reell was for real, and when he became a member of the triad in 1991, he fit right in. For the next seven years he worked closely with Wahlstedt, in particular, as Johnson focused his attention on the new European operation, based in the Netherlands, and the start-up of Vadnais Technologies, a state-of-the-art spring-winding business that was spun out as a Reell subsidiary in 1994. (It was sold in 2004.)

By the mid-1990s, both of the remaining founders were beginning to think about retirement. One of them, Johnson, was planning to cut back to half time as soon as possible. It wasn't clear who, if anyone, should replace him when he decided to retire. Some members of the board were skeptical that the triad could be replicated successfully. They thought it might have worked only because of the unique personalities of, and chemistry between, the particular individuals involved. That didn't necessarily mean other people could do it.

Wikstrom, who had become a convert to the idea of shared leadership, argued that they shouldn't give up on it without at least trying to bring in new players. He suggested experimenting with a leadership team of five current managers on which he would serve as a so-called *prima inter pares*—first among equals, a concept drawn from the servant leadership philosophy of Robert K. Greenleaf (see Chapter 6). The overall leadership responsibility would belong to the entire group, however, not just one person. Wahlstedt, who was chairman of Reell's board, would serve as the team's mentor and adviser, providing what they referred to as the "balcony" perspective. There had always been one member of the triad who was not directly involved in day-to-day operations and therefore brought a more detached view to discussions and decisions. "Nose in, fingers out," Wahlstedt called it. The person in that role had been an important contributor to the triad's success.

The five-person team turned out to be what is usually referred to in business as an important learning experience. That is, it flopped. In hindsight, Wikstrom said there were two factors that ultimately doomed the experiment. The first was the sheer number of people involved. "I learned that the difficulty goes up exponentially as you add people," he said. "It becomes much harder to get the commitment to unity and consensus, and to maintain the relationships needed—the empathy, the communication, and so on, everything it takes to be aligned."

The second problem had to do with chemistry. There was one individual, an engineer, who played a particularly critical role in the company. Wikstrom described him as "our mustang." Bob Carlson, who later joined Reell as co-CEO, said he was "one of the most talented engineers I've ever seen. His fingerprints are all over every new technology we have." But the other members of the team had a tough time with him. The tensions mounted until finally, after two years of trying to make it work, Wikstrom felt compelled to sit down alone with the other three people. Frankly, he told them, the group wasn't functioning the way a leadership team had to, and part of the problem was their relationship with the engineer. Did they think that the company would be better off without him? Two said yes and asked Wikstrom what he thought. He said that parting company with that person was the furthest thing from his mind. "I'm going tell the board that we don't have a viable management group," he said. "I'll ask them what they want to do."

The failure of the five-person team once again forced the board to question whether or not shared leadership really worked. Some of the members doubted that the company needed more than one leader. "Why not have Steve become the sole CEO?" asked one of them. "He has a collaborative style. Everyone will be happy."

But Wikstrom demurred. "Had they asked me in 1981, I'd have said, 'Yes, sure, in a few years, I'd like to be CEO,'" he said. "But in 1998, I no longer felt that a single leader was the way to run this or any other organization. I didn't feel qualified to be the single CEO. I said, 'If I'm offered the job, I will decline. But if we're talking about a co-CEO, and we find someone whose skills are complementary to mine, I'm very interested.'" At the time, he said, he didn't realize what a big decision he had just made. Looking back, he felt it was one of the two things he'd done in which he took the greatest pride. The other was his refusal to cut the mustang loose.

So the search began for a new member of the triad to replace Johnson, who was ready to retire. (Wahlstedt was remaining as chairman of the board.) A hiring committee was formed, including two board members, an engineer, the head of human services, and Wikstrom. In a Reell committee, there is usually one member identified as the "buck stopper," that is, the person with a veto. That person in this case was Wikstrom. He had already sought out the advice of one of the board members on the hiring committee, Margaret Lulic, a consultant who had written a book, *Who We Could Be at Work*, in which Wikstrom and Reell had figured prominently. She had encouraged him to stick with shared leadership. She had also advised him to look outside the company for candidates.

As it happened, one of the other people she'd written about in her book was a West Point graduate, Vietnam veteran, engineer, ex-IBM sales rep, and Wharton alumnus named Robert Carlson. He had worked in sales and marketing for various companies before deciding that he'd had enough of corporate life. At the moment, he had his own consulting business in the Twin Cities, with numerous clients large and small, and was quite content with his situation. When Lulic called in May 1998 to tell him that Reell was looking for an experienced person to share a leadership position with another executive, Carlson said he wasn't interested.

"Do me a favor," Lulic said. "Steve Wikstrom is in my book, too, and I'm on their board. Read his part of the book before you say no." Carlson, who had talked in the book about the kind of company he'd like to lead someday, agreed.

A few days later, he called her back. "Well, it's what I said I wanted," he said. "If it's real, I'm interested."

He proceeded to go through an elaborate vetting process at the company, which included a round of golf with the founders and interviews with a lot of other people. The more time he spent with them, the more he wanted the job. "The values got me," he said. "They had a solid connect with the people. I'd been in a number of companies that did things in ways I wasn't comfortable with, and I could see these people walked the talk." But after his initial round of interviews, he heard nothing for a couple of months and began to wonder if Reell had lost interest in him. Finally, he called Jim Grubs, the head of human services and chairman of the hiring committee, who assured Carlson that he was still in the running.

There were, in fact, seven or eight candidates altogether, including two from inside the company. Wikstrom, for his part, was anxious to move forward. "People on the board and in management were pushing me to clean up some problems," he said. "They said, 'Don't make this new person deal with them.' I said, 'I *want* him to deal with them. That's why I'm hiring him.'"

One issue revolved around the constant torque hinges that Reell had originally developed for Hewlett-Packard in the mid-1980s. They allowed the top of a laptop computer to be moved up and down, or left in one position, without falling. Over time, Reell had modified the design while adding major new customers, notably Apple and Compaq. As computer manufacturing moved to the Far East in the 1990s, and was increasingly subcontracted to other companies, the demand for constant torque hinges exploded. Reell had to decide whether to pursue the opportunity, which would require major investments of time and capital, as well as a serious marketing effort in China, Taiwan, and other countries.

There were also questions about the organizational structure. Now that the gang of five had been disbanded, what would happen with the four people who were no longer part of the senior management team but were still important players in the company? Who would be working with them, and how? And what should be done with the European operation and the new spring-winding subsidiary, both of which were losing money? People inside and outside Reell—including its bankers—were asking when the company was going to stop wasting money on them and close them down.

Wikstrom hoped that the new person would help him think through these issues and come up with good answers, and he liked Carlson, but would people accept an outsider in such a high-level position? Carlson himself recognized the challenge. "It was a big risk," he said afterward. "I had concerns about coming in at this level. I was worried about the reaction of the community." Nevertheless, he was offered the position and accepted it. He and Wikstrom decided they would call themselves coCEOs. Carlson began on October 12, 1998.

The transition went remarkably smoothly. "The founders did a great job of passing the torch," Carlson said. "Some people thought they were still calling the shots. They dealt with that by disappearing for a year. Of course, Dale Merrick had already been out for ten years. Lee Johnson retired. Bob Wahlstedt made a point of not being around a lot. When he was asked about something, he said, 'Go see Bob and Steve.' It was great to have that support. It made things much easier."

It also helped that Carlson and Wikstrom had done their homework. For one thing, they'd spent a couple of half-day sessions working together, walking around, talking about issues facing Reell. They'd taken Myers-Briggs personality tests (as had all the candidates for the job) to identify their complementary qualities and points of potential conflict. They'd even brought in a psychologist to work with them. He'd concluded that they were both emotionally secure extroverts, and more or less opposites in every other way, but with the ability to "reach across the table" to each other.

In any case, they had no trouble working together from the start. Within a short period, they'd dealt with the various problems Wikstrom had been under pressure to resolve. On the organizational front, they developed the matrix structure that showed exactly who was responsible to whom. They also decided to take full advantage of the opportunities in the constant torque hinge business and to stick with the struggling European branch and the spring-winding subsidiary. "Bob was quick to pick up on their potential," said Wikstrom. "The dumbest thing we could have done would have been to drop them. Bob had experience with small companies getting established. He said, 'These things are getting better. Why get out now?'"

"I knew how tough it was to make a new business work," said Carlson. "There were good people at the top of both operations, which was most important."

"He brought a fresh view, and people listened," said Wikstrom. "We took care of all the problems very quickly. I'm glad I didn't try to do it before he came."

The two got along so well, in fact, that they were happy to share an office in the beginning, while new offices were being built for them. Not wanting to lose the ease of communication they'd had in one office, they decided that the new offices would be side by side, separated only by a glass door and a counter with a retractable window that they could slide open when they wanted to talk or close when they wanted privacy.

Carlson and Wikstrom were soon functioning effectively as co-CEOs, with Bob Wahlstedt, who remained chairman of the board, serving as the "balcony" person. To that extent, Reell continued to be run by a triad, although responsibility for the results, both short- and long-term, rested squarely with the dyad. That was the basic leadership configuration they expected to maintain as the company moved forward and they began thinking about the next transition, which wasn't far off. In a few years, after all, Wahlstedt would be ready to retire; and Carlson, who was fifty-seven when he joined the company, would be thinking about cutting back. If he replaced Wahlstedt as the balcony person, the company would need to recruit another dyad member. Both Wikstrom and Carlson preferred to recruit from within, and they began grooming potential candidates almost immediately.

Although three internal candidates eventually emerged, none of them was ready yet for top management when Carlson decided in 2004 that he wanted find a replacement for himself. Fortunately, a strong outside candidate had come along—Eric Donaldson, a Kodak veteran who lived in the area and whom Reell had been courting for four years. On February 1, 2005, he joined the company as vice president of engineering. Two months later, Carlson officially moved on to become CEO emeritus and a member of the board. At the same time, Bob Wahlstedt and the other two founders resigned from the board, thereby completing the transition of leadership.

Meanwhile, an ownership issue loomed, one that no one had antici-pated when the original shareholders' agreement had been drafted: At what point, if any, should the company be allowed to buy back stock from the founders' heirs? People could see that it would become an in-creasingly critical question as time went along. That's because one of Reell's greatest strengths had always been the absolute alignment be-tween the shareholders, the board, the management, and the employees. That alignment was particularly evident in tough times. On four occa-sions, in four different decades, the company had cut salaries rather than lay people off, and shareholders had insisted that dividends be reduced as well. In 2001, the board had issued guidelines: A 10 percent pay cut would trigger a 25 percent dividend cut, and on up from there. Share-holders were even willing to accept no dividends—and no profits—at all if that was necessary to get through a crisis, provided there was no ero-sion of the company's equity. A loss of value was not okay.

It wasn't hard, however, to imagine that bargain breaking down as the founders' stock passed to the second, third, and fourth generations. "In other companies, you see shifts when stock moves from one genera-tion to the next," Carlson noted. "The agenda changes. There's really not much difference between third-generation ownership and public ownership."

Ironically, the managers had expected that their biggest challenge would be to get employees to understand the opportunities and respon-sibilities of ownership, but they discovered that it was the founders' children and grandchildren who had the hardest time coming to grips with what it meant to own stock in Reell. If they didn't have much di-rect contact with the company, their emotional ties to it—and to its unique way of doing business—were weak. People had to experience Reell before they could get it—whether they were family members or employees. "At one of our meetings, we asked people, 'When did you come to believe in the Reell values?' said Jim Grubs, the head of HR. "To a person, they said it was when they experienced the values in their lives. They needed to have a Red Sea experience, a parting of the wa-ters."

"The question is, who owns the sacred trust?" said Carlson. "Is it the legal heirs or the spiritual heirs? That's really the key issue we face now. Are we a family business, or should we buy the family out? Some family members feel it would be an act of betrayal to sell, but there is probably more consensus right now on the not-a-family-business track." In any case, it's a highly emotional issue, especially for the founders who've already had to struggle with a loss of significance following their retirement.

But Wikstrom feels that the issue may resolve itself over time. "Those who want the stock will get it," he said. "Those who aren't so interested in it will give it up. The ESOP is the only shareholder that has a real appetite for stock. That's the overarching dynamic. I think we should make it easy for those who want to leave to leave and for those who want to stay to stay."

We have spent most of this book looking at what founders do to conjure up the magic of mojo, and how they and their successors handle the equally daunting task of trying to make it last. Making mojo last, however, does not mean keeping the company the way it is, or was. Mojo does not insulate a business from the marketplace. Small giants must adapt to changes in the competitive environment just like every other business. Then again, they usually have an easier time of it, thanks to the same practices and beliefs that give them their mojo to begin with.

They have an easier time, that is, in the first generation, while the founders are still around and driving the change. But, ironically, the founders' very success, and the mystique surrounding it, can often become a significant obstacle to the leaders who follow them, especially when it becomes necessary to make fundamental changes in the way a company does business. That was the situation confronting Kent Murdock, the third CEO of O. C. Tanner, in 1997, four years after Obert Tanner passed away. The company's marketplace was changing so fast and so profoundly, Murdock realized, that not only its mojo but its very survival would be at risk unless it underwent a complete makeover. He quickly discovered, however, that to pull it off, he would have to deal with the legacy of the founder.

On the surface, Murdock appeared ill qualified to lead such a transformation. He was a lawyer, not a businessman. As recently as 1991, he had been a litigation partner in the Salt Lake City law firm of Ray, Quinney & Nebeker, which represented O. C. Tanner. He hadn't had much contact with the company until 1990, when Obert got into a shareholder dispute. It was serious enough that Obert feared it might lead to litigation. He brought Murdock in to protect the company in case it did. After reviewing the facts and talking to all the parties, however, Murdock became convinced that there was no need for litigation: The dispute could and should be resolved through negotiation. He proceeded to serve as the mediator, and no suits were ever filed. Evidently, Obert was impressed with his lawyer's work, because—about six months into the process—he suggested that Murdock leave his law practice and become president of O. C. Tanner. Murdock was taken aback, but the more he thought about the idea, the better he liked it. He decided to accept the offer.

"It was just so foolish!" he said, looking back twelve years later. "It was better than a midlife crisis! I talked to our partner who was corporate counsel to O. C. Tanner. He said, 'Don't sell your office furniture yet.'"

The plan was to have Murdock train with CEO Don Ostler and replace him in five years when he reached sixty-five. For Murdock, it promised to be a great adventure, though he had little idea what lay ahead. To all outward appearances, O. C. Tanner was a well-established and fabulously successful company in 1991, with $181.8 million in sales, more than two thousand employees, a solid operating margin, and no debt. It was clearly the leader of its industry. Nevertheless, both Ostler and Obert Tanner realized that the company needed to change. For one thing, the quality movement was revolutionizing American manufacturing, introducing concepts like just-in-time inventory and team-based management, and O. C. Tanner was way behind the curve. It had an old-fashioned, hierarchical, command-and-control structure that was inflexible, sclerotic, and slow. Efficiency had been dropping for forty years, while the number and variety of orders had been steadily growing. The company was being asked to produce thousands of customized awards every day, more and more in quantities of one. Meanwhile, there were increasing complaints about matters like on-time delivery, which reflected both the rising expectations of customers and the company's antiquated ways.

Recognizing the inadequacies of the manufacturing operation, Ostler and Tanner had begun to overhaul it even before Murdock arrived. Among other things, they'd appointed a young manager named Gary Peterson to serve as a "facilitator of change." His first task was to change the mind-set of the people on the shop floor, who had been trained to do what they were told. He began by asking them simply to speak up—with little success. "I went to the polishing department, where two hundred ladies worked," he recalled. "They had lots of physical ailments—carpal tunnel syndrome and the like. We divided polishing into teams of eight ladies each, and they spent the first few weeks looking at each other. I would go to a meeting and ask, 'What happened on Tuesday?' Nobody said a word. Three weeks went by before they began talking, and then it was usually about a beef someone had. It took a very long time before people began to trust and believe."

Murdock quickly picked up on the problems in manufacturing, and he began raising questions about other aspects of the business as he tried to develop his own assessment of the challenges facing O. C. Tanner. His lack of experience probably helped in this regard, mainly by leading him to ask questions about things that an industry veteran might have taken for granted. It struck him, for example, that the company didn't do much of what he would call marketing. "My idea of marketing is that you look at the market and the customers, and you ask, 'What do they need and how can we give it to them?'" he said. "It's not about making something and seeing how to sell it to customers. That's what we were doing. Our marketing was all sales driven. We were a manufacturing company that sold what we made, and we had fetters on our mind. Our attitude was, we sell beautiful, hand-crafted, high-quality symbolic awards, and people better wake up and get it. Everything in the company was organized around selling awards—the accounting, the computer system, the way of thinking, everything. But it was a dated value proposition."

It was dated because the market was in the process of being utterly transformed. To begin with, long-term employment was fast becoming a thing of the past. Amid the downsizing of the 1980s and 1990s, company loyalty was increasingly seen as a quaint idea, both by the corporations that used layoffs as a means to boost their stock price and by the employees who began selling their services to the highest bidder. In that environment, the prospects for O. C. Tanner's core business of long-term service awards did not look bright.

At the same time, the company faced growing competition, as the industry became more of a commodity business. O. C. Tanner had positioned itself as the Tiffany's of awards providers, offering the highest quality as well as the best service and support, for which customers paid dearly. Now it was being challenged by competitors who claimed to offer comparable quality and service at a lower price. As a result, Tanner's margins were being squeezed, and its chief competitive advantage—the perceived value of its products—was being eroded.

There were also demographic issues to contend with. More young people were entering the workforce, and their tastes were different from, and more utilitarian than, those of the employees for whom O. C. Tanner had made awards in the past. The companies they worked for, O. C. Tanner's customers, were becoming more demanding as well, especially in terms of the speed with which orders were filled and the fine details of each award package. All these pressures would soon multiply, moreover, thanks to the dramatic proliferation of Internet sites. Before long, the company would find itself with eighty-two online competitors, each promising to do exactly what O. C. Tanner did but for much less money. And over the horizon lurked China and the other cheap-labor economies of Asia, Latin America, and Eastern Europe, which sooner or later were bound to test Tanner's commitment to keeping its manufacturing in the United States.

The closer Murdock looked at the company's situation, the more convinced he was of the need for fundamental changes in the way O. C. Tanner operated. Everything had to change, from its definition of its business to the expectations of its employees to the capabilities of its computer system. To survive in the next century, O. C. Tanner would have to become a different company, or so Murdock believed, and he wasn't alone. When he raised his concerns with Ostler and other key leaders, they would nod in agreement. They shared his anxieties about the future. But they also recognized the formidable challenge of remaking a company that had been as consistently successful as O. C. Tanner. In the twenty-three years that Ostler had been CEO, it had never experienced declining sales. From what people could see, it was the most stable and profitable company in the industry. Every company, it seemed, was having a hard time financially except O. C. Tanner.

So how do you convince people that fundamental changes are necessary when the old ways appear to be working so well? How do you arouse people to action when they feel comfortable with the way things are? And how do you overcome the reverence people have for their beloved founder, who had died in 1993? The company operated as it did because Obert Tanner wanted it to, and Obert had never been wrong. Why should anyone believe that this new guy, the lawyer, knew what he was doing? In fact, Murdock readily admitted that he wasn't quite sure what to do about the problems he saw, but he had no doubt that something had to be done if the company's success was to continue into the next century. After succeeding Ostler as CEO in March 1997, he set about launching his revolution.

One of his first moves was to open the books to the managers. Up to that point, only a handful of them had known the company's actual profitability. When the others looked at the numbers, they were shocked. They had thought the business was making a lot more money than it was. Murdock pressed them to ask basic questions about where O. C. Tanner was going. He brought fifty-three people together from all over the company and challenged them to define what business they were really in, what value they should be offering customers, and what changes they would have to make for the company to be the best at what it did. Out of the discussions came a consensus that O. C. Tanner had to transform itself from a service-award manufacturer into a company that helped customers set up and operate employee recognition programs. It was a major change in perspective, and it required the company to make a series of seven "strategic bets," as Murdock called them: (1) embrace reality; (2) define the strategy; (3) get the right people in place; (4) get marketing into the company; (5) harness technology first; (6) change the culture; and (7) improve operations.

By "embrace reality," Murdock meant getting people to recognize that the company's competitors were strong and growing stronger and that what had worked in the past would not work going forward. By "harness technology first," he was acknowledging the need to replace the company's antique mainframe with a network system capable of handling the complex technological needs of a twenty-first-century business being rebuilt for speed. That turned out to be the most torturous part of the transformation process. "Our people killed themselves getting the new system up and running," Murdock recalled. "It took us four years from start to finish. We needed technology that would link together all the company divisions on a common platform and give us new capabilities—an adaptive, flexible architecture that would allow us to create and develop new applications. It's called ERP, Enterprise Resource Planning, and it's murder to install. We talked to a professor from Harvard who had done a study of companies with ERPs. Half of them had failed."

Recognizing the huge challenge that lay ahead, Murdock brought in a speaker to inspire the troops. A renowned rock climber named Todd Skinner, had been the first person ever to ascend a Himalayan peak called Trango Tower. "We needed a metaphor," Murdock said. "Todd came and talked to us about how intimidating the peak looked from base camp as they started to sort their gear. He said they realized they could only climb it by getting on the wall. That applied to us, too. He said, 'When we first got on the wall, we weren't capable of making the ascent. It was on the wall that we became capable of it.' That metaphor helped us. We were doing the Trango Tower of computer transitions. We failed to meet our milestones again and again, but we kept going, and we became more capable as we went along."

Like most companies that put in ERP systems, O. C. Tanner initially relied on consultants to do the installation. "At one point, we had eighty-five consultants from Arthur Andersen working on it," Murdock said. "But the consultants had it wrong. They said it was a project with a beginning and an end. It was more than a project. It was a huge transition. They miscalculated the time line. They didn't understand our business or its complexities. Finally, we fired all the consultants and did it ourselves."

Murdock refers to the period from 1997 to 2002 as "the leap-of-faith years." He has a painting in which a mountain goat is shown jumping from one cliff to another, and he says that's more or less how he felt at the time. He tried to keep his sense of humor. In 1999 and 2000—two difficult years—he told the board, "I have great news! We're paying no income taxes this year!" Of course, there were no taxes because there was no income. For five years, moreover, sales were essentially flat. He admits that his faith was severely tested. "At times, my heart was so discouraged," he said. "Others had to pick up the flag and lead. Many people led the company during this period. Sometimes it was a programmer. Sometimes the project leader." He motioned to the figure of a Civil War soldier on his desk—Joshua Chamberlain, the hero of Little Round Top, whose 20th Maine Volunteers held the extreme left flank of the Union line at Gettysburg against a fierce Confederate charge and thereby changed the course of the war. "He's my hero. You step into the breach. You do what needs to be done."

It was in this crucible that Murdock and his team reshaped the culture of O. C. Tanner. "We tweaked it," he said. "We didn't want to touch the core values—the integrity, the commitment to continuous improvement, the customer intimacy. Obert believed in truth, goodness, and beauty, and so did the rest of us. But we had to add some new values, like humility and learning. Those came from me because I didn't know what to do." Murdock also encouraged a level of debate that hadn't gone on previously. "We got into a Hegelian dialectic. I wanted forces to clash so that synergy could emerge. Before, bad news would stay down, out of sight. I wanted a war of ideas, and no silos. Anyone could speak to anyone else."

Most important, he tried to get rid of the mind-set that if you worked at O. C. Tanner, you could count on someone else—read Obert Tanner—to take care of you. To reinforce the message, he gave everybody a special pen embossed with the phrase, "We write the future." "The point was, there was no Obert," Murdock said. "There was no 'them.' There was just us. If we wanted to have bonuses, we'd have to generate them ourselves. That was a tremendous change, and it met a lot of resistance at first. Obert was so generous that people thought they could rely on him, not themselves. Like his practice of giving $100 bills to employees on Thanksgiving. People were used to it. Obert giveth. We had to go beyond that and get to the pride of success, and I think we succeeded. In 2000 and 2001, wages were flat, and bonuses were down, but there was no complaining. By then, people had accepted the idea that we determine our own compensation. We set targets we expect to meet. If we do better, we take the extra money and split it. The company gets 45 percent. If we do worse, there's nothing to split."

It is hard to exaggerate what the company went through. It changed its strategy from selling products to providing customers with solutions. It changed its value proposition from offering beauty to improving return on investment (ROI). It changed its culture from top down to wide open. It changed the way it maintained quality from using audits to having process-based mechanisms. It changed its marketing philosophy from promoting what it made to creating what customers wanted. It changed its technology from a system built around an outmoded mainframe to one based on a state-of-the-art network.

It changed the entire way it did business. And after five very tough years, the company finally emerged from its purgatory, growing 5 percent in 2003, 7 percent in 2004, and almost 10 percent in 2005, while having the most profitable years in its history. The operating details told the story. In 1991, the lead time from ordering to shipping was 12 weeks; by 2003, it had shrunk to 3.3 days, and by 2004, to a single day. On-time delivery had ceased to be a problem, as the percentage of products shipped when promised went from 80 percent in 1991 to 99.7 percent in 2003. Whereas it had once taken two weeks to customize an award, by 2003 the work could be done in two hours. Emblems would be attached to an award with a special adhesive, but 0.14 per hundred of them used to fall off; by 2004, the fall-off rate was down to .0028 per hundred, the lowest of any company using the adhesive. Meanwhile, the overall manufacturing defect rate had plunged to 0.25 per hundred. Communications errors were down to 0.48 per hundred. As for returns, the largest percentage (1 percent) came from customers who'd simply changed their minds about what they wanted.

By all indications, O. C. Tanner was back on the road it had traveled for most of its nearly eighty years in business, its mojo intact. But Murdock was not about to relax. "We are wary of our success," he said. "We know that new problems and opportunities arise every day, and that our best hope is to move forward with humility and courage. We believe we will survive and prosper, but we are never sure of the next step."

There are, of course, some founders in our sample for whom succession is not in the cards. It's pretty much a foregone conclusion that their companies' mojo will last only as long as they themselves are involved because the businesses can't survive without them. I'm talking specifically about the two companies built around the unique talents of artists, namely, Selima Inc., the dress company of Selima Stavola, and Righteous Babe, the music business of Ani DiFranco. Granted, other artists have created businesses that have continued after the founders departed. United Artists, the movie company, was started by actors Charlie Chaplin, Mary Pickford, and Douglas Fairbanks, and director D. W. Griffith. Trumpeter Herb Alpert was the cofounder of A&M Records, and Frank Sinatra launched Reprise Records. All those businesses were eventually sold. If they ever had any mojo, it was lost after the sale.

Selima and Righteous Babe have mojo in spades, but it's almost impossible to imagine either company without its founder. Perhaps a buyer might someday want to acquire their inventory and other assets—the rights to DiFranco's music, for example, or the patterns for Selima's gowns—in the unlikely event that they would ever be put up for sale. The companies themselves are another story. Stavola created Selima as the vehicle for her art. DiFranco created Righteous Babe for the same reason. It would make no sense for other people to buy and continue operating either company. They would do better starting their own. That situation might change in Righteous Babe's case. If the subsidiary businesses (the concert hall, the store, the record label) continue to prosper, the company might eventually be able to exist without DiFranco's active participation, but Selima Inc. will never be viable without Stavola. She has absolutely no interest in turning it into a business that someone else could own. She would first have to destroy everything she loves about the company she has created, a self-defeating exercise if ever there was one.

With that in mind, it's fair to ask whether a company like Stavola's belongs here at all. I had my doubts. Granted, it's a real business, and very successful financially, and it shares many characteristics of the other companies in our sample. You can't get much more intimate than a two-person operation. But isn't the company just the means by which an artist has made her living? Can you really compare the inspiration behind it to the passions that have animated the other companies in this book?

The answer, surprisingly enough, is yes.

8

❋

The Art of Business

Bernard A. Goldhirsh was the founder of *Inc.* magazine and a man who helped redefine entrepreneurship in America. Although it's hard to imagine now, there was a time when it was not considered a compliment to be called "entrepreneurial." Back in the 1950s, 1960s, and 1970s, entrepreneurs were generally looked upon as shifty characters with little or no redeeming social value. The media ignored them, academia deplored them, and their companies got no more respect than they did. When people talked about business, they were referring to large, well-established, publicly traded companies. Smaller, private companies were regarded as fringe elements, and therefore unimportant by definition.

All that began to change in the early 1980s, thanks in no small measure to Bernie and *Inc.* I had the good fortune to go to work for him in 1983, and I was still around in June 2000, when he sold the magazine after being diagnosed with an incurable brain tumor. He died three years later. During the twenty years I knew him, he shaped much of my thinking about business in general, and entrepreneurship in particular.

Like many people who start companies, Bernie had ended up in business almost by accident. An ardent sailor, he had knocked around the

191

Caribbean following his graduation from MIT in 1961. Later he ran a school on a chartered sailboat in South America. After returning to the Boston area, he began producing educational booklets on sailing, which—by 1970—had evolved into a magazine called *Sail*. During the next ten years, *Sail* became the largest circulation sailing magazine in the world.

But that was not what Bernie had had in mind when he started out. He had just wanted to earn enough money to buy his own boat. "I didn't have any intention of staying in publishing," he said in an interview with *Family Business Quarterly* about a year before he died. "I had envisioned a school ship that would sail around the world. The students on board would write about their experiences, and we would publish those experiences in *Sail*. . . . The ship was going to be a model for the planet, in the sense that everybody on board would be working together, not polluting the water supply, conserving all resources, and taking advantage of natural forces. I had this Buckminster Fuller, spaceship-earth model in my mind. . . . I was very idealistic in those days, and young, and I thought this would be a nice metaphor for planet Earth. This little ship would be a model of how people could live cooperatively."

Eventually, Bernie and one of his friends formed a not-for-profit corporation that bought a boat in Europe—a 144-foot square rigger called the *Regina Maris*. In 1976, they sailed it in the Tall Ships transatlantic race from the Canary Islands to Bermuda. They operated it for a while as a school ship, making voyages to the Galapagos Islands and other ports of call, but Bernie soon married, settled down, and put the school ship idea behind him. By then, he had his hands full with *Sail*.

The magazine had taken off, and Bernie had suddenly found himself with a substantial company to run. As sales grew to $12 million, he was confronted with management issues he'd never thought about before. He searched the business press in vain for articles that would help him deal with them. "They're writing about U.S. Steel and its labor problems," he told *Sail*'s publisher, Don Macaulay. "What does that have to do with me?" Figuring that others must be in the same situation, he came up with the idea for *Inc*. Publishing experts warned him that such a magazine couldn't possibly succeed. There was no market for it, they said; and even if there was, who would want to advertise to people in small to midsize companies? But Bernie started *Inc.* anyway—he sold *Sail* about the same time—and its launch turned out to be one of the most successful in magazine history. Within two years, *Inc.* was profitable and, within six years, had a paid circulation of 650,000, along with a readership of more than 2 million people.

I went to work for *Inc.* in the middle of that initial growth spurt. Those were heady times. The personal computer revolution was just beginning to unfold. A whole generation of great new companies—from Ben & Jerry's in Burlington, Vermont, to Microsoft in Bellevue, Washington, to Patagonia in Ventura, California—was being born. But we didn't have to go anywhere to learn about the world we were covering: We were living in it. Our particular corner of that world was located in a building Bernie owned on Commercial Wharf in Boston, a piece of the waterfront he'd acquired long before it became prime real estate. From our offices, we could hear the call of seagulls and the sound of halyards slapping against the masts of sailboats docked alongside the wharf, one of which belonged to Bernie and was available for the staff's use.

Bernie was like no other boss I'd ever had. He had a certain Woody Allenish quality—short, Jewish, a little eccentric, very sharp but also somewhat absentminded, prone to drawing odd connections between remarkably disparate things. An intensely curious person, he loved to get into long, rambling conversations about sailing, modern dance, inner-city entrepreneurship, the writing process, mathematics, celestial navigation, the challenges of parenthood, whatever. Around the office he dressed informally—chinos, polo shirt, and Top-Siders—and he was utterly without pretense. Once, preparing for a meeting with bankers from Goldman, Sachs, he asked *Inc.*'s editor in chief, George Gendron, "Do you think we have to wear socks?" By the same token, he had little regard for rank or status. He seemed to take a personal interest in whomever he came in contact with, be they Nobel laureates or file clerks.

As for *Inc.*, it was a pleasure to work for. Bernie treated us well and was remarkably hands off as owners of publishing companies go, giving the editorial staff free rein to put out the best magazine we were capable of producing. Nevertheless, in his own way, he exerted a profound influence on *Inc.*'s content, mainly by showing us how interesting, exciting, and rewarding business could be—on many different levels. Building a company was a lot like sailing, he would tell us, and *Inc.* was about helping people on the "rocky voyage from the garage to the fully-managed organization." As he wrote in the magazine's tenth anniversary issue, "The part of sailing that I really like is this: when people go to sea, they have a need for self-reliance and at the same time they are dependent on one another. Much of the satisfaction comes from the mutual trust that develops, particularly after coming through a bad storm. . . . It's the same whether you're sailing a ship across the Atlantic or taking your company from start-up to its destination. There are storms, there are calms, and, most important, there are people pulling together to achieve common objectives."

In addition to his sailing analogies, Bernie frequently talked about an aspect of entrepreneurship that other people sometimes overlooked— the intensely creative, almost artistic, part of the process. His thoughts on the subject grew partly out of an experience he'd had as an undergraduate at MIT, when he had taken a semester off to work for Dr. Edwin Land at Polaroid. There he had joined a small group of people charged with inventing the cameras of the future.

"Dr. Land [was] like a hero to me," he recalled. "Here was this fast-growing company, creating all kinds of jobs, created by this one man with an idea. And I thought, 'This is so fantastic, that one person can do so much in terms of creating a business, creating an enterprise, creating jobs, increasing the tax base. So much good comes out of this one person and his idea and his willingness to go ahead and start a business.'"

To be sure, the phenomenon was hardly limited to Dr. Land. Entrepreneurship, Bernie realized, was the means by which an economy continually renewed itself. Without it, a country would lose its vitality, its energy, and become impoverished—just as a culture would become impoverished without the ongoing creation of art. "I kept thinking that the entrepreneur is like an artist, only business is the means of his expression. . . ." he said. "He creates [a business] from nothing, just a blank canvas. It's amazing. Somebody goes into a garage, has nothing but an idea, and out of the garage comes a company, a living company. It's so special what they do. They are a treasure."

That was a point he urged the editorial staff to keep in mind as we put together the magazine each month. When contemplating our reader, he reminded us, we needed to take the whole person into account. "I always tried to tell the editors to think of the business person as an artist using both sides of his brain," he said. "You're not just writing for a rational person. You are writing for someone who has the soul of an artist, and his expression is business." Of course, Bernie himself was as good an example of that person as anyone else who ever appeared in our pages.

As I noted in the introduction, this book is best viewed as a field report on a group of extraordinary companies. By the same token, researching and writing it has been a journey, and as with most journeys, you don't know exactly where you've been—or where you will wind up—until you reach the end. As I look back on my journey, one obvious question comes to mind. After spending time in and around these small giants, what can we say is the essence of the mojo they all have?

The answer, I believe, has more to do with the people than with the businesses. To me, the owners and leaders of these companies stand out for being remarkably in touch with, and focused on, what most of us would probably agree are the good things in life. By that, I mean that they are very clear in their own minds about what life has to offer at its best—in terms of exciting challenges, camaraderie, compassion, hope, intimacy, community, a sense of purpose, feelings of accomplishment, and so on—and they have organized their businesses so that they and the people they work with can get it. When outsiders come in contact with such a business, they can't help but feel the attraction. The company is cool because what's going on inside it is good, it's fun, it's interesting, it's something you want to be associated with. From that perspective, mojo is more or less the business equivalent of charisma. Leaders with charisma have a quality that makes people want to follow them. Companies with mojo have a quality that makes people want to be part of them.

All that starts, however, with the creative impulse that Bernie Goldhirsh was referring to when he talked about entrepreneurs as the artists of the business world. If there's one thing that every founder and leader in this book has in common with the others, it is a passion for what their companies do. They love it, and they have a burning desire to share it with other people. They thrive on the joy of contributing something great and unique to the world.

Listen, for example, to Fritz Maytag as he talks about the "theme" behind Anchor Brewing's beers and ales. "When Winston Churchill was asked at a dinner party what he thought of the dessert, he said, 'Madam, it's a pudding without a theme.' We have a theme," Maytag said in the early days of the American microbrewing renaissance, talking to David Gumpert of the *Harvard Business Review*. "No other beer in the world, and certainly no group of beers, has anything like the theme we have. It is that we make everything as simply as we can with as few shortcuts, adjuncts, and additives as possible, and in a pure, traditional manner. Just as an example, all of our beers are made with malt. We don't use corn or rice or sugars or sugar syrups or other grains. Almost all other brewers in this country and many overseas use them. . . . There's nothing wrong with it. It's not cheating. It's not evil. It's very common these days. There are a lot of advantages, especially in terms of cost and in ease of production. But we prefer to go back to the old way of making ale, the way it was done for thousands of years—with malted barley.

"That's just one part of our theme. We also use nothing but whole hops—the little hop flowers. Traditionally, you pick these, dry them with warm air, pack them in a bag or a bale, and take them to the brewery to put in copper kettles. Our brew kettles are copper, of course. Nowadays, most new breweries don't use copper kettles. They use stainless steel. We wouldn't dream of using stainless. Ask me why, and I can't really tell you. Copper looks good, it feels good. The old brewers say that it affects the flavor. I don't want to find out. The same with air-dried hops. We could use extract, which is what most brewers all over the world do now. Shipping and storing efficiency would be infinitely greater. Many breweries around the world also use a special treatment on the hops; it's something like packing the molecule, a way of getting more yield out of a pound of hops. Almost doubles the yield. A little chemical trick. We wouldn't dream of doing that.

"And there's more. We ferment all of our beers in very strange, old-fashioned fermenters that are very shallow, very large. And we cool the fermenting room with filtered San Francisco air. . . . We don't have coils in the tanks. This apparently is the way beer was made in the old days on the West Coast before they had ice. They just used the cool night air. So here we are with these unusual fermenters and with the air cooled by San Francisco air. Does it make the beer different? I don't want to know. I hope so. Why do we do it? Because it feels good. . . . Part of the joy of Anchor Steam beer is that it comes from this funny old way of fermenting . . .

"Now I think my role is to make sure that everybody here gets the idea that we have a theme and to remind people what we're up to and to set standards. . . . I'm actually a little embarrassed to talk about what I do because I love it so much and it's such a sort of a selfish, quixotic kind of existence I have. But life is short, and if I thought we were being silly, and the beer was a joke, and it was all a con job, then I'd really be embarrassed about what I do. But I have so much fun and do such amazing things, I'm beginning to relax and enjoy it. Because I'm persuaded that the beer is so damn good."

The passion that Maytag feels for his craft of brewing isn't much different from the passion that Selima Stavola feels for her art of clothing design. "I tell you, I wake up in the morning, and it's the best hour for me—because I'm so excited about going to work," she said. "When I lived in New York, I would set the alarm for 3:30 A.M. and catch the 5:04 A.M. train. I would get up, and I'd be wide awake and full of joy because I was going to work. I hear other people saying, 'I can't wait for my vacation.' To me, it's a lost day out of your life when you feel that way. It's such a waste to be unhappy when you can wake up in the morning anticipating the day. Your work should be something you enjoy. My client has to be someone I enjoy. It all comes down to, are you happy with yourself when you tackle a new day?"

There is passion in Jay Goltz's voice, too, when he talks about the renovation of the old factory on North Clybourn in Chicago where he put his home and garden store. "I wanted to keep the grittiness," he said. "Like a prizefighter with a broken nose and a beautiful blond girlfriend on his arm. Before, the floor was black with black cutting oil. We sanded it. I was afraid we wouldn't get rid of the smell, but the smell went away, and the color came out. I didn't want anything to look brand new. There's a French limestone counter, and a tin counter. The designer said to paint the walls white. She said, 'In New York, everyone paints the walls white.' I was afraid I'd lose the authenticity. I wanted the vintage charm. We sandblasted them and left them raw, and we didn't cover the beams. But I was careful not to overdo it. . . . We also put up signs in the parking lot with quotations about art, flowers, and home. I wanted the experience to start when you park your car. That's the art of what we do. We create an experience for the customer. I like doing it. I feel like an artist who has painted a picture. I stand there on Saturday and see customers coming in and know we're making people happy."

And here's Ari Weinzweig explaining to a group of new Zingerman's employees the four steps to selling great food: "The first step is what? Know it. Right. This is a loaf of French farm bread from Zingerman's Bakehouse. Why is it rough on the bottom? Because it's cooked on a stone. Why are there lines on the crust? They come from the basket. How long is it cooked? Eighteen hours versus three to four hours for commercial bread using yeast. And time is money, you know, but the dough needs that amount of time to develop the great flavors, and great bread is all about flavor—and smell. Ninety percent of taste is smell. The other 10 percent is taste. The sweet taste buds are on the tip of the tongue. The salty ones are all over. The bitter ones are in the back. The sour ones are on the side. As a professional, you can't taste food if you take two chews, wash it down, and start talking. You need to appreciate the food. It doesn't matter if you don't like it. I hate peanut butter, but it doesn't matter. I have to learn how to tell what great peanut butter is."

Even Norm Brodsky talks with passion about what many would consider the most mundane business in the world: records storage. "When most people visit my company and look around one of my warehouses, all they see are boxes," he said. "They see hundreds of thousands of boxes neatly arranged on shelves that rise up to the ceiling, almost 56 feet high. But when I look around that warehouse, I see something different. I see a fabulous business that my employees and I have built from scratch. You walk into my place and all you can smell is cardboard. I love it. That smell gets my juices flowing.

"I guess some people don't feel that way about their business, but I don't know how they manage. I think you need to feel in your gut that whatever you do is the most interesting, exciting, worthwhile thing you could be doing at that moment. Otherwise, how do you convince anyone else? If I thought storing boxes on shelves was boring, I never would have been able to attract the great people I work with, and we wouldn't have been able to accomplish what we've done. But I found every aspect of records storage fascinating from the start, and I still love showing off our facility to visitors. I'm sure my enthusiasm is contagious."

I don't believe it's possible for a company to have mojo without leaders who feel that way about what their companies do. If they don't love the business, if they don't feel that what the business does is vitally important, if they don't care deeply about being both great and unique in providing whatever product or service they offer, nobody else will either. Granted, such passion exists to one degree or another in all entrepreneurial ventures, or at least the successful ones, as Bernie noted. The difference between the small giants and everyone else lies in their refusal to let go of the passion and their success in keeping it alive.

So how do they do it? To begin with, they understand that you can't measure the value of what a company does by looking at how big it is and how much profit it generates. A company's record of growth and the consistency of its financial returns may tell you something about the skill of its management team, but they say little about whether or not the business is contributing anything great and unique to the world. Instead, the small giants focus on the relationships that the company has with its various constituencies—employees, customers, community, and suppliers. Why? Partly, no doubt, because the relationships are rewarding in and of themselves, but perhaps also because their strength reveals the degree to which people are inspired by the company, and its ability to inspire them is the best measure of how they perceive the value of what the company does. If they are as passionate about it as the founders and leaders, the financial results are likely to follow.

But the small giants also know those relationships are fragile. They depend on a level of trust and intimacy that's easily lost. All it takes is a little neglect. If you allow yourself to get distracted, if you stop working on whatever it is that ties you to the people you do business with, the intimacy will vanish, the trust will dissipate, and the bonds will erode. That can happen for many reasons. It usually happens, however, when a company's leaders begin focusing on growth or financial return, not as by-products of a well-run business, but as goals to pursue for their own sake. And if you sell equity to people outside the company, you will probably *have* to start viewing them as goals to pursue for their own sake—because you will owe those people a good return on their investment. Hence, the small giants' commitment to remaining private and closely held.

Clearly there's a certain discipline involved here. For any competitive individual—and entrepreneurs are competitive by definition—it becomes quite tempting to chase after growth at a certain point in a company's life. The financial indicators are, after all, the most convenient, and objective, measures of success available. It's easy to fall into the trap of thinking that if you're maximizing growth, you're also maximizing success. It feels like you're winning, and who doesn't like to win?

In addition, getting caught up in the growth game helps to assuage one of the least recognized and most underrated hazards of company building: boredom. That is, I believe, what leads many entrepreneurs to embark on acquisition binges, take their companies public, launch new ventures, become angel investors, and get involved in various other pursuits—some of which are constructive, some of which aren't. Once you move beyond the exhilaration of the start-up stage and the growth phase, you find yourself facing the kind of management challenges that a lot of entrepreneurs consider, frankly, boring. If they're smart, they bring in other people to help. Meanwhile, they themselves try to figure out what to do next, what to do that they really enjoy, what to do that can recapture the excitement they have already begun to miss. The problem is, the move that feels right to them may turn out to be harmful to the company.

Somehow the small giants avoid that trap. I believe it's their passion that saves them. They so love what they and their companies do—and they are so determined to keep doing it—that they develop powerful, protective instincts. They become acutely sensitive to anything that might stop them, or lead them off in the wrong direction, or simply get in their way. Like all successful entrepreneurs, they have to navigate a sea filled with opportunities, temptations, distractions, and dangers. Their passion is their compass. Even if they may stray off course from time to time, their love of their work shows them the way back.

It's worth noting, moreover, that what they love is not limited to the products their companies make or the services their companies provide. Those products and services are obviously important. Just as a great composer must have a passion for music, a great brewery must be built around a passion for brewing, and a great special effects company around a passion for computer graphics, and a great manufacturer of torque-control products around a passion for solving torque-related engineering problems. But in much the same way that a symphony is the end result of a composing process, any great product or service is the end result of its own particular creative process, and whoever is doing the creating must love the process as much as the end result.

For people in companies with mojo, that process is inseparable from the business. It's the business that allows them to pursue their passion, and they strive to ensure that the operation of the business enhances their ability to do so. To the extent that they work on developing their own systems and mechanisms toward that end, managing the business becomes a creative endeavor in itself. Traditional management may be an exercise in rationality, to use Bernie's language, but entrepreneurial management requires "the soul of an artist," and—for its practitioners— the business itself is an evolving work of art (as reluctant as some of them might be to use the term).

Then again, it is more of an art for some people than for others. At one end of the spectrum is Selima Stavola, who devotes virtually all her creative energy to designing her clothing. There is very little left over for the business. That's how she wants it, and why she keeps the company as small as it is. "A big business is no longer art," she said sitting in her living room on a late March day. "If it's a big business, costs would matter, and the public reaction would matter. If cost matters, where am I then? How can I do what I want to do worrying about what it's costing? If I have a big business, I have to answer to people. Anonymous people will buy it—the public. These are my things. When I make them, I care very much about who wears them. How can you market that? You can't market that. In my life, I only made something twice one time, for two friends of mine. Everything else I make for one person only, the person who will wear it.

"I also do my fancy. Last week, I stopped production on work for [a client]. She's waiting for me. Instead I do other things, things that I've cut. I think they will be beautiful. I'm tired of winter, I want summer clothes. How can I do that if I have a company and people want to profit? My work is a joy to me. It's not work. I don't want it to become work."

Stavola is not quite as cavalier about costs, marketing, and profit as she lets on. As a business, Selima Inc. has been consistently and solidly profitable since its founding in 1947, and she is, in her own way, a first-rate marketer. But she is undoubtedly correct that keeping things simple allows her to focus on the art of clothing design, while minimizing the need to be creative in the business realm.

Norm Brodsky is the opposite—partly, no doubt, because records storage is about as far removed from clothing design as you can get. It does not take a whole lot of artistry to pick up a box from a customer, bring it to a warehouse, put it on a shelf, and take it back when the customer wants it. But to build a great business with mojo around those simple activities is a creative challenge of the first order—the sort of challenge that Brodsky loves. "I guess I'm like a lot of entrepreneurs," he said. "When I'm told something is impossible, I want nothing more than to go out and do it. That's what I like, doing things other people think are impossible. It's not so much that I want to prove something, at least not to anyone but myself. But for people like me, business is sort of a puzzle. We believe there's a solution to every problem, and we think we can figure it out if we can just visualize what needs to be done. That usually means coming up with a different way of looking at the situation. You need a kind of peripheral vision. You try this angle and that angle, searching for what everybody else is missing. You don't always find it, but when you do, the experience is tremendously satisfying."

It was this peripheral vision that allowed him to go into a highly competitive, very mature industry with enormous barriers to entry and, within eight years, build the preeminent independent records-storage business in the country. Initially, he had found it almost impossible to sign up accounts. Customers were locked into long-term contracts and wouldn't even consider changing suppliers unless someone was offering a significantly lower rate—something that Brodsky was reluctant to do. He had seen too many companies go out of business by competing on price and letting their gross margins slide. Besides, lower prices wouldn't solve the problem. Those long-term contracts also required customers to pay removal fees of up to $5 per box whenever they decided to take their boxes out permanently. Changing suppliers could thus involve an upfront cost of hundreds of thousands of dollars—a major disincentive, to say the least.

But Brodsky couldn't accept the notion that an industry, any industry, was closed to new competition. He realized that if he was going to get anywhere in records storage, he would have to come up with an approach to the business different from that of the established records-storage providers. That meant using his peripheral vision, looking at the business this way and that until he saw something that everybody else was missing.

It took a little while, but then it came to him. "Out of the blue, it suddenly hit me that we were actually in the real estate business," he said. "We weren't just storing records; we were renting space in our warehouse to boxes. So how do you get more rent out of a building? By fitting more rental spaces into it. Same thing for records storage. If you could accommodate more boxes per square foot than your competitors, you could charge less per box and still have better gross margins. And how do you get more boxes per square foot? By having very high ceilings and racks that go right up to the roof."

Carrying the logic a step further, he asked himself what he would do if he had a brand-new office building in a cold market. How would he attract tenants? For one thing, he might offer rent concessions, say, giving six months free rent if the tenant signed a five-year lease with automatic renewal at a higher rate for another five years. If the tenant couldn't afford to build out the space, Brodsky might offer to do it and raise the rent to cover the cost over the length of the lease. A similar tactic, he realized, would work in records storage. To make it easier for customers to switch suppliers, he could offer to pay the removal fees at the other storage company and make it up later by charging higher rates per box.

Brodsky quickly put his ideas into action. He found a warehouse with unusually high ceilings and installed unusually high racks. Meanwhile, he began offering rates much lower than those of his competitors and paying the removal fees of customers who moved their boxes to his place. Such practices were heresy in the industry. "When we started doing these things, our competitors went wild," he recalled. "They told customers, 'Brodsky's nuts. He can't survive. He won't be around in two years.' Prospects would ask me about it. I said, 'It's very simple. Look at our ceilings. We get more than 150,000 boxes per 10,000 square feet. Our competitors get 40,000 or 50,000. Our warehouse holds three or four times as much as theirs. So I'm really overcharging you.' The customers would laugh and ask for a price break. I'd smile and say, 'No, that's what we have to charge—because we provide so many other services. . . .' Then I'd go on from there." The business took off. Eventually Brodsky's competitors woke up and started doing the same things, but by then his company, CitiStorage, had already passed most of them, and he and his colleagues were developing the mojo-generating systems and practices that would make the business a star of its industry.

To some people, it may seem a stretch to describe what Brodsky does as art, but there is obviously a kind of artistry involved in creating something out of nothing based on an ability to see what everyone else is missing. That is, after all, what artists do. In business as in art, moreover, the end result is an experience, and the quality of the experience reflects the relationships between the different participants, as well as the specific medium of expression. While entrepreneurs may rely on peripheral vision rather than artistic inspiration, it's often hard to tell the difference between the two. They are both critical components of a creative process, and it takes such a process to produce something great and unique—be it a symphony or a restaurant or a records storage company.

The other small giants in this book fall somewhere between Stavola, whose passion is focused on what her business does, and Brodsky, whose passion is the business itself. Although all of them put a considerable amount of creative energy into the design and operation of their companies, they are also deeply engaged in and committed to their specific fields of endeavor—food, music, construction, hospitality, engineering, employee recognition, whatever. Thus, to a greater or lesser degree, the business is both a form of creative expression, as it is for Brodsky, and the means by which people can pursue the activity they love, as it is for Stavola. The trick is to find the right balance between the two. If you focus too much on the activity, you may jeopardize the means. If you focus too much on the means, you may lose what you love about the activity. "We have three bottom lines at Zingerman's—great food, great service, and great finance," said Ari Weinzweig. "Potentially, they could all conflict. We could increase our profit by cutting back on the quality of our food. We could improve our service by having a lot more staff on hand, but then we'd go broke. We want to bolster all three bottom lines, and we have limited time, which is a nonrenewable resource. So we spend it thinking about improving each of the three, one at a time."

At no company is the balance between business and art more clearly defined than it is at Righteous Babe, mainly because of the way the CEO, Ani DiFranco, and the president, Scot Fisher, have divided their responsibilities. As Fisher likes to say, "We are a music business. Ani is the music, and I'm the business."

It's an arrangement that both of them feel has worked remarkably well. "From the early days of this company, I've wanted us to be professional and businesslike," Fisher said, sitting in his office in Buffalo, New York. "Ani has allowed me to be businesslike without compromising what she is and what she stands for. I've allowed Ani to be a pure artist without our being unbusinesslike. I think we've found a common ground where art and business can coexist."

"It is absolutely the synergy between the two of us that is making all of this happen," said DiFranco, sitting in her dressing room before a concert in Chicago. "It's true that the company couldn't exist without me, but at this point it couldn't exist without him, either. I know that fundamentally."

At the heart of the relationship is a mutual respect for, as well as an appreciation of, their respective roles. "Yes, I care about making money and being successful from a business standpoint, but it's not the driving force," said Fisher. "I like to do what Ani wants. When she tells me she wants us to bring out an album of such and such an artist, with such and such a design, and whatever, I think, *How can we do this and still be profitable?*"

From time to time, respect for DiFranco's art means acceding to some of her patently unbusinesslike wishes. "We hired a video company to shoot a show she was doing in Colorado," he said. "It cost us about $40,000. Ani wasn't happy about the show. She had sort of a bad hair day. She didn't like the way the drummer was playing. It was an off night. Our plan was to do 'Two Hours in the Life of Ani DiFranco.' She said, 'I don't want to release it.' I said, 'Ani, we just spent $40,000 and put in all this time. We got to get something out of it.' She said, 'Okay, we can distribute it, but I'll hate you forever.' She was smiling, but she made her point. I said, 'Okay. We'll drop it.' I mean, why be independent if you can't make that decision? That's why you give up the $10 million you could get from being on a major label. For all the money in the world, people can't give you the ability to say, 'No.'"

Then again, it's not as if DiFranco doesn't make sacrifices of her own for the business. She is well aware of her responsibilities to the people who've made it possible for her to do her art the way she wants to. "We have ten or fifteen people who work at the Righteous Babe office at any given time," she said in early 2004. "Then there's ten or fifteen more people who work with me out here on the road. There's also the booking agent. There's my publicist, the manufacturers, all the printers, all the peripheral businesses. And if I stop . . .

"Well, yeah. I've been feeling that responsibility a lot lately, because I've been quite tired, and I've been murmuring to Scot about taking some time off. 'I need a break. I want to stop touring for a little while. Please can I. . . .' He sort of sits there quietly, and then he lovingly keeps booking me shows. On one hand, he knows I go stir-crazy when I don't work. I would probably think I was happy not working for a month or two, but then I would freak out. And also, as he said in his gentle way the other night, 'Okay, if you want to take more time off in the spring, I'll let you know well in advance when we're reaching a financial crisis.' We have that very give-and-take relationship. We both compromise to help each other. I wanted to take the month of May off, but as soon as he said that, I said, 'Okay, okay. How 'bout we do states between here and here.' Because our unified goal is to sustain the company, and all these people, and all of this work, and right now if I don't keep on my hamster wheel, it doesn't happen." (In 2005, tendonitis in her wrists and hands finally forced her off the hamster wheel for a few months. The company survived.)

Obviously it takes an enormous amount of trust for two people to function as DiFranco and Fisher do. The trust they have for each other is particularly extraordinary when you consider that for the first seven years of Righteous Babe, they lived together as a couple. During those years, DiFranco was touring constantly, which took a physical and emotional toll. Hoping to relieve some the pressure, she and Fisher decided in 1995 to hire a sound engineer who could also serve as her road manager and driver. What neither of them counted on was that Ani and the sound guy, Andrew Gilchrist, would fall in love.

DiFranco broke the news to Fisher over dinner one night at a restaurant in Buffalo. "She was very straightforward, as always," he said. "She said it wasn't working out between us, and she was in love with Andrew."

"I told him, 'I guess I have to fire Andrew,'" DiFranco recalled. "Because Scot was my manager as well as my boyfriend. Between a business manager and a road manager, who did I need more? So I said I'd let Andrew go, and Scot said no. He knew how desperately I needed help. He said, 'No, I will not let you fire him. You need that help.' And he dealt with it."

It was, they agree, an extremely difficult situation. "Brutal," she said, "for years." Although Gilchrist skipped the next tour, thereafter he and DiFranco were seldom apart, either on tour or in the studio. In 1998, they got married. Fisher, despite the misgivings of his friends, continued to run Righteous Babe. "Everyone who cared about Scot was telling him it was insane to stay on as my manager and business partner when I'd dumped him as a lover," said DiFranco. "They said he was flogging himself. And he had to ride through that without the respect of the people he was working with. My booking agent was, like, 'Ahh, the jilted boyfriend who won't let go.' It took years for Scot to prove himself and to make the emotional transition."

"It was very hard," said Fisher. "But I thought, if I can do this, I can do anything. I never considered leaving. I believed what Ani was doing was important, so I had a choice. Would I be her ex-boyfriend, or would I be her business partner? It wasn't even a discussion. I just had to accept reality."

He also had to work with DiFranco, which wasn't easy either. "It was strained, so strained," she said. "For years, our conversations were only business, and even then strained. Because the heartache was so great. And all the guilt I felt. 'Am I using him? This person I really don't want to take advantage of.' We'd been everything to each other, as you can imagine. I told him he didn't have to stay. Maybe he should take our friends' advice. But he insisted this was how he wanted to do it. He was determined that our relationship and our common purpose was bigger than our romantic connection."

Somehow they managed to get through the difficult times and emerge with their partnership even stronger. "Scot and I are now just light years closer than we've ever been," said DiFranco. "You know, that romantic grappling, that sort of volatile connection, was certainly not good for the business and probably not good for our relationship either. I mean, once we got over being lovers, we finally became . . ." She paused. ". . . whatever you call it. Family. Just as close as two people can be."

It helps, certainly, that they have a virtually identical understanding of why they are in business, and what role they want the company to play. There is no question that it exists to serve art. That's the reason they decided to start putting out CDs by other artists, even though the vast majority will never do better than break even. "We always had the pipe dream of it growing beyond me," said DiFranco, "and of us being a legitimate label with other artists—independent, renegade artists who need help with distribution. If that can be self-sustaining, and if we can be a mechanism for artists to get their work out to an audience, that's what I want. The only time Scot and I have had conversations with artists about their new record maybe not being the best that it could be, it was out of love and trying to help them help themselves. Like, 'Maybe you should spend more time with this record.' It's never our intent to have them change something to make it more salable, or more radio friendly, or more slick. We don't tell any of our artists what to do for business reasons. Typically at record companies, there's endless negotiation between business people and artists, but Scot is very clear that his purpose is simply providing support for the art."

"They're all very different," said Fisher, referring to the other artists on the Righteous Babe label. "We call them 'the Babes,' although they're mostly men over forty. There isn't really a common thread among them. I'm interested in diversity and people who are good at what they do. You may not like their music, but you can't say they're not good at it. We're creating a home for them, a community of artists."

While the art may come first, there is a balance. Fisher and DiFranco are equally committed to doing what's right for the business within the context of promoting the arts. You can see it perhaps most clearly in the decision to buy and renovate the Asbury Delaware Methodist Church. "I had contemplated investing in a recording studio down in New Orleans," said DiFranco. "We had accumulated a nest egg, and we both understood the need to diversify, because the record business was imploding around us. Then Scot proposed the idea of the church, which made a lot of sense on a lot of levels: our think-globally-act-locally mind-set, a space for the office. You know really, when we thought about it, it seemed much more practical and useful than the studio. And it was a way that we could bring more art to our community. There are stadiums and bars in Buffalo, but in order to get tours to come through, you have to have a midlevel venue."

Not coincidentally, Fisher and DiFranco decided to share the space with Hallwalls Contemporary Arts Center, one of Buffalo's leading arts organizations, which was looking for a new home. So in addition to Righteous Babe's concert hall and jazz club, the building also houses Hallwalls's exhibition galleries, screening room, media arts center, and offices. "It was no surprise that they wound up together," said Ron Ehmke, who had worked for both organizations. "In fact, it makes perfect sense. In the beginning, Scot had looked at Hallwalls as a model for Righteous Babe. He frequently says he's not an artist himself, but really he is. His art is helping artists make their work."

Actually, Fisher wouldn't disagree. "I sometimes tell Ani that business is my art, my canvas, my instrument," he said. "I like looking at spreadsheets and adding up columns. She has a different relationship to the business, but she always knows what's going on. Ani and I talk every day. She's involved in every major decision and many smaller ones—not leasing vehicles, but certainly choosing the colors for the church windows and figuring out how the exterior stairs should look. On little decisions, I just try make sure they're what Ani would want."

Perhaps they complement each other so well because each of them has some of the other's strengths. "It doesn't occur to me as much as it should, how creative Scott is," DiFranco said. "I am actually a very practical and, in my way, a good businessperson, and he is, in his way, an artist."

To be sure, it's unusual to have leaders who embody the two sides of the relationship between business and art as clearly as Fisher and DiFranco, but the need to seek the kind of balance that they have is hardly unique to Righteous Babe. You find a similar balance in all the small giants. If nothing else, they demonstrate that it's possible for the business side and the creative side to live in harmony, rather than constantly fighting each other, as tends to happen elsewhere. What makes it possible are the company's priorities. There is no doubt in anyone's mind that the business is the means people are using to pursue their passion, and not the other way around.

And that, I suspect, is where so many companies that start out with mojo go astray. Somewhere on the rocky voyage from the garage to the fully managed organization, they get it backward. They begin to view the passion as something they can use to build the business. That may well be true, of course. The problem is, if you keep heading in that direction, you'll eventually lose whatever it was that gave the company its mojo in the early days. Contributing something great and unique to the world will become less and less of a priority. By the time the second or third generation of owners takes over, there's a good chance that the passion and the business will have gone their separate ways, and the company will have become just another income-producing property. If it's acquired, it won't be because the acquirer's stockholders share the passion or believe in the mission (whatever the new management may say). They'll want to own it only if they think it will improve their financial returns. People will work there mainly because they need a job. Customers will buy its products and services only if they offer the best value for the money. The company will be an economic mechanism and little more. Pretty much everything else will have been lost.

What's wrong with that? From one standpoint, nothing at all. A healthy economy requires those types of companies, and plenty of them. We would all be considerably worse off without them. They provide jobs. They pay taxes. They sell us the goods and services we need and want. They add value. They contribute to charitable causes. They do all kinds of worthwhile and commendable things. It might be nice if they all operated like the role-model businesses Jim Collins wrote about in *Good to Great,* or that he and Jerry Porras wrote about in *Built to Last,* but that's probably more than we can expect. Still, even businesses that aren't role models contribute an enormous amount to our continued prosperity as a nation, for which we should all be thankful.

But being thankful does not necessarily mean being content. There are some people who want more out of business than the typical company offers. It's too boring for them. It's too limited. It's not worth the sacrifice. They have a passion, or perhaps just a burning idea, and they don't want to let their life slip away without ever getting around to it. So they build companies that allow them to pursue their passion and follow their bliss, and they don't forget why they went into business in the first place and how they got where they are. They make sure that, as it grows, the business continues to be a mechanism for doing what they're passionate about and for contributing something great and unique to the world.

They are the founders, leaders, and employees of the small giants. Even if you're not one of them—and most of us aren't—you can't look at what they've done, how much fun they've had doing it, and how rewarding the experience has been on every level without asking yourself whether you, too, are getting what you want out of whatever it is that you do for a living. If the answer is no, well, the people in this book are living proof that there is a viable alternative.

And they aren't alone. As I mentioned in the first chapter, my research uncovered many more small giants than I could possibly include here. Some of their names are as recognizable as Anchor Brewing and Clif Bar. Others are scarcely known at all outside a relatively small circle of people who come into direct contact with them. Not that small giants are the norm in any place where they can be found, but there are, I would guess, hundreds—maybe even thousands—doing their good work in towns, hamlets, and cities all over the country. All you have to do is look, and you'll start to notice them. For me, it got to the point where I could hardly turn around without discovering another one.

Right as I was wrapping up my research for this book, my wife and I and the couple who share the building we live in—an old Victorian house in Cambridge, Massachusetts—decided that it needed painting. In the twenty years we've lived there, we've had it painted several times, and never by someone we'd think of hiring again. But a year or two earlier, another neighbor had had a paint job done that we all admired. We decided to contact the painter and see what he could do for us.

His name was Peter Power, and his company was called New Hope Contracting. He turned out to be a dark-haired, bouncy, bespectacled fellow with a sunny disposition and a strong religious faith; and he was, without doubt, the most conscientious housepainter I'd ever encountered. He also had a great sense of design and wonderful taste. Under his guidance, we and our neighbors picked out six colors to be used on the front, back, sides, and trim of the house. Shortly thereafter, Powers's crew of eight painters descended on us and went to work.

They ranged in age from twelve to fifty-seven and were, well, motley, as painting crews generally are, but a friendlier and more cheerful—or diligent—group of painters you'd be hard pressed to find. They put in long hours, worked extremely hard, cut no corners, and would drop everything on a moment's notice to carry in the groceries, or move a piece of furniture, or put together a bed frame, or fix a broken window sash. It was sort of like having your own Boy Scout troop around to help out with life's little headaches. As they worked, they joked with one another in a good-natured way and seemed to be having a splendid time whether they were chipping, sanding, filling, painting, cleaning up, or eating lunch. They also did a spectacular job on the house, and they did it with almost no apparent supervision. When Power showed up, it was mainly just to lend a hand.

Only as they were finishing their work did it dawn on me that their company was remarkably similar to the businesses I'd been researching for my book. I think it was one of the crew's veterans, Gene Pettiford, who tipped me off. I happened to ask him how long he'd been working with Power. "Ten years," he said.

"That's a pretty long time for a painting company, isn't it?" I said.

"Oh, yeah," he said, "but I'm not the one who's been here the longest. That would be Steve."

"How long has Steve been here?" I asked.

"Seventeen years," Gene said.

Understand, both Steve Quinn and Gene appeared to be in their mid-thirties. I figured Steve must have started when he was about fifteen. Later, Power and I went through the entire crew. Rob Moreno had been around for nine years, American Chris Pointen for six years, English Chris Howell for four years, and so on. Power's son, Danny, who was twenty-five, had been working for his father since he was nine years old and had no plans to stop. But leave him aside for the moment. Housepainting businesses have notoriously high turnover rates, as much as 50 percent a month, which is understandable given the seasonality of the work and the nature of the workforce. I realized something very unusual had to be going on at a painting company where the average employee tenure was almost ten years. I did a little more investigating and quickly concluded that New Hope Contracting met all the criteria I'd established for deciding which companies to include in this book and had all the telltale characteristics of other small giants.

I mention the episode mainly to make the point that, precious though it is, mojo is not as scarce as you might suppose. Companies that have it are all over. Much has been written about Germany's *Mittelstand*, the small to midsize, mostly family-run businesses that are often described as "the backbone of the German economy." I'm not sure we can say that small giants are the backbone of the American economy, but they certainly are its heart and its soul, and they are setting a new standard for excellence on Main Street.

Perhaps most important, it's a standard that thousands of companies can aspire to, and many can achieve. If they do, they will, in the process, contribute more than the uniquely great products and services for which they will be known. Businesses are the building blocks, not just of an economy but of a whole way of life. What they do and how they do it have an impact that extends far beyond the economic sphere. They shape the communities we live in and the values we live by and the quality of the lives we lead. If businesses don't hold themselves to a high standard, the entire society suffers.

There are no businesses that hold themselves to higher standards than do the small giants. Having more of them can't help but make our world a better place.

FURTHER READING AND RESOURCES

At the top of any small giants reading list is Gary Erickson's book, written with Lois Lorentzen, *Raising the Bar: Integrity and Passion in Life and Business: The Story of Clif Bar, Inc.* (Jossey-Bass, 2004). It is a must for anyone interested in the small giants phenomenon—or, frankly, in business and entrepreneurship generally. Aside from being filled with insights and lessons, it tells an engaging story about Erickson's life as a cyclist, rock climber, jazz musician, wilderness guide, and entrepreneur. For a look at companies with a similar ethic to Clif Bar's, check out *Saving the Corporate Soul & (Who Knows?) Maybe Your Own* (Jossey-Bass, 2003) by David Batstone.

Jay Goltz has also put his business thoughts on paper. In his first book, *The Street Smart Entrepreneur: 133 Tough Lessons I Learned the Hard Way* (Addicus Books, 1998), written with Jody Oesterreicher, he managed to be wise, practical, and entertaining at the same time. He is at work on a second book, tentatively titled *Business Income, Business Outcome: How to Build a Successful Business with Soul.*

Ari Weinzweig has written passionately and prolifically about all kinds of foods. His *Zingerman's Guide to Great Eating* is a classic. But if you want to know more about Zingerman's as a business, you should start with Ari's book *Zingerman's Guide to Giving Great Service* (Hyperion, 2004). You should also check out the seminars—on everything from finance to merchandising—offered by ZingTrain, one of Zingerman's Community of Businesses.

Danny Meyer has written two highly acclaimed cookbooks featuring recipes from Union Square Café. Now he is finishing his first business book, due to be published by HarperCollins in late 2006. As I write, there is not yet a title, but whatever it's called, it's sure to be as insightful as the man himself. In addition, I'd recommend Bruce Feiler's excellent article on Union Square Café, "The Therapist at the Table," which appeared in the October 2002 issue of *Gourmet*.

Norm Brodsky may also have a book out in 2006. In the meantime, you might want to check out the column he writes for *Inc.*, "Street Smarts." I would hope that you'd subscribe to the magazine so that you can read the latest installment every month, but you can also find Brodsky's past articles and columns, coauthored by me, at www. inc.com/magazine/columns/streetsmarts.

While Fritz Maytag has (unfortunately) not written a book, I would highly recommend reading the full interview he did with David Gumpert for the *Harvard Business Review*, "The Joys of Keeping the Company Small," (July–August, 1986). For a vignette of Anchor Brewing in its early days, you should read the excellent profile by Curtis Hartman, "The Alchemist of Anchor Steam," which appeared in the January 1983 issue of *Inc.*

You can get another perspective on Reell Precision Manufacturing in Margaret Lulic's *Who We Could Be at Work* (Butterworth-Heinemann, 1996). The official Reell company history by Bob Wahlstedt is fascinating, but only available in a very limited edition through the company. There have been numerous fine newspaper articles about Reell. They are available on the company's Web site, www.reell.com. In fact, I'd urge you to look at the Web sites of all the companies that have one. (Selima Inc. doesn't.) I've listed them below.

There is no official history of O. C. Tanner Co., but you can get a sense of what the company does from the Carrot books written by Adrian Gostick, its director of marketing and corporate communication, and Chester Elton, its vice president of performance recognition. There are three: *Managing with Carrots* (2001), *The 24-Carrot Manager* (2002), and *A Carrot a Day* (2004), all published by Gibbs Smith, Publisher, in Layton, Utah.

You can get a taste of Ani DiFranco's political philosophy from her music and her poetry book, all available at the Righteous Babe Store, which you can find at www.righteousbabe.com/store. Unfortunately, we'll have to wait for the official guide to her business philosophy. In the late 1990s, the company's in-house writer started work on one, but it was never finished.

As I noted in Chapter 7, Palo Alto's University National Bank & Trust was a small giant in its time, but didn't last. You can find part of its story in Paul Hawken's *Growing a Business* (Simon & Schuster, 1988) and Tom Peter's *Thriving on Chaos: Handbook for a Management Revolution* (Harper Paperbacks, 1988). I still think, however, that the best profile of the business remains Elizabeth Conlin's article in the March 1991 issue of *Inc.*, titled "Second Thoughts on Growth."

There are other books worth reading that have a bearing on the small giants phenomenon, although they don't directly address it. The essential book on employee ownership, for example, is *Equity: Why Employee Ownership Is Good for Business* by Corey Rosen, John Case, and Martin Staubus (Harvard Business School Press, 2005). For the experience of making employee ownership work, you should read *A Stake in the Outcome: Building a Culture of Ownership for the Long-term Success of Your Business* (Currency/Doubleday, 2002), written by Jack Stack with some help from me. For more about open-book management, check out *The Great Game of Business: Unlocking the Power and Profitability of Open-Book Management* (Currency/Doubleday, 1992), also by Jack Stack and me, as well as *Open-Book Management: The Coming Business Revolution* (HarperCollins, 1996) and *The Open-Book Experience: Lessons from over 100 Companies Who Successfully Transformed Themselves* (Perseus, 1999), both by John Case. The writings of Robert K. Greenleaf have had an important influence on many of the small giants—especially his booklets *The Servant as Leader* and *The Institution as Servant*. Both are available from The Greenleaf Center for Servant-Leadership in Indianapolis, Indiana.

Finally, I'd urge you to take a virtual tour of the small giants by visiting their Web sites:

- Anchor Brewing—www.anchorbrewing.com
- CitiStorage—www.citistorage.com
- Clif Bar—www.clifbar.com

- ECCO—www.eccolink.com
- Hammerhead Productions—www.hammerhead.com
- O. C. Tanner Co.—www.octanner.com
- Reell Precision Manufacturing—www.reell.com
- Rhythm & Hues Studios—www.rhythm.com
- Righteous Babe Records—www.righteousbabe.com
- The Goltz Group—www.goltzgroup.com
- Union Square Hospitality Group—www.ushgnyc.com
- W. L. Butler Construction—www.wlbutler.com
- Zingerman's Community of Businesses—www.zingermans.com

INDEX